Hizmet in Transitions

Paul Weller

Hizmet in Transitions

European Developments of a Turkish Muslim-
Inspired Movement

Paul Weller
Faculty of Theology and Religion
Regent's Park College - University of Oxford
Oxford, UK

ISBN 978-3-030-93797-3   ISBN 978-3-030-93798-0   (eBook)
https://doi.org/10.1007/978-3-030-93798-0

Cover illustration: Willy Deganello / Alamy Stock Photo

This Palgrave Macmillan imprint is published by the registered company Springer Nature Switzerland AG.
The registered company address is: Gewerbestrasse 11, 6330 Cham, Switzerland

Özcan Keleş
Former Director of the Dialogue Society
in the United Kingdom of Great Britain and Northern Ireland.

PREFACE

This book has a primary focus on Europe, rather than on the presence and activity in Turkey or other parts of the world of what is known to those within it as Hizmet (meaning in Turkish, "service"). It is also focused much more on the movement than on the Sunni Muslim scholar of Turkish origin Fethullah Gülen, whose teaching and example inspired it. As the first book-length monograph addressing these matters since the events of 15 July 2016 in Turkey and their aftermath (hereafter collectively referred to in abbreviated form as "July 2016"), it aims to offer its readers insight into Hizmet's intensified and accelerated internal debates, developments, possible future trajectories and transitions, especially in Europe.

It is a companion volume to Paul Weller's (2022) *Fethullah Gülen's Teaching and Practice: Inheritance, Context and Interactive Development*, also published by Palgrave Macmillan which focuses on the person and teaching of Fethullah Gülen who inspired Hizmet. While both books can be read independently, when read together in a complementary way they add detail to some things that are not appropriate to discuss in equal detail in both books, given their respective foci. Read together, they even more strongly illuminate the dynamic inter-relationships between Fethullah Gülen's teaching and practice; how that teaching and practice has historically developed and is still developing in a contextually informed way; and how (as exemplified in this volume, in relation to Europe) its inheritance is then taken forward within different contextual trajectories which, within an overall hermeneutical circle, in turn inform Fethullah Gülen's own continued contextually developing reflective teaching and practice.

Oxford, UK   Paul Weller

Acknowledgements

General Acknowledgements

Primary research for this book and its companion volume was conducted during 2017–2020. Bearing in mind the pressures upon those associated with Hizmet not only in Turkey, but also beyond it, and which for some interviewees have ranged from loss of employment, expropriation of property and funds through to imprisonment; the need to undertake irregular and sometimes dangerous migration; threats of violence to persons, family and property; as well as state attempts at legal extradition and/or illegal rendition, acknowledgements for their kind assistance are especially due to the twenty-nine people whom I interviewed.

Among individuals publicly associated with Hizmet organisations in Europe who were interviewed and were also generally content for quotations from what they said to be associated with their names across the book and its complementary volume (Weller 2022) were twelve people, the majority of whose interviews took place in English which, it should be noted, was in most cases not their first or, in some cases, even their second, language. These were Selma Ablak (a member of the Hizmet *overleg*, or co-ordinating body in the Netherlands); Alper Alasag (also a member of the Hizmet *overleg*, in the Netherlands); Abdulkerim Balcı (a leading member of the Hizmet-related London Advocacy, UK); Sadik Çinar (Executive Director of the Dialogue Society, UK); Asen Erkinbekov (working with the Platforme de Paris, France); Mustafa Gezen (previously in the leadership of the Dialog Forum, Denmark); Özcan Keleş (Chair of the Dialogue Society's Board of Trustees and, until 2014, Executive

Director of its staff team); Ercan Karakoyun (a leader in the Forum Dialog, Berlin, Germany); Termijón Termizoda Naziri (President of the Arco Forum, Spain); Ramazan Özgü (responsible within Hizmet for dialogue activities, legal questions and asylum-seeker matters in Switzerland, and an *abi*—or member of the informal leadership structure of Hizmet—in the Zurich region, Switzerland); Özgür Tascioglu (Secretary General of Fedactio, Belgium) and Erkan Toğuşlu (responsible for the Gülen Chair, at the Catholic University of Leuven, and also a volunteer in Fedactio, Belgium). Interviews with those from the UK and Switzerland took place in person in the countries concerned in 2018, while the others were conducted over Skype in 2018–2019.

While readers may have noted that this book is dedicated to one of the forgoing interviewees (Özcan Keleş), neither the fact nor the content of that dedication should be taken as an evaluative endorsement of all or any of the particular positions taken by Keleş in terms of his positioning in relation to debates within the movement. Rather, in both this book and its complementary volume (Weller 2022), these positions are presented alongside those of other interviewees with the aim of giving readers insight into a range of positions being taken and the debate that is ongoing within Hizmet in relation to its future possible trajectories. At the same time Keleş' (2021) unpublished doctoral thesis at the University of Sussex on *The Knowledge Production of Social Movement Practice at the Intersection of Islam and Human Rights: The Case of Hizmet*, and to which this author was kindly given privileged access just prior to submitting the manuscript, is a piece of work that this author evaluates highly as a very important specialist contribution to the field which, in due course when it is translated into published form, is likely also to have a wider impact in facilitating an understanding of both Hizmet and Fethullah Gülen.

From among Fethullah Gülen's close associates who were content for quotations from what they said to be associated with their names across this book and its complementary volume (Weller 2022), acknowledgements are due to nine individuals: Muhammed Çetin, Enes Ergene, Mustafa Fidan, Reşit Haylamaz, Ahmet Kurucan, Mustafa Özcan, Hamdullah Öztürk, Şerif Ali Tekalan, and Hakan Yeşilova. Haylamaz and Özcan have been with Fethullah Gülen since close to the start of his public work; as was Fidan, who was one of Gülen's early business supporters. Tekalan first met Gülen in 1971 when he was a medical student and became an otolaryngologist by profession and later President (2010–2016) of the Hizmet-related Fatih University in Istanbul. Kurucan was a student of Gülen who, although he had students dating back to the 1960s, formed a new circle of students on 23 October 1985, and of which Kurucan was a part. Öztürk was a later student of Gülen's, while Ergene is author of a book on Fethullah Gülen and Hizmet, and Yeşilova is editor of Hizmet's *Fountain* magazine. Çetin was (with the support of Fethullah Gülen and Hizmet, under circumstances discussed further in Sect. 4.1) a Member of Parliament in Turkey between 2011 and 2014.

The great majority of these interviews took place in the USA in December 2017 (with the exception of that with Tekalan, which took place in the UK in April 2019) and were conducted in Turkish, supported by Turkish-English-Turkish translation and interpretation undertaken within research ethics approved protocols. This included two interviews with Fethullah Gülen himself, to whom special thanks must be recorded for allowing me to interview him towards the end of 2017 at a time when he was not physically well.

Acknowledgements are also due to three male Hizmet-related asylum-seekers (identified in the text as AS1, AS2 and AS3), and one female Hizmet-related asylum-seeker (identified in the text as AS4) who is married to AS3, all of whom at the time the interviews took place in November 2018 were based in Switzerland. These interviewees not unsurprisingly requested and were granted anonymity. All of the asylum-seeker interviews were conducted in English.

This was also the case, as was the grant of anonymity, for three other individuals both of whom were male: one is publicly associated with Hizmet in Europe, identified in the text as HE1, and whose interview took place over Skype in August 2018; and one is a Hizmet participant in Italy, identified in the text as HE2 and who was interviewed over Skype in September and October 2019; and one is a participant observer of Hizmet in the Netherlands, identified in the text as HE3, and whose interview took place over Skype in August 2019. A request for anonymity was also made and granted in relation to the attribution of some specific quotations (addressed in Weller 2022) from a male interviewee from among the associates of Fethullah Gülen and which are identified as being contributed by CA1.

All interviewees were given the opportunity to review and, if necessary, correct and/or clarify written draft transcripts of the digital recordings of their interviews. At the same time, it should be noted that the interviewees have not reviewed or approved the selected quotations used by the author from their transcripts or how those selections have been deployed in the text, the responsibility for which lies with the author's professionalism in terms of a best understanding of the overall contributions and intentions of the interviewees, and a commitment to, as far as possible, try to avoid being unrepresentative or unbalanced in use of the materials concerned.

Given that English was not the first language of the vast majority of those interviewed, in the presentation of quotations are sentences that are not completely correct in terms of English grammar or structure but in relation to which the decision has been made, where the intended meaning of the interview seems intelligible, not to correct or "improve" the record of what was said orally, but to leave it as it was originally recorded, thereby reflecting something of its original oral flavour.

Finally, acknowledgements are due to members of the research project's reference group. During the lifetime of the project this included Revd. Professor Dr Paul Fiddes, Professor of Systematic Theology and formerly Research Director, Regent's Park College, University of Oxford; Revd. Dr Nicholas Wood, formerly Fellow in Religion and Culture and previously Director of the Oxford Centre for Christianity and Culture, Regent's Park College; Dr Minlib Dalhl, OP, formerly Research Fellow in the Study of Love in Religion, Regent's Park College; Dr Anthony Reddie, Director of the Oxford Centre for Religion and Culture, Regent's Park College; Mahmut Gunyadin from the Dialogue Society, Oxford; Dr Fatih Isik and Dr Ismail Mesut Sezgin – Dialogue Society volunteers; Mr Sadik Cinar, Executive Director, the Dialogue Society; Mr Cem Erbil, Academic Director, the Dialogue Society; and Mr Özcan Keleş, Chair of the Dialogue Society.

COPYRIGHT PERMISSIONS

The vast majority of this book's content is formed from new primary research data. However, acknowledgements are also due to authors, publishers and creators of websites whose work this book quotes under the generally recognised provisions for "fair dealing ... for the purposes of criticism or review". Every attempt has been made to exclude material in this book that may go beyond such provisions. If, in error, the author has inaccurately or not fully represented or referenced any material and if this is brought to the author's attention, any such mistakes will be rectified in any future editions.

Personal and Professional Thanks

The author wishes to record personal and professional thanks to other colleagues at Regent's Park College, Oxford, and beyond, who supported him by showing an interest in his work on this book and the research that underlies it. This includes the former Principal of the College, Revd. Dr Robert Ellis, who supported bringing the project to the College, and Ms Nichola Kilpin, the College's Finance Officer, who administered the project funds granted through the Dialogue Society, behind which were individual anonymous donors, without whose financial support neither the research project underlying these two books would not have been possible, nor their publication in Open Access format would have been possible.

Personal thanks are due to the author's wife, Marie Adenau, for her patience with and interest in this book and its companion volume, as well as the author's wider work on Fethullah Gülen and Hizmet.

Finally, professional thanks are due to colleagues at Palgrave Macmillan for their patient support and work in bringing this book to publication, including especially to Philip Getz, Senior Editor, Palgrave Macmillan; Amy Invernizzi, Assistant Editor Philosophy and Religion, Palgrave Macmillan; Jack Heeney, Editorial Assistant—Literature and Theatre & Performance, Palgrave Macmillan; and Immy Higgins, Editorial Assistant—BEST (Books Editorial Service Team) Springer Nature: as well as to the copy-editing and production team lead by the Springer Nature production manager, Dhanalakshmi Muralidharan.

Turkish Words

Since Turkish is the first language of both Fethullah Gülen and of many of those inspired by his life, teaching and practice (including many of those in Europe) and it remains an important language in Hizmet's overall milieu, generally speaking key Turkish language terms and concepts are, on first use in this book, referred to in their original Turkish form, followed by an English language translation and/or explanation.

Turkish words are generally used in their modern Latin script form, without diacritics apart from those that are normally present in modern Turkish writing (ö, ü, ğ, ç) which contains several letters that are not present in the English alphabet. These are pronounced as follows:

Ç, ç "ch" as in "chime"
ğ which lengthens the sound of the vowel that appears before it; except
   that when it appears between two vowels it is not pronounced
I, ı the sound of the "a" as pronounced in "attack"
Ö, ö same as the sound of "u" in "Turkey"
Ş, ş "sh" as in "shoot"
Ü, ü same as "u" in "tube"

CONTENTS

ABOUT THE AUTHOR

Paul Weller When conducting the research that lies behind the writing of this book, and during its substantive writing, Paul Weller was part-time Research Fellow in Religion and Society and Associate Director (UK) of the Oxford Centre for Religion and Culture, Regent's Park College, a Baptist Permanent Private Hall of the University of Oxford, where he is an Associate Member of the Faculty of Theology and Religion. He retired from his employed Research Fellowship at the end of November 2021, and from 1 December, his Research Fellowship became a non-Stipendiary one. He is also Emeritus Professor of the University of Derby and a Visiting Professor in the Research Institute for Peace, Security and Social Justice of Coventry University.

CHAPTER 1

Introduction

1.1 THE FOCUS OF THE BOOK

This book sets out to offer the reader an understanding of the origins and development of what it argues is one of the most dynamic Islamically inspired civil society movements in contemporary Europe and of how this movement, known among those who seek to live it as Hizmet (from a Turkish word meaning 'service'), is currently undergoing a period of what could be quite significant transitions for its present and future.

Inspired by the teaching and practice of the Turkish Sunni Muslim Islamic scholar of the Hanafi school, Fethullah Gülen, this movement began in Turkey in the 1960s. Following the collapse of the Soviet Union in 1991, Gülen encouraged the spread of Hizmet into the Turkic world of Central Asia and then beyond, including into other continents. Hizmet has therefore developed a global footprint, including in Europe. During the early 1960s, large numbers of people of Turkish origin had migrated to Europe to fill the labour shortages of the post–Second World War period (Abadan-Unat 2011). Some of these sought to connect with the Hizmet initiatives that were developing a considerable momentum in Turkey and, by the early 1970s, Fethullah Gülen and other leading figures from Turkey originally inspired by him visited Europe.

Although this book is not focused on Hizmet's original homeland of Turkey, Hizmet has always been subject to some degree of contestation there, including instances and phases of social, political and legal attack (Weller 2022, Sect. 5.2). Within what has often been the highly fractured

© The Author(s) 2022
P. Weller, *Hizmet in Transitions*,
https://doi.org/10.1007/978-3-030-93798-0_1

nature of Turkish social, political and religious life, this has variously included from politicians and movements of the political left; from those on the nationalist right; from 'Islamist' groups; and from the military. However, following the emergence of the AKP (*Adalet ve Kalkınma Partisi* or, The Justice and Development Party) into national government in the 2002 elections, the social and political reach and influence of individuals and of organisations associated with Hizmet grew considerably. This was especially so in the early 2000s, during which it seemed to many external observers, as well as to some 'insiders' in both the AKP and Hizmet, that there might be at least some confluence of interest (see Sects. 4.1 and 4.2) between the value orientations of the Hizmet and the strategic positions apparently adopted by the AKP around such matters as the need to overcome Turkey's cycle of repeated military coups and to strengthen its democratic structures, as well as an orientation towards full Turkish membership of the European Union (EU).

However, divergences gradually became clear and the history of contestation around Hizmet intensified exponentially from around 2013 onwards when, in reaction to charges about corruption concerning then Prime Minister Recep Tayyip Erdoğan and some of his family, and the statements made by Fethullah Gülen in support of the Gezi Park demonstrations (see Sect. 4.4), the AKP government started to take increasingly restrictive and repressive actions against Hizmet organisations, especially its schools, accusing it under a derogatory and threatening name of being a *Paralel Devlet Yapılanması* (PDY or, Parallel State Structure). Attacks on Hizmet reached a new level intensity following the events of 15 July 2016 and following (see Sects. 4.4 and 4.5) with the, by then President, Erdoğan and the AKP government charging Fethullah Gülen and Hizmet with responsibility, naming Hizmet as *Fethullahçı Terör Örgütü* or FETÖ (Fethullahist Terrorist Organization), a charge which Fethullah Gülen and Hizmet strongly deny.

As a result of the campaign waged against it by the Turkish authorities and agencies, including beyond the borders of Turkey (Alliance for Shared Values 2016), Hizmet has, perhaps ironically, become even more well known internationally than previously. In many ways, the significance of Hizmet is highlighted not only by those sympathetic to it, but also by those who see it as potentially dangerous. Writing, for example, even from before July 2016, Holton and Lopez (2015) refer to Hizmet as "one of the best organized Islamic grass-roots organizations in the world" (p. 21) which is, however, now "attracting some long-overdue scrutiny" (p. 9).

They refer to "claims from former members of a cult-like structure; a highly segregated role for women; and a lavishly funded travel program to Turkey for selected officials from academia, government and law enforcement" (p. 10), while in the foreword to their work, the President of the Washington DC–based Centre for Security Policy, Frank Gaffney Jnr. (in Holton and Lopez 2015), evaluatively summarised the movement as being a "mix of sophisticated influence operation and Islamist supremacism guised as Turkish nationalism" (p. 5).

While this book focuses on the development and transition of Hizmet in Europe, a range of the issues being faced by it there are also occurring in other parts of the world. In parts of the Two Thirds World, the Turkish government and state has deployed economic, diplomatic and other pressures designed to discredit and close down or take over Hizmet-related organisations. Turkey's Eurasian geopolitical context and significance as a member of NATO (North Atlantic Treaty Organization), its Customs Union arrangement with the EU and its long-standing candidacy for accession to membership of the EU means that how Hizmet emerged into global presence and activity; how it is dealing with extra-territorial pressures from the Turkish government and how it is charting a course for its future in Europe and beyond—a matter of wider economic, political and general public interest.

Thus far, the majority of studies on Hizmet have focused either on its birth and development in Turkey; its expansion into the Turkic former Soviet Republics; or more globally—often concentrating on its schools and pedagogical practice. The present book covers Hizmet in Europe in a broader way than other single-authored publications up to now. It is also the first monograph to address Hizmet's development in Europe that has been completely researched and written following July 2016. It contends that to properly understand Hizmet in Europe, one has to situate it contextually in its Turkish historical and geographical origins; its emergence within the forms taken by Turkish diaspora in the European countries within which it has sought to integrate and, finally, its ongoing interactive engagement with the inspiration coming from Gülen's teaching and practice as worked out within an overall hermeneutical circle of engagement in which Hizmet, in ways increasingly informed by critical reflection on the impact of and lessons to be drawn from what has happened to it in Turkey, feeds back again into the contextually influenced further development of Gülen's teaching.

1.2   A Religious Studies Approach
and the "Politics of Naming"

The disciplinary approach of Religious Studies provides the main framework for this study. Within this approach is what is known as the "insider-outsider" problem in the study of religion (McCutcheon Ed. 1999) in which scholarly problems and opportunities are not seen as being exclusively associated with either "insider" or "outsider" perspectives. Indeed, in contrast to much mainstream of Sociology of Religion, where religions tend to be approached according to the kind of prior sociological theory adopted for understanding them, or of Theology, which usually entails the making and application of normative evaluative judgments, in the non-confessional study of religion known broadly as "Religious Studies" there has been a well-established tradition of phenomenological approach to the understanding of lived religion among individuals and groups (Smart 1973).

Although this overall approach has been critiqued (Flood 1999), it argues that it is important, as far possible, to avoid imposing one's own interpretative (whether theological or sociological) framework without first having sought to understand phenomena as fully as possible according to how they present themselves. Taking such an initial approach does not mean one can or should completely avoid responsibility for making evaluative judgements (as discussed in detail later in this chapter; in Chap. 6 of this book; and in Weller 2022, Chap. 6).

However, even before getting into matters of substance, it will be evident that such an approach has significance for the "politics of naming" in relation to what this author has chosen to call "Hizmet"—which is how the movement is known by those who are engaged in it, and sometimes also by those sympathetic to it. By contrast, the Turkish government, state authorities; the now nearly exclusively state-supporting media; as well as reports produced by government-aligned bodies, refer almost exclusively to the Fethullahist Terrorist Organization or FETÖ (*Fethullahçı Terör Örgütü*); or the Presidency of the Religious Affairs of the Turkish Republic's (2017) variant reference to the "Gülenist Terrorist Organization".

Perhaps the most widespread description used by "outsiders" who are neither completely hostile, nor fully aligned with it, is that of "The Gülen Movement"—thereby very much linking it to the person of Muhammed Fethullah Gülen, the Turkish Muslim teacher who inspired it. Indeed, one finds this usage among diverse "outsider" and "insider" monograph authors including, for example, Yavuz (2013); Ebaugh (2010); Tittensor (2014); Tee (2018) and Alam (2019). Some authors, such as El-Banna (2013), use a compound name such as "The Gülen-Inspired Hizmet". Others have, on occasion, tried to promote a different kind of terminology, most notably Gürkan Çelik's and Pim Valkenberg's (Eds. 2010) promotion of the use of the phrase in Dutch of *Vrijwilligersbeweging* (The Volunteers' Movement) on the basis that this is "how Gülen himself describes it" (p. 10—English translation by the author of this book).

Nevertheless, even when a conscious politics of naming is at work, the terminology used is far from absolutely consistent, due to authors' changing understandings over time; the context for, or readership of, a particular publication; and the position taken by the marketing departments of various publishers. However, many authors directly involved in Hizmet would be wary of any over-identification with the person of Fethullah Gülen that might be taken to be implied by use of the descriptor "The Gülen Movement". This is on the basis of a concern that such terminology may imply that Hizmet has a much more centralised and directed organisation than is, in reality, the case. However, some "insiders" are more flexible and do use this phrase (as in Çetin 2010), although within that book the text often switches to the (at least apparently) more straightforward epithet of "The Movement", a usage that, albeit without capitalisation, is also sometimes used in this book and its companion volume. At the other end of spectrum, Reşat Petek's (2019) hostile to Gülen and Hizmet book incorporates "The Hizmet Movement" into its title, while seeking to link this more "insider" usage with the more negative and conspiratorial tropes of "The Puppet" and "The New Tool of the Global Forces" that characterise the rest of the title.

Such issues are not unique to the specific phenomenon being discussed here, in the sense that setting Hizmet within a wider comparative theoretical framework for understanding movements in general, and religiously inspired initiatives in particular, can arguably help to illuminate also aspects of its particular developmental trajectory. One such example might be taken from that part of the Christian tradition out of which the present author comes, and which is now generally known as "Baptist" (see also Weller 2017). Like those within Hizmet, the early Baptists did not call themselves that or understand themselves as founders of a new movement within Christianity but, rather, as trying to bring about the restoration of a more authentic expression of the Christian faith in comparison with what had resulted from the adoption by the Roman Emperor Constantine of Christianity as the official religion of the Roman Empire.

The label that was applied to Baptists and intentionally used with the aim of inciting hostility towards them was that of "Anabaptist"—a word which, in itself, contained a theologically interpretive critique of the baptismal practice of those to whom it was applied by placing the Greek root prefix *ana* (meaning, again) in front of the word "Baptist." Theologically and sociologically speaking, this was intended to evoke fear of the kind of unbridled religious and social "enthusiasm" unleashed by a group of adult baptising theocratically oriented Christians who took part in the 1534–1535 German city of Münster experiment to establish a new society on the basis of the direct application of scriptural injunctions to hold all property in common, but which ended, among other things, in enforced polygamy (Kautsky 1879).

Just like the early Baptists, Gülen and those inspired by him to do Hizmet have always wanted to insist that they are not "innovating" in the sense of trying to create some kind of idiosyncratic version of Islam, still less to create some kind of a "cult" around Fethullah Gülen as an individual. At the same time, there are aspects of the respect shown to Fethullah Gülen by numbers of those who have been inspired by him that, especially when looked at from outside a (Turkish) enculturated and more broadly traditional Muslim understanding, could lead to such interpretations (see Weller 2022, Sect. 3.2).

Because of this, among those associated with Hizmet there can be considerable discomfort with a word such as "Gülenian" which, on occasion, the author of this book has used "for convenience" (Weller 2017, p. 134). However, Fethullah Gülen's thinking and teaching (Weller 2022) are concerned with trying to uncover, develop and apply, in ways appropriate to the contemporary context, particular aspects of the Islamic tradition that is rooted in the sources of the Qur'an and the Sunnah of the Prophet Muhammad which have arguably become buried relative to other aspects, for both Muslims and others. Indeed, even where commentators identify a strongly Sufi flavour in Gülen's approach, Gülen himself has been at pains to stress that Sufism is the inner dimension of Islam itself and is therefore not to be separated from the *Sharia'h*. However, just as the epithet "Baptist" was one with which the "insiders" generally in time came to live, and eventually to adopt, on the basis of explaining what for them it does and does not mean, so also there are signs that, even if it is not felt by "insiders" to be ideal, a descriptor like the "Gülen Movement" is becoming an increasingly widespread shorthand way to describe a specific phenomenon within the development of a broader religious tradition.

1.3 SITUATING IN THE AUTHOR'S PREVIOUS RESEARCH AND THE WIDER LITERATURE

Not least because of the controversies that have developed around Hizmet, it is important to situate this study of Hizmet transparently within the author's previous research on Hizmet and Fethullah Gülen, as well as the wider literature about Hizmet. This includes two previously co-edited books: the first edited by Weller and Yılmaz (2012a), containing two co-authored chapters by the co-editors (Weller and Yılmaz 2012b, c) and two chapters by the author (Weller 2012a, b); the second co-edited by Barton et al. (2013a), containing two co-authored chapters by the co-editors (Barton et al. 2013b, c) and one chapter by the author (Weller 2013). The majority of these chapters were based on papers that had first been presented in international conferences.

In addition, the author has acted as Director of Studies for a University of Derby doctoral thesis discussing the Hizmet movement in relation to social movement theory written by Muhammed Çetin (2010), to whom Weller 2022 is dedicated. In this overall field, the author has also published a co-authored booklet, Weller and Sleap (2014), as well as four single-authored book chapters (Weller 2006, 2015a, b, 2017), the latter of which specifically focused on the development of Hizmet in the UK.

The contentious nature of literature on the movement is highlighted in a number of places. These include the hostile website *Turkishinvitations.*[1] Its section on "Essential reading on the Gülen Movement"[2] states that "A large mass of printed matter and web material about the Gülen Movement has been published, but much of it is self-promotional propaganda. Often, sources that appear independent of the Movement are in fact not". The website goes on to claim, "Further, even reports from outside the Movement have at times made misleading or inaccurate statements" and that, "To save the reader time in sifting through all this, a list of the most genuinely insightful publications is provided below". However, despite this claim, the website goes on to list what are largely journalistic materials (albeit including from reputable publications, such as the German magazine *Der Spiegel*) and blogs, along with a number of master's and doctoral dissertations, with the only significant published scholarly work cited being Turam's (2007) now quite dated book.

However, the claim of *Turkishinvitations* does point to an issue that is frequently discussed in the scholarly literature. For example, Hakan Yavuz (2013), who wrote one of the early seminal scholarly works on Fethullah Gülen and Hizmet, referred to what he called "four genres of literature or approaches" (p. 12) in literature about the movement. The first genre he called "academic" (p. 12) which he saw as being valuable but limited due to its being largely focused on educational aspects of the movement and based on case studies. The second genre he called "journalistic" (p. 13), which he saw as being based either on journalistic interviews or on secondary sources. The third genre he called "promotional and apologetic", on the grounds that such publications were produced either by members of Hizmet or by scholars invited, with expenses paid, to attend what he called "the movement's promotional conferences" (p. 13). The final genre he called "alarmist and militantly anti-Gülen writings" (p. 13) which, at the time of his writing, he identified as tending to be associated with hardline Kemalist approaches.

Particularly in the Turkish language, there are a considerable number of publications, albeit of a more journalistic or popularist kind that are fundamentally designed to attack and discredit Fethullah Gülen and Hizmet, rather than to evaluate him, his teaching and the movement inspired by him in a sober and properly critical way. As discussed in more detail in the companion volume to this book (Weller 2022, Sect. 1.3), Doğan Koç's (2012) book examines such literature from its earliest appearance in Turkish, in the early 2000s, up to the time of his book's publication when such materials were also increasingly appearing in English, especially online.

Since Koç's analysis, such works have been added to by authors aligned with and/or supporting the ruling AKP party. Although the majority of such works are published in Turkish, among recent examples that have also appeared in English are Reşat Petek's (2019) *The Puppet. The New Tool of the Global Forces: The Hizmet Movement*. Petek was Chair of the Turkish Parliamentary Inquiry Committee into the events of July 2016 and, given the position taken by that Committee in reflecting the overall stance on those events taken by the President and the government, it is perhaps not surprising that in the title of his book alone, one can see a confluence of nationalist perspectives and conspiracy theories in the context of which Gülen is portrayed primarily as a political operator at the head of a hydra-headed "well established terrorist organization" (p. 159) dedicated to the overthrow of Turkey's constitutional order. Other publications attack Hizmet on religious grounds, as with the recent publication of Presidency of Religious Affairs of the Republic of Turkey (2017) which portrays Gülen as an at least heterodox "cult leader" engaged in strategic deception of a kind that hides behind religious justification (p. 5).

There is also a wide range also of scholarly relevant literature that reflects sometimes quite radically different religious, political and academic disciplinary approaches and evaluations of both Fethullah Gülen and of Hizmet. These include hundreds of journal articles, conference proceedings papers and book chapters, as well as master's and doctoral theses, representing a variety of disciplinary approaches. In relation to scholarly literature David Tittensor argued, in the Preface to his 2014 study of the movement, that "I found that there are seemingly only two camps, members and sympathisers in the one group, and those that are against them in the other. In short, a battle to define the Movement as either paragons of virtue or deceivers is at hand" (p. ix). If there was at least some truth in this judgement before the events of July 2016, such tendencies have subsequently become more acute even if not all scholarly works fall into one or the other category.

A range of relevant scholarly publications on Hizmet is also reflected in the Oxford University Press's online bibliography of *Muhammed Fethullah Gülen* by Alparslan Açıkgenç (2011). However, since this was last updated only in 2011, its coverage is now somewhat out of date. More recently, the (recently deceased) Dutch scholar Karel Steenbrink (2015) wrote what he called a "bibliographical essay" (pp. 13–46) on "Fethullah Gülen, Hizmet and Gülenists", while a 2016 edition (3.4) of the *Hizmet Studies Review* (linked with the movement-funded Gülen Chair at the Catholic University of Leuven) was devoted to a *Hizmet Index, 1996–2015*.

An important part of the research project that underlies this book was a systematic review of research and other literature with which this volume and its companion volume engage. Indeed, the present author is currently working together with Ismail Şezgin on an annotated bibliography project[3] with the aim of creating a new and comprehensive annotated bibliography of publications on Hizmet and Fethullah Gülen, initially covering English and Turkish language publications, but with the future possibility of extending its coverage also to other languages.

In relation to work by some Hizmet "insiders", Yavuz (2013) argues in a footnote that "their works while informative tend to lack a critical edge" (p. 251). This debate is arguably further complicated by contention over the role and status of "external" scholars who have presented papers at what Tittensor (2014) describes as the "deeply problematic and ultimately counterproductive" flurry of "in-house books and conferences", and which he sees as "little more than a public relations campaign that seeks to capture the field" (p. x). Indeed, in a more recent book chapter on "Secrecy and Hierarchy in the Gülen Movement and the Question of Academic Responsibility" Tittensor goes on to develop further his concerns in this regard referring to what he describes as "a major push by the GM to effectively co-opt Western scholars into writing 'academic lite' articles that overlook its more problematic aspects" (pp. 217–218).

To put the Hizmet-related specificity of this issue into some wider context, around two to two and a half decades ago, similar debates took place in relation to the work of scholars of the Unificationist Movement who took part in conferences out of which came publications that were sponsored by the Unificationist movement—the various dimensions of, and issues related to, which are discussed in a paper by one of those scholars, George Chryssides (2004), who reflects honestly that "The researcher's role involves several areas of conflict, which are difficult, if not impossible, to resolve" (np).

Clearly, as with conferences of many kinds where scholars are given an honorarium for preparing and presenting a paper, there are ethical issues to consider in relation to expectation and independence. However, while respectful of Tittensor's work on Hizmet, and understanding the potential grounds for his concerns, this author does not ultimately share Tittensor's scepticism about the nature of these conferences or value of the literature produced out of them. This is not only because of what could be seen as the potentially self-interested reason that the author's two co-edited books on Hizmet originated largely from papers presented at movement-sponsored conferences, albeit the books were published by "mainstream" scholarly publishers. Rather, it is that in the current book and in its companion volume, all scholarly publications—including those published by publishers related to Hizmet and those published by commercial academic publishing houses; those written by "insiders", as well as those written by "outsiders"; those that aspire to objectivity and those which are clearly of a strong positionality—are all seen as offering different kinds of valuable insight into Fethullah Gülen's teaching and practice and how it is received by others, including by those in Hizmet that his person, teaching and practice have inspired.

Indeed, despite Tittensor's (2018) strictures in relation to movement-funded conferences and publications, he concludes his own discussion of academic responsibility in relation to studies of Hizmet by saying, "I wish to stress that I am not seeking to impugn the scholarship or the place of insider research but simply counsel that it is important that scholars maintain a critical distance" (p. 232). In relation to such concerns, it is this author's experience of participating in editorial work for Hizmet conferences that he has been freely able to review and score papers for inclusion or otherwise and that Hizmet has given "outsiders" invitations to offer critiques with a consistency and to a degree that is rare among religious groups. And for those of us who are outside Islam and/or Hizmet the fact that we do not always take the opportunities afforded to us and the invitations made to make our honest, and including properly critical, input is not the fault of Hizmet, but is rather a matter of our scholarly and/or religious/ethical responsibility.

Of course, to operate in a way in which one can engage with, and evaluate, texts at multiple levels requires a methodologically sophisticated and critical hermeneutical engagement with the texts concerned. In relation to Hizmet, such a theoretical discussion linked with worked examples can be found in Florian Volm's (2017) German language book *Die Gülen-Bewegung im Spiegel von Selbsdarstellung und Fremdrezption*[4] (or, in English translation by the author, *The Gülen Movement in the Mirror of Self-Representation and External Reception*). Taking an approach of this kind, while no scholarly literature will be excluded from consideration in this book, there will be a transparent acknowledgement of both the locus and type of the publications concerned.

Among monographs from publishing houses connected with Hizmet[5] and which focus on Hizmet more generally, including Hizmet in Europe, are more general works such as Ergene (2008); Çetin (2010); El-Banna (2013); Michel (2014); and Alam (2019). Those from publishing houses not aligned with Hizmet include Ebaugh (2010); Çelik (2010); Yavuz (2013); Tittensor (2014); and Cıngıllıoğlu (2017). Finally, for published works that focus specifically on Europe, see Sect. 3.1 and, for individual countries within it, Sects. 3.2, 3.3, 3.4, 3.5, 3.6, 3.7, 3.8, 3.9, 3.10 and 3.11.

Alongside these authored and edited books are many hundreds of journal articles and book chapters representing a variety of disciplinary approaches and evaluative stances in relation to Hizmet and Fethullah Gülen. From among these, one new edited collection of book chapters should particularly be noted—both because it was published following

July 2016, and because of the critical (albeit varied) perspectives it contains on the question of the involvement or otherwise of the Fethullah Gülen and the Hizmet movement in those events. This is published under the title of *Turkey's July 15th Coup: What Happened and Why?*, edited by Hakan Yavuz and Bayram Balcı (2018). However, while generally relevant to the question of the futures of Hizmet, that book is much more concerned with Turkey and is not specifically focused on the European context.

Smaller and more journalistic pieces can be found on Hizmet in various European countries. But, overall, the literature specifically focused on Europe as a whole remains relatively limited. In addition (with the exception of some more campaigning reports) the vast majority of the above were written and published prior to July 2016, the impact from and evolution of Hizmet following which is the main focus of the current book. Indeed, this is the first book-length scholarly publication to take a European overview of the interaction between Hizmet and its European environment following July 2016 and the subsequent persecution, imprisonment, asset-stripping and civic deprivation of individuals and organisations associated with Hizmet in Turkey. One of the by-products of this period has been a growing re-assessment, not only by external observers, but also and in many ways especially by those associated with Hizmet both about how it developed in Turkey, and also about its future trajectory and the implications of it increasingly operating outside the historical inheritance of the Turkish social, religious and political environment.

At the time of writing, the only other scholarly published sources that have specifically engaged with this in relation to Europe are the series of articles published in the 2018 special edition of the journal *Politics, Religion and Ideology* called "Ruin or Resilience? The Future of the Gülen Movement in Transnational Political Exile"[6] which includes overview articles by Watmough and Öztürk (2018a, b). This, as well as covering a more general discussion of exile and transition, includes articles that centre on Hizmet-related case studies including in relation to Europe, on France, the UK and Italy.

In addition to all the above there are a range of magazines through to newspaper articles which also form part of the context for the debates that rage around this movement and the figure who inspired it. In so far as these in themselves form part of what might be called relevant "social data", they will also be engaged with where appropriate, albeit also on a basis informed by transparency concerning their locus and modes of production.

1.4 Evidence, Aims and Methods

Research and scholarship undertaken into movements and people involved in religious and political contention can be subject to many challenges, some of which are informed by real issues; while others can be more to do with perceptions, whether accurate or inaccurate; and still others (including also among scholars) can be the product of ideological or prejudicial stances of which there has been insufficient reflexive and self-critical awareness.

In the Preface to his 2014 book on Hizmet, David Tittensor (2014) explains his aim to "make a serious empirical contribution" that provides "insight into the lived realities of those that work within the movement and those that are touched by it" (p. x). By gathering primary research data through interviews with individuals publicly associated with Hizmet in Europe, this book, like Tittensor's, aims also to provide such empirically informed insight into the lived realities of Hizmet, albeit in this instance focused geographically on Europe.

Alongside being able to draw upon two decades' worth of informal knowledge of, and conversations and interaction with, those associated with Hizmet, this was achieved by means of conducting twenty-nine semi-structured in-depth narrative interviews that, through participants' stories, collated evidence of underpinning cultural milieux, social contexts and personal attitudes. Initial selection of the European countries was made in order to cover locations that would be as geographically, historically and demographically varied as possible, while also having differing histories with regard to the Turkish diaspora in general and Hizmet in particular. In the end it did not prove possible to secure interviews that had originally been hoped for in Austria and Poland, but interviews did take place in relation to nine European countries, namely Belgium, Denmark, France, Germany, Italy, the Netherlands, Spain, Switzerland and the UK.

One limitation of the fieldwork, and therefore potential criticism of the book that must be acknowledged and taken seriously, is that the vast majority of the formal interviews that inform this book took place with men. This partly reflects the reality (as discussed in Sect. 5.7 of this book) that Hizmet is still quite strongly reflective of patriarchy in terms of both its Turkish and Muslim heritages. When coupled with the choice made to give significant voice to those who have been Fethullah Gülen's historically close associates and to interviewees in Europe who have had public roles within Hizmet-related groups (primarily on the grounds that in the post-2016 context interviewees already known to be publicly aligned with Hizmet might be less hesitant to go on the record) this inevitably had further gender-related consequences.

Acknowledging the gender imbalance limitations of the interviews, the author has tried in terms of other published sources, to pay special attention to those that concern the position and perspectives of women within the movement (for example: Curtis 2010, 2012; Hassencahl 2012; Pandaya 2012; Rausch 2012, 2014). Nevertheless, despite these mitigating factors, it remains the case that it is likely that both companion volumes will, in due course, need complementing, critiquing and quite probably correcting by primary interviews with emergent women leaders in Hizmet, and also by a conscious and systematically applied specifically feminist perspectives and approaches, some work on which has been contributed, among others, by Raja (2013) and Fougner (2017).

Despite these acknowledged limitations, it is to a large degree the "raw" nature of the contributions made by interview participants—and who, in this book, are frequently given voice in direct quotations as well in summarised form—that brings a particular focus and power to the wider discussions of the book. Of course, when it comes to a more analytical consideration of the raw interview data and the observations of the researcher, neither can straightforwardly be taken as having any especially privileged status that is not itself subject to further analysis. Therefore, as a matter of transparency, it should be stated that this research was conducted in the course of the author's employment at Regent's Park College, where it was funded through charitable donations made by anonymous donors for this purpose and channelled via the Dialogue Society, a UK registered charity (No. 1117039) which, on its website, acknowledges its inspiration from Fethullah Gülen.[7] The Dialogue Society therefore has had a material interest in this book and research that lies behind it. That interest was also represented in the project's reference group, of which some representatives of the Dialogue Society were a part, along with senior scholars from the College.

However, in relation to research on religion (as in other fields) in a university context it is quite possible for it to have an ultimate funding source that may or may not have expectations for, and/or be welcoming or not of the work that is actually produced, while having confidence in the academic integrity and rigour of the publication and its underlying research. In contrast with consultancy, in which the contractual relationship is directly between the commissioner of the research and the person, persons or company that conducts it, higher education institutions have systems in place that control for potential challenges to the integrity of research results, and the funders of research who work through higher education institutions accept such controls.

In this instance, the funding agreement with the College for the research included a clear statement relating to the College's academic independence and the author's academic freedom, thus safeguarding the independence, integrity and results of the project. In addition, the project went through a rigorous research ethics scrutiny and approval process at the University of Oxford, as one of the world's leading research universities, and which took account of the University's Conflict of Interest policy. Within these processes the funding source and arrangements governing the research were made transparent and within which the approaches to be taken to the research were set out and discussed in a detailed way, resulting in the formal ethical approval that undergirded the rigour and integrity of the research.[8]

However, it remains the case that those who conduct research and write for publication are necessarily affected by their disciplinary, religious and civil society backgrounds and commitments. Transparency in relation to such is particularly important when research deals with individuals and groups that have been the focus of controversy. In this case, it should therefore be made clear that the author works broadly in the study of religion rather than that of political science, the latter of which, along with sociology, are the disciplines from within which many scholars have hitherto approached these matters. When dealing with phenomena which, at the least, present themselves to others in terms of a religious inspiration, the epistemological presuppositions and social understandings that the researchers inevitably bring to their disciplines and the subject matter of their research entail both potential benefits and limitations. One of the lessons that has been pressed home by, among others, advocates of feminist and decolonising epistemologies and methodologies is that, however rigorously scholars seek to operate within their disciplinary norms, neither they nor their disciplinary traditions are neutral—even, and perhaps are especially not so, when they purport to be.

Thus, in terms of personal positionality it should be acknowledged that the author is a religious believer and practitioner, albeit within (the Baptist tradition of) Christianity rather than within Islam. Thus, for all that it is the case that the research lying behind this book and its companion volume draws on social scientific methodologies and literatures, informed by over two decades of personal knowledge of, and interaction with, Hizmet and an extensive engagement with the literature about Fethullah Gülen and Hizmet, it is ultimately the author's professional judgement that, in order to understand Fethullah Gülen and Hizmet in as fully an adequate a way as possible, one needs to recognise and acknowledge the primarily religious register in which they at least understand themselves to be operating.

According to the African historian Achille Mbembe (2016), it is both possible and important to work within a "a process of knowledge production that is open to epistemic diversity" (p. 37). At the same time, in advocating this, Mbembe is quick to anticipate the critique that such an approach might lead to an epistemological, cultural and ethical relativism by arguing that such an approach "does not necessarily abandon the notion of universal knowledge for humanity", but rather that pluriversity itself embraces the possibility of a universal knowledge for humanity *"via a horizontal strategy of openness to dialogue among different epistemic traditions"* (italics in the original).

In terms of the relationship between one's position and approach as a scholar and one's engagements and responsibilities as a citizen, the author should also acknowledge his both being and having for a number of years been a member of the Board of Advisors of the Dialogue Society. A readiness to act in such a capacity is, of course, distinct from being in membership or having similar categories of direct personal alignment. Nevertheless, readiness to act in this capacity signals the fact that, evaluatively speaking, overall the author takes a critically sympathetic approach to the practice of Hizmet and the teaching of Fethullah Gülen. It also means that, in addition to any ways in which one's academic work may impact upon and influence the development of Hizmet, in the context of his role in the Society's Board of Advisors the present author has, on occasion, either individually and/or as part of the wider Board, made recommendations to it on matters that are discussed later in this book, including that of transparency around the inspiration for the Dialogue Society's work as having been drawn from the person and teaching Fethullah Gülen (see Sect. 5.4), and encouragement to the Society to engage with other organisations of Muslim inspiration (see Sect. 5.6).

Such a role also enables the possibility of having an awareness of, and perhaps more access to, some important and sometimes sensitive internal discussions and debates. At the same time, ethically, it is important to differentiate such informal knowledge from data that is collected when one is acting formally as a researcher which is only used here within the principles and practice of informed consent.

Finally, in the light of a note on the *Turkishinvitations* website that "there is no such thing as a free Turkey trip",[9] the author should also acknowledge, in 2008, taking part in a study visit to Turkey and Hizmet institutions there at the invitation of the UK's Dialogue Society. Nevertheless, as with the author's previously noted experience concerning Hizmet-sponsored conferences, participation in such a trip certainly did not preclude the asking of sharp and robust questions. Details of some of those that were posed by the author in an 18 July 2008 paper, circulated to participants as part of the preparations for the trip, are set out in detail in the companion volume to this one (Weller 2022, Sect. 6.1), to which the reader wanting more detailed evidence is referred.

As Tittensor (2014) acknowledged when arguing for the importance of trying to make an empirically based contribution, his approach was also "not value-neutral" (p. x). In all of this, therefore, awareness of oneself and transparency before others are the main means by which there can be control for potentially problematic bias. This is, in turn, a part of what the widely acknowledged parent of the discipline of Religious Studies, Ninian Smart (1973), used to call the importance of "axioanalysis" in the study of religion, and particularly in relation to any attempt at a cross-cultural approach to religion, where one "should stimulate some degree of self-awareness. It is as though we should undergo axioanalysis—a kind of evaluational equivalent to psychoanalysis: what has been called more broadly 'values clarification'. Or perhaps we might call it 'own-worldview analysis' " (Smart 1973, p. 265). Especially in such hotly debated areas as those that are under discussion in this book, both the contributors to the research and researchers themselves are inevitably actors in a social process.

In relation to this, one of the anonymous interviewees, HE1 (see Acknowledgements), who is publicly associated with Hizmet in Europe, said, "For me it was really a good reflection" and of which the person concerned commented that they and others previously "didn't have time for." Finally, because of the extensive number of imprisonments without trial, deprivation of employment and assets, and actions pursuing guilt by mere association with Fethullah Gülen and/or Hizmet which followed July 2016, in contrast with Tittensor's (2018) counsel, "it is important that scholars maintain 'a critical distance' " (p. 232) as between "two polar-opposite narratives" of what "actually transpired" (p. 218), there is at least a case to be argued that such a context calls rather for scholars to be ready to take the risk of adopting a clear overall position in terms of (consciously, rather than in any case it already being so, even without explicit consciousness) becoming a social actor in relation to the human issues at stake.

Adopting such a conscious position as a scholarly social actor entails a willingness to accept the responsibility that in doing so, one's evaluations and associated choices might be wrong. Therefore, in moving beyond critical distance alone, and incorporating positionality in a way that is academically and ethically responsible, this can only be undertaken on the basis of being as informed as possible through the aspiring to gain as much empirical insight as possible into lived realities of what is being researched alongside being as self-aware as possible of one's own value and epistemological positionalities through the application to oneself and one's academic approach of a rigorous axioanalysis.

NOTES

1. The website is produced by C.A.S.I.L.L.I.P.S. (Citizens Against Special Interest Lobbying in Public Schools), a group critical of, and campaigning against, Hizmet, especially in relation to its so-called Charter Schools in the United States. https://turkishinvitations.weebly.com/who-is-fethullah-gulen-and-what-is-the-gulen-movement.html, 9.6.2010, last updated 4.3.2012.
2. https://turkishinvitations.weebly.com/essential-reading-on-the-gulen-movement.html, 28.7.2013, last 3.5.2014.
3. This project is also being conducted at Regent's Park College, a Permanent Private Hall of the University of Oxford, where the author is a Non-Stipendiary Research Fellow in Religion and Society. Like the project behind this book and its companion volume, this is also being funded by donations deployed through the Dialogue Society, but also crowd funding contributions, for details of which, see: https://www.youtube.com/watch?v=oVvFkDKQsOM, 29.11.2019.
4. In English, *The Gülen Movement in the Mirror of Self-Representation and External Reception* (translation by author).
5. Hizmet's current main English language publishing arm is Blue Dome Press, based in New Jersey, USA. Its English language publishing houses have included The Light, The Fountain and others.
6. *Politics, Religion and Ideology*, Volume 19. Issue 1. 2018 https://www.tandfonline.com/toc/ftmp21/19/1

7. http://www.dialoguesociety.org/about-us.html, 2021.
8. University of Oxford Humanities and Social Sciences Divisional Research Ethics Committee Reference No: R52855/RE001.
9. https://turkishinvitations.weebly.com/the-interfaith-dialog-bubble.html, 3.10.2010.

REFERENCES

(All web links current at 20.11.2021)

Abadan-Unit, Nermin (2011). *Turks in Europe: From Guest Worker to Transnational Citizen*. Oxford: Berghan Books.

Açıkgenç, Alparslan (2011, last modified). *Muhammed Fethullah Gülen*. Oxford Bibliographies Online. Oxford: Oxford University Press. https://www.oxfordbibliographies.com/view/document/obo-9780195390155/obo-9780195390155-0106.xml.

Alam, Anwar (2019). *For the Sake of All: The Origin, Development and Discourse of the Gülen Movement*. New Jersey: Blue Dome Press.

Alliance for Shared Values (2016). *The Failed Military Coup in Turkey and the Mass Purges*. Brussels: Intercultural Dialogue Platform. https://afsv.org/wp-content/uploads/2020/04/A-Civil-Society-Perspective-on-The-Failed-Military-Coup-in-Turkey-Digital.pdf

Barton, Greg, Weller, Paul and Yılmaz, İhsan (Eds) (2013a). *The Muslim World and Politics in Transition: Creative Contributions of the Gülen Movement*. London: Bloomsbury.

Barton, Greg, Weller, Paul and Yılmaz, İhsan (2013b). Fethullah Gülen, the Movement and This Book: An Introductory Overview. In Greg Barton, Paul Weller, İhsan Yılmaz (Eds.), *The Muslim World and Politics in Transition: Creative Contributions of the Gülen Movement* (pp. 1–12). London: Bloomsbury.

Barton, Greg, Yılmaz, İhsan, and Weller, Paul (2013c). Towards a Conclusion: Fethullah Gülen, the Hizmet and the Changing 'Muslim World'. In Greg Barton, Paul Weller, İhsan Yılmaz, *The Muslim World and Politics in Transition: Creative Contributions of the Gülen Movement* (pp. 209–216). London: Bloomsbury.

Çelik, Gürkan (2010). *The Gülen Movement: Building Social Cohesion Through Dialogue and Education*. Delft: Eburon Publishers.

Çelik, Gürkan and Valkenberg, Pim (Eds. 2010). *Fethullah Gülen und de Vrijwilligersbeweging*. Amsterdam: Dialoog Akademie.

Çetin, Muhammed (2008). *Collective Identity and Action of the Gülen Movement: Implications for Social Movement Theory*. Doctoral thesis, Derby: University of Derby. https://derby.openrepository.com/handle/10545/254792.

Çetin, Muhammed (2010). *The Gülen Movement: Civic Service Without Borders*. New York: Blue Dome Press.

Chryssides, George (2004). 50 Years Unification: Conflicts, Responsibilities and Rights. Paper presented at 2004 CESNUR international conference at Baylor University, Waco, Texas, June 18–20. https://www.cesnur.org/2004/waco_chryssides.htm.

Cıngıllıoğlu, Salih (2017). *The Gülen Movement: Transformative Social Change*. Cham: Palgrave Macmillan.

Curtis, Maria (2010). Reflections on Women in the Gülen Movement: Muslim Women's Public Spheres, Yesterday, Today, and Tomorrow. In Gurkan Çelik and Martien Brinkman (Eds.), *Mapping the Gülen Movement: A Multidimensional Approach, Conference Papers from Felix Meritis, Amsterdam, The Netherlands, October 7th 2010* (pp. 162–86). Dialog Academie and VISOR Institute for the Study of Religion, Culture and Society,

Curtis, Maria (2012). Among the Heavenly Branches: Leadership and Authority among Women in the Gülen Hizmet Movement. In Tamer Balcı and Christopher Miller (Eds.). *The Gülen Hizmet Movement: Circumspect Activism in Faith Based Reform* (pp. 119–154). Newcastle: Cambridge Scholars Publishing.

El-Banna, Sanaa (2013). *Resource Mobilisation in Gülen-Inspired Hizmet: A New Type of Social Movement*. New York: Blue Dome Press.

Ebaugh, Helen (2010). *The Gülen Movement: A Sociological Analysis of a Civic Movement in Moderate Islam*. Dordrecht: Springer.

Ergene, Enes (2008). *Tradition Witnessing the Modern Age: An Analysis of the Gülen Movement*. New Jersey: Tughra Books.

Flood, Gavin (1999). *Beyond Phenomenology: Rethinking the Study of Religion*. London: Bloomsbury.

Fougner, Tore (2017). Fethullah Gülen's Understanding of Women's Rights in Islam: A Critical Reappraisal, *Turkish Studies*, *18* (2), 251–277. https://doi.org/10.1080/14683849.2016.1245582

Hassencahl, Fran (2012). Framing Women's Issues in the Fountain Magazine. In Sophia Pandaya and Nancy Gallagher (Eds.), *The Gülen Hizmet Movement and Its Transnational Activities: Case Studies of Altruistic Activism in Contemporary Islam* (pp. 117–132). Boca Raton: Brown Water Press.

Holton, Christopher and Lopez, Claire (2015). *The Gülen Movement. Turkey's Islamic Supremacist Cult and its Contributions to the Civilization Jihad*. Washington DC: The Center for Security Policy. https://centerforsecurity-policy.org/book-release-the-gulen-movement-turkeys-islamic-supremacist-cult-and-its-contributions-to-the-civilization-jihad/

Kautsky, Karl. 1879 (2013 reprint). *Communism in Central Europe in the Time of the Reformation*. Theclassics.Us.

Koç, Doğan (2012). *Strategic Defamation of Fethullah Gülen: English v. Turkish*. Lanham, Maryland: University Press of America.

McCutcheon, Russell (Ed.) (1999). *The Insider/Outsider Problem in the Study of Religion: A Reader*. London: Continuum.

Mmembe, Achil (2016). Decolonizing the University: New Directions. *Arts and Humanities in Higher Education*, *15* (1), 19–45. https://doi.org/10.1177/1474022215618513

Michel, Thomas (2014). *Peace and Dialogue in a Plural Society: Contributions of the Hizmet Movement at a Time of Global Tensions*. New York: Blue Dome.

Pandaya, Sophia (2012). Creating Peace on Earth through Hicret (Migration): Women Gülen Followers in America. In Sophia Pandaya and Nancy Gallagher (Eds.), *The Gülen Hizmet Movement and Its Transnational Activities: Case Studies of Altruistic Activism in Contemporary Islam* (pp. 97–116). Boca Raton: Brown Water Press.

Petek, Reşat (2019). *The Puppet. The New Tool of the Global Forces: The Hizmet Movement*. Gaithersburg, Maryland: Kopernik.

Presidency of Religious Affairs of the Turkish Republic, The (2017). *Gülenist Terrorist Organization: A Sponsored Exploitation of Islam and Muslims (Volume One)*. Ankara: The Presidency of Religious Affairs of the Turkish Republic.

Raja, Aamir Hanif (2013). Role of Women in Hizmet and Feminist Movement: A Comparative Analysis. *Pakistan Journal of Social Sciences*, *33* (2), 321–329. https://www.bzu.edu.pk/PJSS/Vol33No22013/PJSS_Vol33%20No%202_2013_08.pdf

Rausch, Margaret. (2012). Gender and Leadership in the Gülen Movement: Women Affiliates' Contributions to East-West Encounters. In Sophia Pandaya and Nancy Gallagher (Eds.), *The Gülen Hizmet Movement and Its Transnational Activities: Case Studies of Altruistic Activism in Contemporary Islam* (pp. 133–59). Boca Raton: Brown Water Press.

Rausch, Margaret (2014), " 'A Bucket with a Hole': Hizmet Women and the Pursuit of Personal and Professional Progress Through Sohbetler (Spiritual Conversations). *Hizmet Studies Review 1* (1), 73–79.

Smart, Ninian (1973). *The Phenomenon of Religion*. Basingstoke: Macmillan.

Steenbrink, Karel (2015). Fethullah Gülen, Hizmet and Gülenists. A Bibliographical Essay. In Gürkan Çelik, Johann Leman and Karel Steenbrink (Eds.), *Gülen-Inspired Hizmet in Europe: The Western Journey of a Turkish Muslim Movement* (pp. 13–46). Brussels: Peter Lang.

Tee, Caroline (2018). The Gülen Movement in London and the Politics of Public Engagement: Producing 'Good Islam' Before and After 15 July. *Politics, Religion & Ideology*, *19* (1), 109–122. https://doi.org/10.1080/21567689.2018.1453269

Tittensor, David (2014). *The House of Service: The Gülen Movement and Islam's Third Way*. New York: Oxford University Press.

Tittensor, David (2018). Secrecy and Hierarchy in the Gülen Movement and the Question of Academic Responsibility? In Hakan Yavuz and Bayram Balcı (Eds), *Turkey's July 15th Coup: What Happened and Why?* (pp. 217–236). Salt Lake City: University of Utah Press.

Turam, Berna (2007). *Between Islam and the State.* Stanford: Stanford University Press.

Volm, Florian (2017). *Die Gülen-Bewegung im Spiegel von Selbsdarstellung und Fremdrezption: Eine Textuelle Performanzanalyse der Schiften der BerfürterInnen (Innenperspektive) und KritikerInnen (Aussenperspeckive)* [English translation by the author of this book: *The Gülen Movement in the Mirror of Self-Reflection and External Reception: A Textual Performance Analysis of the Writings of the Proponents (Internal Perspective) and Critics (External Perspective).* Baden Baden: Ergon Verlag.

Watmough, Simon and Öztürk, Ahmet Erdi (2018a). The Future of the Gülen Movement in Transnational Political Exile: Introduction to the Special Issue. *Politics, Religion and Ideology, 19* (1), 1–10. https://doi.org/10.1080/21567689.2018.1453244

Watmough, Simon and Öztürk, Ahmet Erdi (2018b). From 'Diaspora by Design' to Transnational Political Exile: the Gülen Movement in Transition. *Politics, Religion and Ideology 19* (1), 33–52. https://doi.org/10.1080/21567689.2018.1453254

Weller, Paul (2006). Fethullah Gülen, Religions, Globalization and Dialogue. In Robert Hunt and Yüksal A. Aslandoğan (Eds.), *Muslim Citizens of the Globalized World: Contributions of the Gülen Movement* (pp. 75–88). Somerset: New Jersey, The Light Inc. and IID Press.

Weller, Paul (2012a). Dialogue and Transformative Resources: Perspectives from Fethullah Gülen on Religion and Public life. Paul Weller and İhsan Yılmaz (Eds.), In *European Muslims, Civility and Public Life: Perspectives on and From the Gülen Movement* (pp. 3–19). London: Continuum.

Weller, Paul (2012b). Robustness and Civility: Themes from Fethullah Gülen as Resource and Challenge for Government, Muslims and Civil Society in the United Kingdom. In Paul Weller and İhsan Yılmaz (Eds.), *European Muslims, Civility and Public Life: Perspectives on and From the Gülen Movement* (pp. 143–59). London: Continuum.

Weller, Paul (2013). Fethullah Gülen, Turkey and the European Union. In Greg Barton, Paul Weller and İhsan Yılmaz (Eds.), *The Muslim World and Politics in Transition: Creative Contributions of the Gülen Movement* (pp. 108–125). London: Bloomsbury.

Weller, Paul (2015a). The Gülen Movement in the United Kingdom. In Gürkan Çelik, Johan Leman and Karel Steenbrink (Eds.), *Gülen-Inspired Hizmet in Europe: The Western Journey of a Turkish Muslim Movement* (pp. 239–251). Brussels: Peter Lang.

Weller, Paul (2015b). Islam in Turkey as Shaped by the State, its Founder and its History: Insight through Baptist Eyes and Three Key Muslim Figures. In Raimundo Barreto Jnr, Kenneth Sehested, Luis Rivera-Pagán and Paul Hayes (Eds.), *Engaging the Jubilee: Freedom and Justice Papers of the Baptist World Alliance (2010–2015)* (pp. 193–209). Falls Church, Virginia: Baptist World Alliance.

Weller, Paul (2017). Religious Freedom in the Baptist Vision and in Fethullah Gülen: Resources for Muslims and Christians. In John Barton (Ed.), *A Muslim Sage Among Peers: Fethullah Gülen in Dialogue with Christians* (pp. 133–156). New Jersey: Blue Dome.

Weller, Paul (2022). *Fethullah Gülen's Teaching and Practice: Inheritance, Context and Interactive Development*. Cham: Palgrave Macmillan.

Weller, Paul and Sleap, Frances (2014). *Gülen on Dialogue*. London: Centre for Hizmet Studies.

Weller, Paul and Yılmaz, İhsan (Eds.) (2012a). *European Muslims, Civility and Public Life: Perspectives on and From the Gülen Movement*. London: Continuum.

Weller, Paul and Yılmaz, İhsan (2012b). Fethullah Gülen, the Movement and This Book: An Introductory Overview. In Paul Weller and İhsan Yılmaz (Eds.), *European Muslims, Civility and Public Life: Perspectives on and From the Gülen Movement* (pp. xxi–xxxiv). London: Continuum.

Weller, Paul and Yılmaz, İhsan (2012c). Conclusion: Fethullah Gülen and the Hizmet: Towards an Evaluation. In Paul Weller and İhsan Yılmaz (Eds.), *European Muslims, Civility and Public Life: Perspectives on and From the Gülen Movement* (pp. 199–210). London: Continuum.

Yavuz, Hakan (2013). *Toward an Islamic Enlightenment: The Gülen Movement*. New York: Oxford University Press.

Yavuz, Hakan and Balcı, Bayram (Eds.) (2018). *Turkey's July 15th Coup: What Happened and Why?* Salt Lake City: University of Utah Press.

PART I

Hizmet in Turkish Origins and European Development

CHAPTER 2

Turkish Origins and Development

2.1   Hizmet: The Emergence of a Phenomenon

Movements and groups, both civil and religious, do not exist in either a contemporary or an historical vacuum. What is today known to those who are engaged in it as Hizmet (the Turkish word meaning "service") emerges out of the conjunction of a particular set of geographical, historical, cultural, political and religious factors and their interplay which have all had a part in Hizmet's emergence onto the European (and world) stage.

In terms of geography, history, culture, politics and religion, what is seen as belonging to Europe and why, and by whom, is a matter of ongoing debate. The landmass that is currently recognised in international law as the Republic of Turkey was historically only a part of the multi-national Ottoman Empire. This geographical area was, and often still is, seen by many in these debates (see Aydın-Düzgit 2012) around Turkey's potential membership of the EU—and especially among those in the EU who are opposed to this—as belonging culturally to "the East" rather than "the West". A part of this debate relates especially to the perception of Turkey, despite its state secularism, being seen as belonging culturally to what is, by many, called "the Muslim world".

All of these matters are the subject of contestation, with some seeing Turkey's relationship with, and orientation towards, Europe as having been decisively addressed in Atatürk's revolution and the dominant political Kemalism that followed it (including its very specific form of secularism). Within Turkey itself, some have dreamed of potentially restoring the

© The Author(s) 2022
P. Weller, *Hizmet in Transitions*,
https://doi.org/10.1007/978-3-030-93798-0_2

historical role of the Caliphate in global Islam and some have denounced the EU as being basically a "Christian Club". Others, including Gülen himself in his capacity as Honorary President of the Journalists and Writers Foundation, in a message sent to the Abant Platform meeting in the European Parliament in Brussels on 3–4 December 2004, have argued that "A Turkey in the EU will more successfully realize its function to establish a bridge between the Islamic world and the West" (Gülen 2004). And all of these debates, in turn, both shape and are shaped by debates more specifically on the nature of the Hizmet movement in its past, present and potential future(s).

Hizmet has been described in a variety of ways by a range of external scholars, commentators and critics, as well as by internal participants. Some, using classical Turkish terminology that was historically utilised in relation to Sufi expressions of Islam, have both described and sought to understand Hizmet in terms of it being a *cemaat* (meaning "community"). Others have argued that such a description does not do justice to the distinctive features of Hizmet. Still others, and especially those seeking to locate Hizmet more in terms of civil society than in relation to the more religious and Islamic, have couched it in terms of "movement" terminology, including debate about the extent to which Hizmet can either be described and/or at least in part analysed and explained as a so-called New Religious Movement and/or by reference to social movement theory (Çetin 2010).

It is the argument of this book that one can, in many ways, best characterise Hizmet as a network of congregants, recordings, books, *sohbets* (or, meetings) that has developed in interactive engagement with the emergence of Fethullah Gülen as a figure who has religiously inspired, intellectually articulated and practically initiated a distinctive action- and reflection-oriented hermeneutic of Anatolian and Sufi-inflected Sunni Islam into a dynamic and organic set of networked initiatives including dormitories (often known as "lighthouses"), schools, businesses, media enterprises, business and other initiatives that have a relationship with one another in terms of mutual engagement, learning and challenge.

In contrast to the approach by many political scientists and sociologists, while an understanding of Hizmet can certainly be enhanced by locating it within its social and political contexts, this book argues that an appreciation of the fundamentally *religious* nature of the origins of Hizmet is of central importance to understanding it. And this religious character has been attested to by those who have from early times been close associates of Fethullah Gülen, such as interviewee Mustafa Öztürk (see Acknowledgements) who, when interviewed, testified concerning Fethullah Gülen that:

> Since he came to Izmir in 1966 – except one period, which is the March 12 1970 military Memorandum and interference – during that time in the 70s, except for seven months he never ever gave up teaching and running the circle with the students of reading the authentic texts of Islam on theology, *hadith*, *sunnah*, jurisprudence, whether they are young students or not according to their understanding.

The richness and innovation of this period as described by Öztürk is described and discussed in Weller 2022 Sect. 2.4. It provided structural opportunities for the realisation of a key part of Fethullah Gülen's vision which concerned the creation and the moving into all parts of society of what he called a "Golden Generation" (Sunier 2014) of young, pious Muslims who were at the same time equipped to engage with the natural sciences and with social modernity. In this one can see the influence of the vision of Said Nursi, the Kurdish Islamic scholar (Mardin 1989; Turner and Hurkuç 2009) since, from the beginning, Hizmet has been characterised by its aim to tackle the three evils of ignorance, conflict and poverty which were initially identified by Nursi.

2.2   TURKEY'S NEED FOR MORE SCHOOLS, NOT MORE MOSQUES

The earliest forms of Hizmet that connected with the wider Turkish society were the schools that were sponsored initially by businesspeople inspired by Fethullah Gülen's articulation of Islam and his radically formulated argument that Turkey had a greater need for the foundation of schools than it did for the building of further mosques. Thus, these schools addressed the first of the three evils identified by Nursi that were taken up as a focus by Gülen and Hizmet, namely, that of ignorance. In time, as graduating students began to move through these schools from primary to secondary levels, an organic need developed for informal, supplementary education support that would better prepare existing students and others wishing to gain entry to higher-level schools and, ultimately, for entry to Turkish higher universities in general, eventually including also to the higher education institutions founded by Hizmet.

According to the Presidency of the Turkish Intelligence Department's, a source not sympathetic to Hizmet 1998 Bulletin 70, under the title of *The Radical Right and Reactionary (Fundamentalist) Activities*, the following schools (*lise*, lyceum) and colleges (*kolej*, college) were among those that were run by Hizmet. These included: İzmir Yamanlar Fen Lisesi, İstanbul Fatih Koleji, İstanbul Safiye Sultan Kız Lisesi, Mersin Yıldırımhan Lisesi, Ankara Samanyolu Lisesi, Van Serhat Lisesi, Denizli Server Lisesi, Erzurum Aziziye Lisesi, Erzincan Otlukbeli Lisesi, Eskişehir Ertuğrul Gazi Lisesi, Sakarya Işık Lisesi, Manisa Şehzade Mehmet Türk Lisesi, Aydın Nizami Erkek Lisesi, and Fatih Üniversitesi (founded November 1996).[1] While in this source the list was deployed as part of an argument against what it identified as a growing cause for concern about the widespread nature of Hizmet's influence, there is no doubt that this commitment to developing educational institutions was foundational and central in the development of Hizmet, again Öztürk explained this by situating it in the wider social and political context out of which Fethullah Gülen developed his commitment to educational opportunity (which wider context is also explained in more detail in Weller 2022, Sect. 2.6):

> If you just look at the 1960s and the '70s at that time it was always the same story, coup d'etats, coalitions, failing coalitions, street fights and skirmishes, and interference of the state apparatus in all government issues and the people, but no matter what happened, Hojaefendi didn't give up his idea of education.

2.3   TURKEY'S DEEP FISSURES, NEED FOR DIALOGUE AND HIZMET RESPONSES

The deep social and political fissures highlighted by Öztürk as having been part of the context for Fethullah Gülen's commitment to educational development were also very much part of the context for Hizmet's addressing the second of the evils identified by Nursi: namely that of disunity and conflict and the need for dialogue as a means of overcoming that. Thus, Hizmet initiatives became concerned with facilitating dialogue in the context of an otherwise ideologically deeply divided Turkish society. In this context, the Gazeteciler ve Yazarlar Vakfı (GYV) or, as it is more internationally known in English, The Journalists and Writers Foundation (JWF), founded in 1994 with Fethullah Gülen as its Honorary President, played a very important role. In 2012, the JWF became the first Turkish institution to be accorded General Consultative Status with the United Nations Economic and Social Council (ECOSOC) which gives NGOs various privileges of access and engagement within the United Nations system, including the right to be represented at designated meetings, and the right to have their documents translated and circulated as official UN documents.

Its Board of Directors made annual Tolerance and Dialogue Awards to public personalities, and the JWF organised a number of regular events, including the International Family Conferences (2010–2016); the Women's Perception Workshop in Media (2011–2016); Cohabitation Awards (2011–2016) and the Antalya Forum (2012–2016) which was held bi-annually by the Dialogue Eurasia Platform (see further below). According to the Forum's preserved historic website,[2] among the topics addressed were Lack of Dialogue and Prejudices; Youth within the Process of Change in Eurasia; Globalization; The Future of Local Cultures in the Process of Globalization; Tolerance and Dialogue in Education; The Role of Media in the Process of Establishing Dialogue in Eurasia; Tolerance and Discrimination in Peace Education; A Meeting of Eurasian Intellectuals; Family as a Value and Rethinking the Global Economic Order.

The JWF largely carried out its work through a number of specifically focused "Platforms". These included the Abant Platformu (or, Abant Platform). Named after a freshwater lake in northwest Anatolia's Bolu Province, it created openings for contact and dialogue between individuals and groups who otherwise had very little, if any, social or intellectual contact (Uğur 2013). Its aim, as stated on its historic website, was:

> To bring together academicians, journalists, civil society representatives and decision-makers from different parts of society to create grounds where polyphony will be resolved. Religious – state relations, education, clash of civilizations, human rights, Alevi and Kurdish issues, and the Middle East were discussed in the Abant meetings.[3]

Many of the early Abant Platform meetings sought to engage especially with the pivotal question for the Turkish Republic of how far, in a society operating within the social and political legacy of the founder of the Republic, Kemal Mustafa Atatürk, but also with a long and rich Muslim civilisational heritage, it might or might not be possible to develop a consensus around the social and political meaning of the "secular" in a way that could be inclusive for all citizens of the Republic (both religious and non-religious). In a context within which social, political and ideological cleavages had developed of a kind that made it difficult for people to communicate in terms of even some basis for a shared understanding of each other's life worlds, the Platform played an extremely important role in building the possibility of social cohesion between people holding at least apparently radically different perspectives, and in laying foundations for a more creative shared future. As interviewee Özcan Keleş (see Acknowledgements) from the UK put it, commenting on the Abant Platform events:

> The best way to judge that is to look at the comments of people who were part of them but were not Hizmet-related: whether they were left or right, they were expressing their shock at being able to share the same room with some of their ideological rivals and arch-enemies. So, it was quite extraordinary and the first few topics were very significant – Islam and secularism; Islam and democracy; and Islam and human rights. And you had a very wide-ranging group of people coming there.

While focused primarily on Turkey, from 2004 onwards the Platform's work expanded internationally, with meetings also being held in Washington, Brussels, Cairo, Erbil and Addis-Ababa. Towards the end of its work in Turkey, the JWF also held meetings under the theme of "Different Perspectives on Turkey" and, following the events of Gezi Park in which protestors clashed with police (for more details see Sect. 4.4), Abant Taksim meetings were also regularly held in Istanbul.

Other platforms of the JWF included the Diyalog Avrasya (or, Dialogue Eurasia Platform, in brief DA Platform) which was founded in 1998 and was taken forward by the platform's broadcaster, *The Dialogue*, as well as by the magazine *DA* (meaning 'yes' in Russian), a Turkish and Russian magazine providing also publications in Kazakh, Kyrgyz and Ukrainian and distributed widely in Eurasia, as well as regional special editions that aspired to be a point of reference for the region in relation to art, history, archaeology, literature, life, global thought, politics, religion and ideas.

The Kültürlerarası Diyalog Platformu (KADİP), or Intercultural Dialogue Platform, was another platform of the JWF. According to its historic website: "The Intercultural Dialogue Platform (GAD) carries out projects that encourage communities of different religions and denominations to create deeper, richer and stronger ties between different cultures or different segments of society" and that "The platform seeks to contribute theoretically and practically to the culture of living with its activities in social, cultural and religious fields by combining communities that are not in dialogue, or who avoid being side-by-side with common themes".[4] For example, in 2015 it held an international panel on "The Compassion of The Holy Prophet (PBUH)" and another on "The Compassion of Hazrat Mary in the Holy Qur'an and in the Book of Holy Book".

The Kadın Platformu (or, Women's Platform) was founded in 2010 not only to engage with issues specific to women (although it included this), but also to bring a female perspective to bear onto wider shared issues with the aim of producing new solutions. The Medialog Platform's historic preserved web page explained about Medialog that it "carries out programs aimed at creating a consensus in the media and spreading principled and accurate journalism within the framework of press freedom, a multivoice in the press, media ethics, democracy and human rights" and that "The platform aims to contribute to the development and solidification of human rights such as freedom of thought and expression, the right to information, information and free criticism".[5] For example, in 2014, in Istanbul, it held a "Turkey-Jordan Media Workshop" and also a "Turkey-Japan Media Workshop", as well as in Moscow, a "Turkey-Russia Media Workshop".

Returning to the Abant Platform, its thirty-fourth and final meeting was held in Bolu between 31 January and 2 February 2016 under the title "The Problem of Democracy in Turkey". Its sessions focused on a range issues noted in the meeting's *Summary and Evaluation Text*.[6] This concluded that "Our democracy is experiencing one of the deepest crises in its history. This crisis consumes human, moral and conscientious values quickly, laying the groundwork for lawlessness and the settlement of one-man rule". The summary also included what eventually turned out to be the somewhat prophetic warning that "We are going through a period where everyone who is seen as opposed to political power is targeted and lynched through the media. These lynchings show that the concept of 'internal enemy', which we have been critical of for decades in our democratization processes, has returned to our lives".

Indeed, immediately following the events of July 2016, the JWF and all its previously associated Platforms were targeted for closure by the Turkish authorities under Decree No. 667 of the National Security Council, dated 23 July 2016. The JWF does, however, continue in renewed international form, now based in New York. Its current website says that it is "an international civil society organization dedicated to culture of peace, human rights and sustainable development"[7] with its main "Working Areas" identified as: Culture of Peace, Human Rights, and Sustainable Development; and its "Projects" identified as She4All; Commission on The Status of Women; Young Peace Ambassadors Academy; Women's Development Summit and UNGA Conference and Reception.

2.4   RELIEF OF POVERTY

Completing the Nursi-inspired triad of education, dialogue and a focus also on the relief of poverty was the Hizmet-inspired initiative, Kimse Yok Mu (in English, Is Anybody There?). As Gülen's close associate, Reşit Haylamaz (see Acknowledgements) explained it:

> This appeared for the first time when we had this huge earthquake on 17 August 1999, when our TV network, STV called on people to help. Thousands of people were killed. Some gave money, some people gave clothing, some people furniture, so they had to organise this under the roof of a relief organization and there came Kimse Yok Mu.

Trust in Kimse Yok Mu was big factor because many people did not have such trust in the Red Crescent organisation, which was widely believed to be corrupt. Therefore, as Haylamaz summarised it:

> Based on that trust, people started opening new branches all over the country and it actually became the biggest relief organization because of the trust our nation had in it. So you can these services actually are emerging out of need. Yes, we cannot ignore the fact that Hojaefendi was certainly involved as the main trigger and the main source of inspiration, and people certainly took courage from his message. But things emerge in the field out there where people decide where we need to invest, or where we need to divert our services to.

By 2002 Kimse Yok Mu had become as an international not-for-profit Humanitarian Aid and Development Organization. According to a promotional video on its historic Facebook site, and entitled, *+40 Things You Didn't Know About Kimse Yok Mu*,[8] by 2015 it had 40 branches in Turkey, with 130,000 registered volunteers, and was working in 113 countries around the world. It had a special disasters team called Asya, which had worked in over 114 disaster zones, using training experts in search and rescue, medical counselling and trauma. Overall, its work included the creation of clean water wells, orphans and orphanages, cataract operations, hospital projects, vocational training for women and schools.

On 4 October 2014, as part of the ongoing tension between the AKP government and Hizmet in this period the Turkish government revoked its licence to collect funds[9] and, as with other Hizmet-related initiatives, in the wake of July 2016, it was closed. On 13 February 2018 it was reported[10] that, on 9 February 2018, arrest warrants had been issued by the Anatolia Chief Public Prosecutor's Office for twenty-one foundation officials linked with Kimse Yok Mu, and of which thirteen had been detained. Since 2010, Kimse Yok Mu, like JWF, had held Special Consultative Status with ECOSOC in the United Nations. Like JWF it has managed to continue in a new form and is now known as KYM International[11] and functions as a non-governmental international humanitarian relief and development organisation.

2.5   BUSINESS LINKS

Given the early role of individual businesspeople in the overall development of Hizmet, it is perhaps not surprising that, in due course, out of the until then seven informal business networks, in 2005, a national business network was established. This was known as TUSKON—the abbreviated Turkish title of Türkiye İşadamları ve Sanayiciler Konfederasyonu (or, in English, the Turkish Confederation of Businessmen and Industrialists). By 2014, it included 7 regional federations which, between them, listed 186 affiliated organisations, of which 90 per cent were small or medium establishments with fewer than 50 employees. Many of the businesspeople involved in TUSKON were linked with Hizmet, and from 2012 it, too, had Special Consultative Status with the United Nations Economic and Social Council, although as with JWF, and Kimse Yok Mu, following representations from the Turkish government, on 19 April 2017 the Council cancelled its membership.[12]

TUSKON engaged in lobbying with decision-makers at the local, regional, national and global levels. As one can see from pictures of its meetings at the time, and reflective of the structures of Turkish society, TUSKON and its affiliates were predominantly composed of male businesspeople. However, out of 186 primary-level member organisations within TUSKON, five of these were specifically businesswomen's organisations, including: the Gaziantep Silk Business Women's Association; the

Kahramanmaras Businesswomen's Association; the Pearl Business Women's Association; the Istanbul Business World and Women's Association; and the Koza Business and Women's Association. TUSKON was already under considerable pressure from the authorities prior to July 2016 with the police, on 6 November 2015, already having raided TUSKON buildings in Ankara, reportedly on the orders of the Ankara Public Prosecutor's Office which was reported to be "investigating crimes against constitutional order".[13] Following July 2016, TUSKON was closed.

Another important example of Hizmet-related initiatives that extended into the business sector was Bank Asya. The bank was established under the original name of Asya Finans Kurumu Anonim Şirketi (Asya Finance Incorporated Company) on 24 October 1996, with its head office in Istanbul. On 20 December 2005, its name was changed to Asya Katilim Bankasi Anonim Şirketi (Asya Participation Bank Inc.). It grew rapidly, and the present author visited its headquarters during a visit to Istanbul in 2008. Recognised for its innovation, AsyaPratik DIT, which was the first pre-paid bank card of Turkey, came into use in 2009. In 2011, Bank Asya received World Finance's award for Best Commercial Bank in Turkey.[14]

However, with the tensions that opened up between the government and Hizmet in the years following 2013, the bank lost a large number of contracts with government agencies. By April 2014, Bank Asya was reported to be facing serious government interference, in particular in relation to its issue of bond debt. In the second quarter of 2014, its net income fell dramatically by 81 per cent. On 25 August 2014, the international credit rating agency Moody's downgraded the bank's status citing "sharp deterioration trends in financial fundamentals".

In early 2015, its top executives were dismissed and replaced with Turkish government nominees and the bank was reported[15] to have been taken over by the Turkish state-run Savings Deposit Insurance Fund, responsible directly to the Prime Minister. Finally, on 22 July 2016 the Turkish Banking Regulation and Supervision Agency (BDDK) cancelled its banking permissions. A year and a half later, action was still being taken against those who had been closely involved with the bank. As reported in the Turkish newspaper, the *Hurriyet Daily News*,[16] forty-nine of the sixty-eight shareholders in Bank Asya were detained across nine cities in Turkey in an operation carried out from Istanbul. According to interviewees for the research behind this book and its companion volume, simply having an account with the bank became grounds for suspicion of links with what the Turkish authorities were by now identifying as FETO.

2.6   THE MEDIA

The media was another area of interface with the wider society into which Hizmet in Turkey extended in relation to what Turam (2007) called Hizmet's "window sites" to the wider world, in comparison with its more internal "private sites". In terms of print media, the newspaper *Zaman* (meaning, time or era) was of particular importance. It was founded in 1986 and, in 1995, was the first Turkish daily newspaper to go online. The paper was printed in eleven countries and distributed in thirty-five, while regional editions were printed and distributed in Australia, Azerbaijan, Bulgaria, Germany, Romania, Kazakhstan, Kyrgyzstan, Macedonia, Turkmenistan and the USA. It originally also had an English language edition, the role of which, from 2007, was taken over by the English language daily newspaper *Today's Zaman*. In 2008 the present author visited its headquarters during a trip to Istanbul. *Zaman* was both very well produced and very popular, becoming the highest-circulation newspaper in Turkey, passing its one million subscribers target in 2011. Although sometimes the accusation was made that its circulation numbers were inflated due to the distribution of free copies, BPA Audits[17] supported its claims and showed that, in Europe, it had one of the largest subscriber bases.

On 4 March 2016, the newspaper was taken over by Turkish authorities,[18] and Abdülhamit Bilici, who had been editor-in-chief since October 2015, was deposed. The front page of *Zaman*'s last edition quoted Article 30 of the Turkish Constitution to the effect that "Printing house, its annexes and press equipment duly established as a press enterprise under law shall not be seized, confiscated, or barred from operation on the grounds of being the instrument of a crime". For two days after the takeover, the *Zaman* website was inaccessible, with a message posted stating that the site was being updated. Archived news and content then became generally inaccessible, although it is now possible to access some historic pages using the *Way Back Machine* internet archive.[19] Government-controlled editions of the paper then followed, in the first edition of which there was no mention of the events relating to newspaper's seizure, while its front page carried a series of pro-government articles and a picture of a smiling President Erdoğan.[20] On 27 July 2016, *Zaman* was closed by the Turkish government under decree No. 668 as published in the *Official Gazette*.

In relation to the broadcast media, Hizmet's presence included the Samanyolu TV which was founded in 1999 as an international Turkish language TV station, with its headquarters in Istanbul. Samanyolu TV's first satellite broadcasts were directed towards Central Asia, but by 1999, it was also broadcasting into the USA, with Turksat as its new mainstream satellite operator. During 2005–2013, Samanyolu TV went into online streaming with the creation of two official websites—one targeted to North American audiences, and the other to Turkish audiences, along with the creation of a range of related social networks such as Twitter, Facebook and YouTube in 2005–2013. The other Hizmet-related TV station, Mehtap TV, began broadcasting on 19 June 2006 via the Turksat 2-A satellite. On 19 July 2016, both Samanyolu TV and Methtap TV's licences were revoked and the channels were closed by the Radio and Television Supreme Council on the basis of their links with Hizmet.

2.7   Spread to "Turkic" Republics of the Former USSR and to the Western Balkans

In the early 1990s, after many of the educational initiatives of Hizmet had become well-established in Turkey itself, wider global events combined to bring about a new opening for Hizmet self-consciously to move beyond Turkey. This was, in the first instance, especially via its educational initiatives in the post-Soviet Turkic republics that emerged out of the collapse of the former Soviet Union (see also Weller 2022, Sect. 2.7).

As explained by close associate of Gülen, Mustafa Özcan, emphasising the contextual situation: "Communism collapsed at that time. This was nothing to do with us but this provided new opportunities, the collapse of the Iron Wall and especially the disintegration of the Soviet Union, provided new opportunities for the community". In relation to this Özcan explained that:

> At that time, neither the Turkish state nor the Turkish intellectuals had … any projects to go to those countries or to contribute to those countries. To convince the Turkish people, then, Hojaefendi said these are our fathers, these are our relatives, these are our kin folks, and these are also (to convince people) saying that they are having the same faith with us. So they have had the suppression and oppression of Communism and they have very limited resources. So now we have to go and help them so that they can stand on their own foot and that they would not be again prone to any imperialistic or exploitative system. From 1989 to 1992, in all his lectures, sometimes he

was really having the true pain of it, and this is shown in his tears. He convinced people to go there, to establish or to help support such projects and initiatives.

As time went on, these post-Soviet Turkic beginnings led to Hizmet volunteers becoming increasingly globally widespread. Emphasising the fundamentally religious motivations of many of those who migrated out of Turkey, even when combined with what were also new business opportunities, the businessman and close associate of Fethullah Gülen, and interviewee, Mustafa Fidan (see Acknowledgements) explained that:

> The Qur'anic message is not only for us, it's a universal message and belongs to everyone. It's a part of the entire humanity, and we may be a means for that message to go across and, for instance, the idea of leaving one's home, it is a Qur'anic prescription. You do move away from your home to migrate as the Prophet did, not just for the sake of growing your business as thousands or perhaps millions of Turks did in the 1960s when they went to western Europe and first and foremost Germany.

Interpreting this migration in terms of the Islamically classical paradigm of *hijrah*, Fidan went on to say:

> I was thinking to myself, this idea of *hijrah*, emigrating away from your home, this is an Islamically virtuous thing to do, because this message you have to carry to other people because those virtues belong to everyone. So if anyone, can they do it really just for the sake of God, so that they can have the pleasure of God, because they don't go only to earn their money, but also go to be there because this is the will of God. And this is why I moved to the US, for these motivations in my heart.

In practical terms these developments happened through Hizmet groups in Turkish cities beginning to sponsor educational initiatives in various "adopted" countries. Citing the participation of the schools in the International Science Olympiads, Özcan said of the sponsoring cities that "they started to compete with their success now" instead of only in relation to the number of schools supported. These schools became popular because, among other things, they taught in English alongside the local language(s), therefore opening up international opportunities to their students. During this period, as noted by Özcan "for a couple of years up to 1995 in these Central Asian countries and a couple of Balkan countries, the number of schools went up to 100" and then it snowballed as it "became such a model for cities, for Turkish people and countries, and Turkish origin people already living in those countries or businessmen, up to 2000, including then schools in Africa and Australia, the number of schools came up to 350 outside Turkey".

Until a certain critical mass was reached, Özcan noted that at that time in Turkey "there was such a competition that the cities and the businessmen were competing almost, you know, how many schools do you have, the neighbouring cities? And even the towns started having one school in those parts of the world, and it becomes a matter of competition". Also, according to the previously noted Presidency of the Turkish Intelligence Department's Bulletin No. 70, in relation to the countries of the former Soviet Union, seventeen institutions were mentioned in Uzbekistan; one university and thirteen secondary schools in Turkmenistan; together with thirty lyceums and one university in Kazakhstan.

More generally speaking, beyond the schools, Gülen's close associate and interviewee Şerif Ali Tekalan (see Acknowledgements) said of Gülen that "Meanwhile, he visited western countries, European countries, Australia and the UK. He regularly updated himself on some details such as methods of explaining some topics, methods of discourse and so on". As time went on, Öztürk said that "Hojaefendi himself is not going but he also asks his students to also go to Europe to start a life in western Europe too".

NOTES

1. Fatih University (https://www.facebook.com/fatihedutr.en/?brand_redir=163510853677769, created 26.02.2016) was founded in November 2016, but closed in July 2016 as part of the Turkish authorities' purge of Hizmet-related institutions.
2. For the Antalya Forum's historic website, see the Way Back Machine for 2.2.2013 at: https://web.archive.org/web/20130202115008/http://www.antalyaforum.org/en/tarihce/
3. The Abant Platform's historic website from 24.4.2016 is accessible at: https://web.archive.org/web/20160424230819/http://www.abantplatform.org/Hakkimizda/Detay/183/Abant%20Platformu
4. Its historic website from 2.3.2016 is accessible at: https://web.archive.org/web/20160302014337/http://kadip.org.tr/Hakkimizda/Detay/62/Kültürlerarası%20Diyalog%20Platformu%20(KADİP)

5. Mediadialog Platform's historic website from 28.3.2016 is accessible at: https://web.archive.org/web/20160328162317/http://www.medialogplatform.org/Hakkimizda/Detay/70/Medialog%20Platformu

6. See its historic website for 31.1.2016, via the Way Back Machine at: https://web.archive.org/web/20160501161016/http://www. abantplatform.org/Haberler/Detay/4202/34%20Abant%20 Toplantısı%20Özet%20ve%20Değerlendirme%20Metni

7. The Journalists' and Writers Foundation current website is at: http://jwf. org/, 2021.

8. https://www.facebook.com/KimseYokMuEN, 8.8.2014.

9. *Hizmet Movement News Archive*, Alí Aslan Kiliç, "Abrupt gov't decision to revoke status of Kimse Yok Mu draws criticism", 6.10.2014. https:// hizmetnews.com/13651/abrupt-govt-decision-revoke-status-kimse-yok-mu-draws-criticism/#.Xs95cEBFw2w

10. *Turkish Minute*, TM, "13 Kimse Yok Mu aid foundation officials detained over Gülen links", 23.2.2018. https://www.turkishminute.com/2018/ 02/23/13-kimse-yok-mu-aid-foundation-officials-detained-over-gulen-links/

11. https://www.facebook.com/kymintl/, 8.6.2010.

12. *Hurriyet Daily News*, Anadolu Agency, New York, "UN body drops consultative status of groups with Gülen links upon Turkish request", 20.4.2017. https://www.hurriyetdailynews.com/un-body-drops-consultative-status-of-groups-with-gulen-links-upon-turkish-request-112216

13. *Daily Sabah*, "Ankara police raid Gülenist business confederation TUSKON over links with FETÖ terror organization", 6.11.2015 https://www.dailysabah.com/investigations/2015/11/06/ankara-police-raid-gulenist-business-confederation-tuskon-over-links-with-feto-terror-organization

14. World Finance, https://www.worldfinance.com/awards/2011-banking-awards

15. *Wall Street Journal*, Emre Peker, "Turkish Authorities Seize Bank Asya," 31.05.2015. online at http://www.wsj.com/articles/turkish-authorities-seize-bank-asya-1433102306

16. On 23.01.2018.

17. Originally standing for Business Publications Audit of Circulation Inc.; is now BPA Audits of BPA Worldwide https://www.bpaww.com/about/, 2021.

18. BBC News, "Zaman newspaper: Defiant last edition as Turkey police raid", 5.3.2016. https://www.bbc.co.uk/news/world-europe-35735793

19. https://web.archive.org/

20. SBS News, "Turkish paper prints smiling leader pic", 6.3.2016. https:// www.sbs.com.au/news/turkish-paper-prints-smiling-leader-pic

References

(All web links current at 20.11.2021)

Aydın-Düzgit, Senem (2012). *Constructions of European Identity: Debates and Discourses on Turkey and the EU.* Basingstoke: Palgrave Macmillan.

Çetin, Muhammed (2010). *The Gülen Movement: Civic Service Without Borders.* New York: Blue Dome Press.

Gülen, Muhammad Fethullah (2004). Ataturk's Contemporary Civilization Aim Reaches a new Horizon with EU. *Zaman,* 12th April.

Mardin, Şerif (1989). *Religion and Social Change in Modern Turkey. The Case of Bediüzzaman Said Nursi.* New York: New York State Press.

Presidency of the Turkish Intelligence Department (1998), *The Radical Right and Reactionary (Fundamentalist) Activities,* Bulletin No. 70.

Sunier, Thijl (2014). Cosmopolitan Theology: Fethullah Gülen and the Making of a 'Golden Generation'. *Ethnic and Racial Studies, 37* (12), 2193–2208. https://doi.org/10.1080/01419870.2014.934259

Turam, Berna (2007). *Between Islam and the State: The Politics of Engagement.* Stanford: Stanford University Press.

Turner, Colin and Hurkuç, Hasan (2009). *Said Nursi: Makers of Islamic Civilization.* London: I.B. Tauris.

Uğur, Etga (2013). Organizing Civil Society: The Gülen Movement's Abant Platform. In Greg Barton, Paul Weller and İhsan Yılmaz (Eds.), *The Muslim World and Politics in Transition: Contributions of the Gülen Movement* (pp. 47–64). London: Bloomsbury.

Weller, Paul (2022). *Fethullah Gülen's Teaching and Practice: Inheritance, Context and Interactive Development.* Cham: Palgrave Macmillan.

CHAPTER 3

Hizmet in European *Hijrah*

3.1 HIZMET AT EUROPEAN LEVEL AND ACROSS EUROPE

Prior to this book there has been no single-authored book-length treatment of the development of Hizmet across Europe, although Çelik, Leman and Steenbrink, eds. (2015), and Weller and Yılmaz, eds. (2012), are edited English language collections of chapters that focus on Hizmet in Europe. The former has chapters on Hizmet in France, Germany, the Netherlands, Northern Ireland and the UK, while the latter has chapters on the historical development of Hizmet in Belgium, France, Germany, the Netherlands and the UK, together with some brief consideration of Romania, Bosnia, Kosovo and at more length, albeit focusing on educational institutions alone, Albania.

Yükleyen and Tunagür (2013) have a book chapter that discusses Hizmet in Western Europe in comparison with Hizmet in the USA, while Sunier and Landman (2015) have authored a book that examines Hizmet within an overall discussion of other transnational Muslim movements of Turkish Muslim origin active in Europe. These include larger organisations and networks such as the Diyanet; the Süleymanlıs; the Millî Görüş and the Alevis, but also the smaller organisational umbrellas at European level of the AÜTDK (Avrupa Ülkücü Türk Dernekları Konfederasyonu, or Confederation of Idealist Turkish Associations—known, in short, as the European Turkish Confederation); the Milliyetçi Haraket Partisi (MHP, or National Movement Party); the Avrupa Türk Birliği (ATÍB, Turkish

© The Author(s) 2022
P. Weller, *Hizmet in Transitions*,
https://doi.org/10.1007/978-3-030-93798-0_3

Islamic Movement in Europe) and the Kaplan movement now expressed in the Islâmî Cemiyet Cemaatlar Birliği or ICCB, Union of Islamic Associations and Communities.

With regard to Hizmet's network in western Europe, Yükleyen and Tunagür (2013) gave an estimate of around 40,000 "participants and sympathisers" (p. 224). This, they explained, was based on numbers of *Zaman* subscribers in Europe at the time of writing. (p. 230). They also estimated a total of 300 educational and interfaith dialogue initiatives in Germany and the Netherlands alone (p. 225). According to Sunier and Landman (2015), although taking the overall position that "There is little information about the size of the movement in Europe" (p. 90), they expressed the judgement that "Hizmet is probably the most successful in establishing a genuine network of activities across borders" (p. 88).

Prior to, during and after the Hizmet's intentional activities in founding schools in the Turkic former Soviet Republics and the Western Balkans, Hizmet had been present in Western Europe. In the first instance this was connected with the post–Second World War Turkish labour migration to help rebuild the devastated Europe, as a consequence of which the profile of those first migrants was generally similar in the different countries, largely reflecting those who were less well educated and looking for work in manual labour (Abadan-Unat 2011).

As Tekalan explained it, "In the early 1960s, Turkish people had gone to work especially in European countries. And unfortunately, the first generation didn't get to high school, college. After completing their primary school education, they started working as their fathers". In this context, Gülen started challenging young teachers to go to France, Germany and other European countries. Primary, secondary and middle school children were initially reached through small cultural centres in these countries and the importance of going to high school and college was impressed upon them. In the course of what he described as visiting "almost every European country", Tekalan said, "I've observed the congestion in the education system of young people. They were having big problems, unemployment, domestic problems, some of them. But after these young people came to our cultural centres and contacted our friends, their interest in education increased". As Tekalan put it:

> The courses given in these cultural centres such as mathematics, physics and chemistry were the cause of these children to go to university. The intervening time passed, the children who went to university graduated and they

wanted to spread this system in Europe, Germany, France and Switzerland. The students who graduated from universities were now engineers, doctors and more.

Generally speaking, however, fewer schools were founded in Europe than in Turkey, which needs to be seen in the context of Tekalan's observation that, in comparison with Turkey, "some things are too expensive". More generally, of Gülen himself in the 1970s, Tekalan said that "Meanwhile, he visited western countries, European countries, Australia and the UK. He regularly updated himself on some details such as methods of explaining some topics, methods of discourse and so on". As time went on, Öztürk said that "Hojaefendi himself is not going but he also asks his students to also go to Europe to start a life in western Europe too". Operating for Hizmet today on a European, and especially (but not exclusively) European Union, level is the Dialogue Platform.[1] The anonymous interviewee, HE1, who is publicly associated with Hizmet in Europe, explains that the Platform was, in fact, originally "founded in 2000 to promote inter-faith dialogue in Belgium and they did a lot of inter-faith activities for more than five years all around Belgium". However, on the basis of reflecting on its work and its increasing knowledge of Belgian society "they came to the conclusion that, in Belgium, there a lot of people who do not have a faith. Therefore, they decided to change the name and change the mission into a more inter-cultural dialogue one so that the activities might be more appealing to other people who don't have faith". Indeed, under its former Director Ramazan Güveli, the Platform had already decided that, given its location in Brussels, there was a strong need for a Hizmet interlocutor on the level of European institutions such as the European Parliament, the European Commission and also the Council of Europe. As interviewee HE1 explained it, "Of course, after 2016, after the coup attempt, I think they were most active for being the mouthpiece of Hizmet and also Fethullah Gülen in Brussels".

The Platform's website explains about itself that it is "a platform of Hizmet inspired dialogue organizations in Europe" and that it is:

A non-profit organization located in Brussels. The association acts as a mouthpiece for the European dialogue organisations associated with the Hizmet (a.k.a. Gülen movement). The platform also serves as the main information channel of Hizmet and Fethullah Gülen, who is the honorary president of the association. Inspired by the teachings and example of the

Muslim/Turkish scholar Fethullah Gülen, these organisations aim to advance and promote intercultural understanding, dialogical interaction and social cohesion in their respective societies. While each partner organisation retains its institutional independence, the Dialogue Platform supports coordination among them to ensure the exchange of best practice and experience. It also works to give a louder voice at the EU level of the initiatives carried out by its partner organisations. Dialogue Platform, moreover, fosters debate and analysis on various issues concerning a peaceful and respectful coexistence in European societies. By so doing, it aims to make practical contributions to the decision-making processes on relevant developments and issues impacting on community relations in Europe.

It notes that the Platform is especially interested to develop ideas and projects in relation to the fields of "Social and Community Cohesion"; "Citizenship and Democratic Engagement"; "Identity and Intercultural Understanding"; "Inter-Faith Dialogue and Religious Studies"; "Muslims in Europe"; "Peace-Building and Diplomacy"; "Education and Youth". From the list of the Platform's partner organisations, one can gain a good, although not fully, comprehensive sense of the range of Hizmet-related organisations in the European continent listing, as it does, organisations in Belgium, Denmark, Germany, the Netherlands, Spain and the UK as "our partners", as well as noting other dialogue organisations in Europe linked with Hizmet including (see Sect. 3.11 in this chapter) Austria, the Czech Republic, Hungary, Poland, Portugal, Slovakia and (see Sect. 3.6 in this chapter) Switzerland.

Since July 2016, in common with many Hizmet organisations in Europe, the paid staffing base of the Intercultural Dialogue Platform has shrunk in size because of the reduction in funds flowing from Hizmet-supporting businesspeople in Turkey such that by 2019, the Platform had only three people working for it. However, the Platform has not been the only Hizmet-related organisation working on a cross-European level. There has also been the European Professionals' Network,[2] founded in 2009 and also based in Brussels (Hazırlyan ed. 2012, pp. 58–59), and of which interviewee HE1 explained: "That association was actually promoting professional life, promoting students to have a professional occupation and also promoting the professionals with migrant backgrounds in both their private and professional lives". There was also UNITEE—The New European Business Federation[3]—that was created in April 2011 and linked national federations and member associations representing entrepreneurs and business professionals from among the "New Europeans" across all major sectors of the European economy, including in Belgium, Denmark, Germany, the Netherlands, Norway, Sweden and the UK.

3.2   HIZMET IN THE NETHERLANDS

People began migrating from Turkey to the Netherlands in the early 1960s, with the Dutch government signing a "recruitment agreement" with Turkey in 1964. Among Muslim religious groups of Turkish origins, the Süleymanlı community was, in the early 1970s, the first to open mosques and to provide Qur'an courses for children (van Bruinessen 2013). However, from the late 1970s onwards, mosque associations supported by Turkey's Presidency of Religious Affairs (Diyanet) increasingly developed. Following the 1980 coup in Turkey, part of the leadership of the politically Islamist Millî Görüş movement moved to Germany, from which base they developed a European-wide mosque-based network including in the Netherlands. In response, the Diyanet tried to exert influence through a network of state-sanctioned mosques and congregational centres. In the Netherlands (as in Germany) this resulted in a significant number of conflicts around the control of mosques. As a by-product of this, Islam in the Netherlands developed quite an extensive range of institutional actors (Canatan 2001; Doomernik 1995; Yükleyen 2012). In relation to this, as van Bruinessen notes, "The GM was a latecomer to this scene" (van Bruinessen 2013). Nevertheless, the Netherlands was also one of the earliest locations for the development of Hizmet in Europe.

Key scholarly publications that trace the history and activities of Hizmet in the Netherlands include Van Bruinessen's (2013) article on "The Netherlands and the Gülen Movement" and Steenbrink's (2015) book chapter on "Gülen in the Netherlands Between Pious Circles and Social Emancipation", while Peppinck's (2012) book chapter discusses aspects of the communication to, and reception by, the wider Dutch society of some of the key aspects of Gülen's teaching. Among other publications on Hizmet in the Netherlands are Canatan's (2001) doctoral thesis that examines matters of organisation and leadership within Turkish Islam in the Netherlands, including some discussion of the Hizmet movement. From a position hostile to Hizmet in the Netherlands there is a dossier compiled by Fähmel (2009).

Today there are a large number of organisations in the Netherlands that are associated with Hizmet. These include the educational foundation Cosmicus;

the entrepreneurial association HOGIAF[4] (Helpt Ondernemers Groeien in Alle Facetten, or Helping Entrepreneurs to Grow in all Aspects); the Kennisplein (or, Knowledge Place) educational centres; the *Zaman Today* and *Zaman Hollanda* newspapers; and the charitable organisation Time to Help. One of the key Hizmet organisations is the dialogue-focused Platform INS.[5] This is based in Amsterdam and was founded in 2012, having emerged out of a previous Foundation Islam and Dialogue that was originally established in Rotterdam in 1998. The name "INS" derives from the Arabic word *'iinsan* (meaning person or human being), of which the website of Platform INS explains that "InS is about what people can do together and how we learn to understand the art of living together".

Platform INS is registered in the Netherlands as a Public Benefit Institution. According to its website, its overarching purpose is that "we see it as our goal to counter the divisions in society and to join forces with everyone who also wants to contribute to this". To achieve this, Platform INS focuses on the aim to "Facilitate meeting between people who don't normally meet"; through serious engagement to "Establish the dialogue in an attempt to get to know each other in depth"; and through co-operation to "Establish partnerships and work together to solve shared problems". Having engaged in dialogue over many years, the Platform is now seeking to break out of the circle of dialogue with only like-minded people into establishing a dialogical engagement with those that, in Dutch, it describes as *andersdenkenden* (or, as often translated into English, "dissenters").

For its governance, Platform INS has a Board consisting of a Chair, Secretary and Treasurer, whose names are published on its website and an Advisory Board which the website explains "meets several times a year" and "advises Platform INS on the policy", while noting that this advice in "not binding". At the time of writing the organisation had four paid positions: a Director, a Programme Manager, a Public Relations Officer and a Communications Officer. It advances its work through "Friends" who volunteer and can give money and who, its website notes, are active in twenty-six cities in the Netherlands, as well as through "Partners" who share in collaborative planning and initiatives.

A key interviewee in relation to the developmental history of Hizmet in the Netherlands is Alper Alasag[6] (see Acknowledgements) from the Netherlands *overleg* which, as Alasag explains, is "the group which comes together every couple of weeks to discuss things about Hizmet. *Overleg* means coming together and discussing things and then taking decisions".

Reflecting on the development of Hizmet in the Netherlands, Alasag says that "Hizmet started here in the late 1970s. When Gülen came to Germany, he met some people and they asked him to send an *imam* who would tell the same way how they can integrate in the society and be a part of it as a Muslim". As he recounts it, this was because although the people very much warmed to Gülen, "Gülen was sent by Diyanet only for Ramadan and he went back". In response to this, Alasag recalls that Gülen "asked a friend of his, Necdet Başaran" if he was willing to go and stay in Düren, a city in the German state of North Rhine–Westphalia close to the border with the Netherlands.

However, the original plan encountered difficulties because, as recalled by Alasag, there were differences of opinion in the Düren mosque arising from the fact that "Gülen was part of Diyanet, part of the system". Therefore, although "Başaran was not sent by the Diyanet" but rather "It was Fethullah Gülen's own request", in the end Başaran had to leave the Düren mosque. From what might be called this "false start", Alasag said of Başaran that "if I remember it correctly he went to Brussels and then he came to Holland" and when in Schiedam, near Rotterdam, he "had some people from his own town in Turkey, so they helped him and he was giving lessons to their children, Qur'an lessons, and he was preaching". Alasag noted that, from this base, by the beginning of the 1980s, they had rented "a small place where they could preach but also give lessons to the children". Therefore that, with regard to the origins of Hizmet in the Netherlands, "it started in this way".

The organisation that was founded in 1981 was called the Akyazılı Foundation (named after the institute founded by Fethullah Gülen in Izmir, in 1972), and of which Yükleyen and Tunagür (2013) note that it "had its own prayer hall open to the public" (p. 228), but also that within a year the focus of its work was changed to that of education only. What is also clear from Alasag's testimony is the wider role played by Başaran in the early European development and networking of Hizmet. As Alasag put it "Başaran had been to many places so people knew him". Therefore, just as in Schiedam in the Netherlands:

> The same was also in Belgium. In Brussels was also a dormitory. In Ghent was also one. And in Germany, in a couple of places, like in Düsseldorf, in Köln, there were small places where people came together to read. So, they rented 100 square metre rooms where they could come together and read books etc.

To this Alasag added that "There were also people from Switzerland". Başaran was clearly a nodal point in this developing network in relation to which, as Alasag explained it, "They were all coming to Holland, because Holland was a kind of centre because Başaran was living in Rotterdam. All came to Holland to visit him".

When he himself first arrived in the Netherlands in 1989, Alasag recalls that what Hizmet consisted of at that point was "people coming together reading books, listening to the sermons of Gülen, and engaging with children. And dormitory for youngsters, helping their homework, giving extra lessons, and helping each other. So that was the Hizmet". Building on that, Hizmet people began to take other kinds of initiatives which, in 1989, included the development of the first dormitory in the Netherlands in relation to which Alasag notes that "The dormitory in Rotterdam was also bought with the money of all these people from these countries, as well. So, they contributed. It was not only a Dutch initiative. It was the first Hizmet initiative, so people supported it from all over Europe".

From the beginnings of this dormitory, "In 1990, the *dershanes*, student houses started. And it spread very quickly. In the first year there were, like, six houses. At the end of the third year eleven, and then it was thirty-three, and then it was more up to one hundred or so". At the same time, "people were coming to Rotterdam visiting and saying we would also like a dormitory". One of the unforeseen consequences of such growth in the number of dormitories is that the number of *dershanes* reduced, partly because "All the students who kind of had the ability to talk to other students and help them out—who could be a role model and could work in the dormitory—they went to the dormitories to help in this initiative". In summary, Alasag's evaluation was that:

> This dormitory was a kind of an answer in the Dutch context, because the dormitory gave the children the possibility to have a good education and integrate in the Dutch society, and this was a good solution for the parents who were kind of afraid that they lose their identity. Because we are Muslims the parents were trusting us their children, if they wanted to pray, or whatever their needs were for their education, they could get all the help they wanted from us, and also that we would guide them and help them in the Dutch society in the schools and in other areas of the society.

In fact, the idea of these dormitories became more widely inspirational in Europe beyond the Netherlands with Alasag saying, "I know that in the

1990s and in the beginning of the 2000s, even from Germany, even from Belgium, from different municipalities, people were coming—the local government were sending people to see this initiative and to promote it in their own municipality". And in the Netherlands itself "it was appreciated and so much so that, in the mid-2000s, these initiatives had received money from the government, as a support and appreciation, to improve the conditions of the dormitories". This was because, at the time, "other groups were sending their children still to Turkey" which was largely because:

> The parents who couldn't speak Dutch, and didn't know the Dutch society very well, and came from a lower class, from a village for example, and didn't have a good education, they couldn't control or help their children. So, they were anxious and afraid that the children would do drugs or whatever, and they couldn't protect their children from such things. So, they were sending their children to their families in Turkey. In all different levels of the society Turkey was seen as a kind of remedy, or solution for how to take care of our children.

As Yükleyen and Tunagür noted in their 2013 chapter on the movement in Western Europe, there were at that time seven student dormitories co-ordinated by the Landelijk Overleg Schoolinternaten (LOS). From these beginnings in the 1990s, other educational initiatives began to take shape because the community was "getting bigger and bigger each year and had other needs than only taking care of the children". As Alasag recalls it, one of the first was "a business association for the Turkish businessmen" and that "after that came a student organization" and then,

> In the second part of the 1990s they came together and also opened platforms. So, there were national platforms for education, for student initiatives, for business associations or whatever. Some of them like Business Association was national, and then opened departments in different cities, smaller initiatives. Some of them were local and then opened platforms.

From the relatively early times of Hizmet in the Netherlands there had also been dialogue initiatives. Thus, Alasag recounts that "People think that dialogue had started in the 1990s. It isn't true". Rather "when the Muslim people from different countries and asylum-seekers and other immigrants came here, the Churches took the initiative and tried to involve all those Muslims in these dialogue settings". What, however, many in the Christian Churches who took part in these early initiatives discovered was that:

> They couldn't find many people who were willing, apart from the Dutch people who became Muslims. So, they were kind of representing the Muslims in the dialogue. And the only group who took part in dialogue besides the Dutch people—or Surinami people, or the Indonesian people who were already integrated and knew the Dutch society and could speak Dutch—the only group as immigrants was as far as I know, our group in the 1980s, and in the 1990s, it continued.

Again referring to his personal experience in 1989, when he first arrived in the country, "there was an interfaith group which came together every couple of months in the church and sometimes in our centre". In the Netherlands, there has been a long history of engagement with religious difference that was traditionally framed within the historical model known in the Dutch language as *Verzuiling* (often translated into English via the rather clumsy word, "pillarisation"). In the early days of increased religious diversity, there were attempts to "stretch" this historic tradition in order also to accommodate Islam and Muslims (Rath et al. 1997). Commenting on the legacy of *Verzuiling* Alasag noted that "Now it is weaker" but that, nevertheless, "In Holland, inter-faith dialogue is a way of living, because half of the population is Catholic and the other half Protestant, and the Protestants are also divided".

Out of this active early "pre-history" of Hizmet dialogue in the Netherlands, Alasag noted that in 1989 the organisation Islam and Dialogue emerged, which he described as "the only active Muslim dialogue organization in Dutch society which was engaging in dialogue in Dutch". Its growth was exponential, with Alasag reflecting that, "when we started in 1998, immediately thirty-five organizations with which we were in touch came to us and they said let's organize something. In the next year it was around seventy. And in the year after 9/11 it was three hundred". The impact of the 9/11 terror attacks on the USA and their aftermath meant that there was an increase in demand from the wider society for reliable dialogue partners. Alasag attributes this successful development to the fact that "we could give information in Dutch, and had our documents in Dutch, and we were willing to engage in dialogue".

Among the range of organisations that emerged in the mid-2000s was, as also happened in many other European countries, the previously mentioned business association HOGIAF, set up in 2006. However it was the opening of a Hizmet school which Alasag characterised as being a watershed moment to the extent that "when the school opened, everything changed". As Alasag describes the history of this, "In 2006, the students' organization came into contact with the Ministry of Education and asked that they done so many things in the field of education, if it isn't time to open a school". The context for this was that in the Netherlands the majority of schools are so-called "charter schools" which means that if one has an educational vision it is, in principle, possible to open a school based on that vision using public funding. In this context:

> Our student association, its name was Cosmicus, they had developed an educational vision on world citizenship. So, on that vision they approached the Ministry to open a school and the Ministry received this very openly and very positively. But some civil servants advised to open the first school with another educational organization, a Dutch one, as a co-operation. So, it opened with another Dutch school in co-operation.

What was important about this for Hizmet's wider development in the Netherlands was that this school was not only for Hizmet children. However, due to this initiative Hizmet found that it had come into wider public view and scrutiny including, from some quarters, opposition. In this context, uniquely in Europe, a whole period of successive investigations (see Sect. 5.2) into the nature of Hizmet followed which, in turn, stimulated a range of responses concerned with transparency (see Sect. 5.4) out of which Alasag says that because of what he calls "the Dutch dynamic of pushing" in the end "we became more Dutch and part of this dynamic. We played the game according to its rules. I feel because of all these developments of the last twelve years, I feel myself more Dutch, more integrated, and a part of this society than before. So, it helped us". Indeed, overall, it was Alasag's view that "The dialogue had helped us, but this process helped us a lot more". Therefore, in summary, through all the suspicions and scrutiny, their experience had been that "the more negative was the news about us, the more positive were the results. The bigger the accusation, the more positive the reaction was from the society, and also from the government".

3.3   Hizmet in Germany

People of Turkish background from Turkey itself, but also from the Balkans and from Cyprus, together form the largest minority ethnic group in Germany, and Germany has the largest population of people of Turkish origin outside of Turkey. Following West Germany's so-called *Wirtschaftswunder* (or, economic miracle), the construction of the Berlin Wall in 1961 led to a fall in the number of labour migrants from the former East Germany. Therefore, on 30 October 1961, the West German government signed a labour recruitment agreement with Turkey. Soon after that, German employers pressed the government to end that agreement's original two-year limitation on workers staying in the country. In 1974, the introduction of family unification rights led to a large increase in the number of people of Turkish origin. After German re-unification in 1990, and subsequent outbreaks of violence against *Ausländer* (or, foreigners), an intense social and political debate took place that led to the gradual acceptance of the principle of Germany being a multi-cultural society, with many people of Turkish origin becoming German citizens.

The Turkish Islamic organisational scene became quickly developed in quite an extensive way, with a range of institutional actors (Doomernik 1995; Yükleyen 2012). These include the Türkisch-Islamische Union der Anstalt für Religion e.V. (Turkish-Islamic Union for Religious Affairs)[7] often referred to as the DİTİB (after the initial of its Turkish name of Diyanet İşleri Türk-İslam Birliği), founded in 1984. With its headquarters being at the Cologne Central Mosque in Cologne-Ehrenfeld, it funds many of the mosques in Germany. There is also the Zentralrat der Muslime in Deutschland (Central Council of Muslims in Germany).[8] Other important Turkish Muslim organisations include the Islamische Gemeinschaft Millî Görüş,[9] which is close to the Islamist Saadet Partisi in Turkey and has its base in Kerpen near Cologne. There is also the Jamaat un-Nur, Deutschland, which is the German branch of the Risale-i Nur Society; the KRM, Co-Ordinating Council of Muslims[10]; and the DIK, the Deutsche Islam Conference.[11] Finally, there is the Deutsche Muslimische Gemeinschaft,[12] which is primarily composed of Arab Muslims and is close to the Muslim Brotherhood. Finally, beyond the boundaries of Sunni Islam, there is the Islamische Gemeinschaft der schiitischen Gemeinden Deutschlands (IGS)[13] which links Shi'ite mosques and associations in Germany.

In relation to the emergence of Hizmet in Germany, key publications that trace this include Karakoyun and Steenbrink's (2015) article on "The Hizmet Movement and Integration of Muslims in Germany", while there is also Emre Demir's web article on "The Gülen Movement in Germany and France".[14] Demir's (2012) book chapter on "The Emergence of a Neo-Communitarian Discourse in the Turkish Diaspora in Europe" covers both France and Germany in its discussion of "the implementation strategies and competition logics" of the movement, while Agai's now more dated (2004) book on *Zwischen Netzwerk und Diskurs: Das Bildungsnetztwerk um Fethullah Gülen* (or, *Between Network and Discourse: The Educational Network around Fethullah Gülen*) focuses primarily on Hizmet-related educational initiatives in Germany (and Albania). In relation to more recent developments, there is Koçak's (2019) magazine article on "Hizmet und die Flüchtlingsfrage in Deutschland: Initiativen aus dem Raum Mitteldeutschland" (or, in translation by the present author, "Hizmet and the Refugee Question: Initiatives from Middle Germany").

Already in the early 1970s Gülen had travelled to and within Germany. According to Öztürk, this was Gülen's "initial encounter with the western world". As previously noted, this visit was organised by the Diyanet in Turkey which traditionally arranged someone as an official imam to travel and preach to the Turkish faithful during the month of Ramadan. According to another of Gülen's close associates, he returned to Germany again during Ramadan in 1977.

According to Ercan Karakoyun (see Acknowledgements), who is a key interviewee in relation to the developmental history of Hizmet in Germany, "when the first people of Hizmet came to Germany, of course at that time everything was very much Turkey orientated". Initially there was a largely invisible informally networked and associational structure. However, "In the 1990s, the first institutions were founded in Germany: tuition centres, dormitories, so-called 'lighthouses', and after that of course many people who were born in Germany became engaged and active in the Hizmet movement". As an anonymous Hizmet-related asylum-seeker interviewee AS1 (see Acknowledgements) from Turkey, and who had previously worked in Germany after finishing his education in Turkey, explained it:

> I got acceptance from German universities and I attended one of them and I stayed four years in Germany. During that time in Germany, in so-called Nachhilfe Centers belong to the Hizmet Movement, I was a volunteer and

I tried to teach the migrant children. This was in the Baden-Württenberg region. I was generally in Offenburg, Freiburg and in Stuggart. I tried to teach the children English and to help in their maths/mathematics problems. And, in free times, we also made some social activities, always trying together with them to be a good model for them.

Today in Germany there are a wide range of organisations and initiatives that are associated with Hizmet. As often the case elsewhere, many of the early initiatives were educational ones, with Yükleyen (2012, p. 50) noting that, at the time of his writing, there were around 200 tutoring centres in Germany. Building out from these individual educational initiatives were bottom-up organisational fora for the sharing of experience. Similarly, in relation to business, in 2009 eight historically separate individual associations merged to become the BUV, Bundesverband der Unternehmervereinigungen (or Federation of Entrepreneurs' Associations, Germany), which now links around twenty bodies under its umbrella.[15]

In the field of dialogue, various associations that had begun from 2001 onwards were linked under the umbrella of the Bund Deutscher Dialog Institutionen (or, Federation of German Dialogue Institutions)[16] which today consists of fifteen member organisations. These include the Forum für Interkulturellen Dialog (or, Forum for Intercultural Dialogue), in Berlin (which Karakoyun was tasked to found in 2008), and of which Karakoyun says, "You can say it is one of THE dialogue institutions in Berlin". It also includes the Forum Dialog[17] (or, Dialogue Forum) formed from a number of dialogue organisations from different Germany Bundesländer coming together in 2015. These include FID RLP e.V; Forum für Interculturellen Dialog e.V., based in Frankfurt am Main[18]; Forum Dialog Schleswig-Holstein; Idizem: Interkulturelle Dialog e.V; Idizem: Interkulturelles Dialogzentrum e.V, in the Munich area[19]; Idizem: Interkulturelles Dialogzentrum e.V. Nord Bayern; AID e.V.; Ruhr Dialog e.V.[20]; Gesellschaft für Dialog Baden-Würtenburg Region Ulm; Gesellschaft für Dialog Baden-Würtenburg Region Stuttgart; Gesellschaft für Dialog Baden-Würtenburg Region Manheim; Forumdialog Hamburg; Forumdialog Kiel; Forumdialog Niedersachsen.[21]

The Society for Education and Promotion of Non-Profit GmbH (GEBIF),[22] which especially aims to work with school leaders, teachers, trainees and pedagogical specialists in the school and pre-school sector, organised International Conferences on Peace Education in 2013 and 2015. The Federation has also sponsored a number of projects on its collaborative level such as, in 2013 and 2014, the German Dialogue Awards, while since 2015, it held an annual Dialogue Akademie.[23] In 2019, this met around the same theme as the sixth *Materialen zu Dialog und Bildung* (author translation: *Materials for Dialogue and Education*), namely that of "Group-Related Hostility". Previous Akademies focused, in 2018, on "Gender Justice and Empowerment: Current Discourses and Strategies"; in 2017 on "Freedom of Thought, Conscience and Religion in the Immigration Society"); in 2016 on "Extremism Prevention" and on "Turkey-Germany Relations"; and in 2015 on "Universal Values and Youth Work". Another initiative of the Federation was (the until 2015 so-called) German-Turkish Cultural Olympiad. Starting in 2013 and developing quite quickly from having only seventeen participating countries, what is now known as the International Festival of Language and Culture[24] involves 145 countries with more than 2000 participants.

There is also the Islam Kompact—Muslims Tell,[25] that was initiated by the Bund Deutscher Dialog Institutionen, but with participation also from Ruhr Dialog, which aims at profiling factually sound information about Islam and Muslims; Tulpe,[26] a platform for youth and family, founded in 2007 and based in Essen; *die Fontäne*,[27] the German language edition of Hizmet's *Fountain* magazine, published since 2008 by Main-Donau Verlag GmbH, based in Frankfurt am Main, and serving a German language readership of over 20,000 people across Germany, Austria and Switzerland; and the VHS: Volkshochschule Leipzig, a municipal further education college.[28]

Among the wider projects in which the Federation is collaboratively involved through the work of its partner organisation, the Muslim Dialogue Initiative Forum Dialog e.V., is the so-called House of One in Berlin,[29] and of which Karakoyun is an Advisory Board member. This works together with the Evangelical parish of St. Petri-St. Marien (which initiated the idea), and the Jewish Community of Berlin in conjunction with the Rabbinical Seminary Abraham-Geiger-Kolleg. As stated on its website, this is intended to be "A house of prayer and exchange about religions – open to all". It is a grassroots project that aims to build under one roof a synagogue, a church and a mosque, with each built around a central space for encounter. In this regard at least, it has some resonances with Haus der Religionen—Dialog der Kulturen,[30] based in Bern, Switzerland.

In terms of Hizmet's public profile on a national level in Germany, the Stiftung Dialog und Bildung (or, Dialogue and Education Foundation),[31] which was founded in 2015, has come to fore. As Karakoyun (who has been its chair since the beginning) explained, it was founded "with the aim to be something like a spokesperson for the Hizmet movement in Germany because there were very critical newspaper articles in Germany about Hizmet and then we decided to make a step towards transparency in Germany". Nevertheless, as Karakoyun clarified its role: "The Foundation is not the 'roof' of all institutions, but it speaks in terms of ideas and values of the Hizmet movement. So, I don't speak for a special institution, or for different institutions, but for the idea that is behind all institutions, so for the idea of Hizmet". Or, as the Stiftung's website puts it:

> The foundation provides information on Hizmet's origins, development and activities in Germany, as well as on the ideas and work of Fethullah Gülen. If necessary, it provides contact with educational associations, dialogue initiatives, business associations, or refugee initiatives on the ground. In particular, the media and the political and social public are invited to enter into dialogue with the Foundation. The foundation advises and mediates scientific studies on Hizmet in Germany and serves as an important contact person, especially for scientists.

The Foundation publishes a magazine, *Materialen zu Dialog und Bildung* (or, for short DuB, in English, *Materials on Dialogue and Education*).[32] The six editions of this, up until the time of writing this book, have been on the themes of: Gülen and Democracy[33]; Interreligious Dialogue[34]; Hizmet and Education[35]; Hizmet and Universal Values[36]; Responsibility and Engagement in Hizmet[37]; and Group-Related Hostility.[38]

In recent years in Germany, both vertical and horizontal organisational structures have developed, with the vertical ones professionally co-ordinating the voluntary commitments to particular areas of work, such as dialogue, in what aspires to be a transparent way. Horizontal networking exists in three state associations, which embrace all Hizmet associations across all topics in each of the states of Nord-Rhein Westfalen, Baden Wurtenburg and Berlin. These are the Verband engagierte Zivilgesellschaft in NRW e.V (Association of Committed Civil Society in NRW e.V.) in Nord-Rhine Westfalen, founded in 2014 and with over sixty member organisations[39]; the Landesverband für bürgerschaftliches Engagement e.V. (State Association for Citizenship Engagement)[40] in Baden-Württemberg, now with over forty member organisations;[41] and the

Verband für gesellschaftliches Engagement (Association for Social Engagement) in Berlin, founded in 2014 by bringing together around twenty organisations from the capital and the surrounding areas.[42] Hessen, Bavaria and North Germany do not yet have any registered associations but there are state-level meetings, and leaders from all these structures now meet together in a Hizmet Germany working group where the focus is on the mutual exchange of knowledge and experience.

3.4 Hizmet in Belgium

Systematic migration of what were originally Turkish "guest workers" in Belgium originally began when, in 1964, Turkey and Belgium signed a mutual agreement. The majority came from rural areas of central Anatolia, especially from Afyon, Eskisehir and Kayseri. Following settlement in Belgian industrial areas, when Belgium began to encourage family reunion as part of addressing its challenge of a low population growth, many also brought their families. In the 1970s, many Turkish people came on tourist visas and stayed to find work, with the Belgian government improvising to regularise their status on a number of occasions. Early on in this period associations were founded that focused on language, folklore, cultural, educational, funeral and, to some extent, religious needs. In the 1970s, students, intellectuals and trade unionists who had fled from Turkey's fractured and often violent left-right conflicts established themselves especially in university cities such as Gent, Liège and Brussels, with their associations focused primarily on the politics of Turkey.

By the 1980s, primary migration was no longer possible, but only for family reunification or as an asylum-seeker, a number of whom (including Kurds) came from Turkey itself, while others were ethnic Turks from Bulgaria or Macedonia. By this time, Turkish civil society organisations began to emerge that were more concerned with forging their future within Belgium, a process that accelerated by the 1990s. This included catering for religious needs. Religiously speaking, the majority of people of Turkish Muslim background in Belgium are Sunni Muslims, with the Millî Görüş and Süleymanci groups predominating, but also with a Nurcu presence and the official Diyanet, which controls most of the Turkish-related mosques in Belgium. In terms of legal identity, the Diyanet in Belgium dates back to 1983. It was originally known as the Turkish Islamic Religious Foundation of Belgium; then as the Turkish International Islamic Religious Association of Belgium; and is now known as the

International Diyanet Association of Belgium. Until 2018, an attaché of the Turkish Embassy presided over it.

Beyond the Sunni Muslim presence in Belgium there is also an Alevi one, while following Bulgaria's entry into the European Union, the numbers of people of Turkish heritage originating originally from Bulgaria increased still further. In relation specifically to the development of Hizmet in Belgium, Leman's (2015) book chapter on "Belgium's Gülen-Hizmet Movement Histories, Structures and Initiatives" provides a useful overview, while an important historical source for this book has been the interviewee, Özgür Tascioglu, the Secretary General of the organisation, Fedactio (Hazırlyan ed. 2012, p. 14), who explained that:

> In the 1990s, the first people of Hizmet came to Belgium and they started to unite with each other to form a Turkish community. There were three problems here within this new generation Turkish community in the 1990s: education, integration and identity-forming. So, the second and third generation was a bit torn between their Belgian and their Turkish identity. That's why Hizmet created education centres to help people with this process. Within a few years, with the support of businessmen these educational centres became schools.

For example, on 1 September 2005, L'école des Etoiles (or, School of the Stars) opened as a primary school started by some Turkish entrepreneurs, parents and teachers (Hazırlyan ed. 2012, pp. 46–49). However, such was the parental demand for places, the school moved into new and larger, former industrial premises in Haren. From 2007, it linked also with the L'école L'Avenir (School of the Future) in Charleroi, and then became known as L'école des Etoiles de Charlerois. Today, its website states that it is "a free non-denominational school open to all" that "is subsidized by the Wallonia-Brussels Federation", being "subject to the decrees and prerogatives set by the Federation and respects its curriculum". Also, "It respects all philosophical and religious convictions, leaving parents free choice of philosophical courses that will be given to their children".[43] In 2012, it was able to open the secondary education College of Stars, also on the Haren site. In 2014, the School of the Stars of Liège was started in Chênée, while a College of Stars was also added to the Charleroi site. Overall, the Star School Centre now operates with a total of 1000 students and 45 teachers in 5 separate schools. Its vision is one of global education built around intellectual, personal and social development.

Alongside education as a major focus, businesspeople of Turkish origin were also concerned with dialogue between the Turkey and Belgium, and in 1996–1997, the Belgian-Turkish Entrepreneurs' Association was formed by twelve businessmen operating in various Belgian cities. In 2008, the Association supported the establishment of Prisma, an after-school supplementary education and youth centre based in Schaerbeek (Hazırlyan ed. 2012, pp. 50–51). In 2008, the Association came together with other organisations that had "similar missions like Unaco, Uniekon, Ashea, Mercury, Action, and the European Professional Network", in a general assembly to federate as the Betiad, the Federation of Active Entrepreneurs[44] (Hazırlyan ed. 2012, pp. 40–45). Betiad today offers services to around 1200 entrepreneurs through six associations which are based in Brussels, Charleroi, Limburg, Gent, Antwerp and Liege. Betiad, in its turn, started a dialogue with other organisations and groups and, on 30 May 2010, twenty-five organisations active in various fields came together across Belgium under the name of Federation of Active Organizations—Fedactio.

Fedactio's website states that "Together we want to encourage all citizens to actively participate in society and we strive, amongst others, for a more democratic and inclusive society" and that towards such an end "it initiates, encourages and supports meaningful projects on different domains such as women's rights, education, social cohesion, multiculturality and interreligious dialogue".[45] In relation to ethnicity and religion, the website states that "Fedactio is not an ethnic organization. Although Fedactio has its roots in the Turkish community, the organization directs its activities towards all Belgian citizens", and also that "Fedactio is not a religious organization, but our founders derive their motivation from their faith. As an organization, Fedactio adopts an independent and neutral approach".

Nevertheless, Fedactio acknowledges that "Initially, our founders were drawn to one another by their shared sense of responsibility towards society, inspired by the ideas of Muslim-intellectual Fethullah Gülen". At the same time, it also makes clear in relation to "the Gülen-movement" that "The movement is represented by 'Dialogue Platform' and not by Fedactio". With regard to the ideals of Hizmet, interviewee Özgur Tascioglu from Belgium (see Acknowledgements) says that "Fedactio endorses the most important ideals conveyed by the Gülen-movement, among which are the combat against poverty, ignorance and conflicts", but with regard to the people involved in Fedactio:

They are not only Hizmet people, they are also community volunteers. For example, all the Gülen schools in Belgium are schools funded by the state and most of the Directors are Belgians. So, the founders and the people who support it financially are inspired by the Gülen movement, but the schools in themselves are funded and implemented by the state.

Tascioglu explained that, at the time of the interview, in September 2019, Fedactio had forty-five affiliated organisations across six cities. Its way of working is that "we co-ordinate and mostly work together on concrete projects. Sometimes we do different co-ordinations on projects and then we communicate around them". In relation to its affiliates "We share the same objectives but Fedactio has a more global approach than the local organizations. Fedactio has also been founded from the outset to showcase its members' activities". Tascioglu's role helps to develop new projects and to co-ordinate Fedactio's regional managers in the different cities of Belgium where Fedactio is based, namely: Antwerp, Brussels, East-Flanders, Hainault, Liège and Linders.

Before becoming Fedactio's Secretary General, Tascioglu had been a regional co-ordinator in Charleroi in Belgium. Prior to migrating to Belgium in 2016, he had worked as a journalist for the *Zaman* newspaper in Switzerland. In summary, Tascioglu explained Fedactio as follows: "Fedactio is like an umbrella federation for different organizations and was started in 2010. It works mainly on educational and multi-cultural projects and also inter-religious dialogue projects. It has different platforms and each platform initiates different projects which they work on". Its Platforms originally included Culture, Arts and Media; Education and Youth; Entrepreneurs and Professionals; Social Cohesion and Dialogue; and Woman and Society (Hazırlyan ed. 2012, pp. 28–37). They are now structured as Art and Culture; Education; Entrepreneurs; Professionals; Social Cohesion and Dialogue; Solidarity and Human Aid; and Youth. Among the large number of organisations still operating today under these Platforms are those noted below, albeit that in addition to these were also many others that no longer exist, hence giving some idea of the organisational range and vitality generated under Fedactio's umbrella.

The Art and Culture Platform includes: La Tulipe, a cultural initiative oriented towards neighbourhood level togetherness and based in Charleroi,[46] Liège[47] and Mons[48] (Hazırlyan ed. 2012, pp. 92–93). The Education Platform includes: BS—Belgium Student Platform, which was founded in 2011 as an umbrella organisation for Oxgyene Plus in Brussels;

Academic Vision in Antwerp; Synergy in Ghent; Integraal from Limburg and Uniwaal from Wallonia, which came together (Hazırlyan ed. 2012, pp. 54–57). BS is now based in Brussels, Antwerp,[49] Limburg[50] and Charleroi (Hainault) and Liège; Compass Onderwijs en Begeleiding scentrum (or, Compass Education and Guidance Centre) founded in 2004 (Hazırlyan ed. 2012, p. 78) in Willebroek, Antwerp; Francolym piades,[51] based in Brussels and has organised a range of educational Olympiads for French-speaking children (Hazırlyan ed. 2012, pp. 68–69).

Meridiaan Gemeenschaptscentrum vzw[52] (or Meridiaan Community Centre) is based in Gent and was originally founded in 1999 as a supplementary education centre, in 2010 merging also with the Gouden Generatie (Golden Generation) association becoming the Gouden Meridian (Hazırlyan ed. 2012, p. 80), and then in 2016 further merging with three other non-profit organisations in Aalst, Sint-Niklaas, Zele to extend its original educational and youth work also into socio-cultural and charitable works. Then there is also Prisma, an education and youth centre providing supplementary education, based in Brussels, and founded in 1998 (Hazırlyan ed. 2012, pp. 50–51); Turkse oudervereniging in België (or, Belgian Turkish Parent Association), based in Brussels, Antwerp and Limburg (Hazırlyan ed. 2012, pp. 70–73); Vlaamse Olympiade Vereniging (or Flemish Olympiad Association) which has organised science, mathematics and social science Olympiad competitions for children (Hazırlyan ed. 2012, pp. 66–67). Finally, there is Vuslat Gemeenschaptscentrum[53] (or Vuslat Community Centre, the Dutch word *Vuslat* meaning "come together, find each other") with its head office in Hasselt (Limburg), but also having centres in Genk, Maasmeschelen, Heusden and Beringen, all in Limburg.

The Entrepreneurs Platform includes Betiad, the Federation of Active Entrepreneurs, based in Brussels, but also present in Antwerp, Charleroi (Hainault), Liège and Hasselt (Limburg).[54] The Social Cohesion and Dialogue Platform includes Academie New Generation[55] education and youth centre (Hazırlyan ed. 2012, p. 74), which was founded in 1996, is based in Merksem, Antwerp, and provides supplementary tutoring for primary and secondary school–age children; ASBL Dialogue,[56] established in 2008 and based in Charleroi (Hazırlyan ed. 2012, pp. 98–99); Beltud, the Belgian-Turkish Friendship Association, founded in 2010, based in Brussels (Hazırlyan ed. 2012, pp. 60–63), and also represented in East Flanders in Gent, in Antwerp and Limburg,[57] and in Hainault, where it is present under the Francophone name of Cedicow—Centre pour la

Diversité et la Cohésion en Wallonie and was founded in 2008 (Hazırlyan ed. 2012, pp. 96–97); Vlaams Intercultureel Dialoog, Gent began as a resource for religious and spiritual needs and an information centre for those interested in Islam (Hazırlyan ed. 2012, p. 82); and, finally, the Vuslat Gemeenschaptscentrum which are also part of the Education Platform (for further details see above).

The Women and Society Platform includes the Golden Rose[58] that supports women's participation in the wider society (Hazırlyan ed. 2012, pp. 52–53). This was founded in 2009 by eighteen women and has over two hundred active members, with bases in both Brussels and Hasselt (Limburg). It also includes Inspiration,[59] launched in 2009 and based in Antwerp (Hazırlyan ed. 2012, pp. 76–77); and Khoza,[60] based in Gent and founded in 2005 (Hazırlyan ed. 2012, p. 84). The Youth Platform includes For Youth,[61] based in Brussels and Antwerp and the BS—Belgium Student Platform, which is also part of the Education Platform.

Among Fedactio's projects are Colours of the World,[62] an international music, dance and poetry festival that is under the patronage of UNESCO, and is run in Belgium by Fedactio in partnership with its member organisation Beltud[63] (Association d'Amitié belgo-turque/Vereniging voor Belgisch-Turkse Vriendschap, or Association for Belgian-Turkish Friendship). Beltud was founded in 2010 with an aim of promoting dialogue and of strengthening friendship between different communities living in Belgium and especially Belgian-Turkish relations. Iftarmee[64] is a national project in which non-Muslims are welcomed by host families to share in Iftar meals during Ramadan. Then, in the field of education, there is SOWO[65] (Sociale wetenschappen Olympiades, or Social Science Olypiads) for pupils of third-grade secondary education; Pangeawiskundequiz[66] (or, Pangea Mathematics Quiz); as well as the Tekenwedstrijd: Kunst van het samenleven[67] (or, Art of Co-Existence Drawing Contest). Overall, the diverse work of Fedactio is promoted via its own YouTube channel.[68]

An important institutional presence of Hizmet in Belgium is that of the Gülen Chair at the Catholic University of Leuven, established in 2010. Interviewee and scholar at the University, Erkan Toğuşlu, from Belgium (see Acknowledgments, section 1), is responsible for this, while at the same time having a voluntary role in Fedactio. In relation to this voluntary role, Toğuşlu said:

I sometimes helped to co-ordinate the dialogue activities and social cohesion activities under the Fedactio umbrella. So, what I do is organise some of the events, for example, with other colleagues within Fedactio, for the whole of Belgium: what kind of activities can we organise; what we need; what the movement needs. So, these are some of the activities in which I take part for almost six or seven years, from the beginning of Fedactio.

With regard to the Gülen Chair, Toğuşlu explained that it is a joint initiative between the Intercultural Dialogue Platform and Leuven University and that:

They came together from before 2010 to establish a kind of Chair or research unit to do some research on, especially Islam and Muslim countries living in Europe, specifically in Western Europe. This was the basic idea because at that time still, I think, Islam became a hard topic, and nowadays as well. But the specialists of the university discovered that there wasn't such a unique programme or research centre that focused specifically on Muslim communities, or on Muslim participation in social, political and economic life in western Europe, so there was a need. And in that sense they thought that the Gülen movement may be a good partner and also interlocutor, as they are coming from the Muslim community, they know the field, and they are very active in education as well.

Toğuşlu went on to further explain that, at its beginning, three specific areas of research were emphasised. These were dialogue or social cohesion between Muslim communities and the wider society; the economic participation of Muslims, and specifically of Muslim entrepreneurs; and, finally, Muslim women. As the Chair developed and other issues emerged, new foci around radicalisation and the media have also been added. Within this overall framework, the Chair organises lecture series and international conferences; it publishes books with the Leuven University Press; and it publishes its own journal, *Hizmet Studies Review*, the inside covers of which state that it is:

A scholarly peer-reviewed international journal on the Hizmet Movement. It provides an interdisciplinary forum for critical research and reflection upon the development of Fethullah Gülen's ideas and Gülen Movement (Hizmet movement). Its aim is to publish research and analysis that discuss Fethullah Gülen's ideas, views and intellectual legacy and Hizmet Movement's wider social, cultural and educational activities.

Every year the Chair has tried to secure one new PhD student that it can financially and educationally support in various different departments within its Faculty at KU Leuven. The Chair is based in the social sciences, but it also invites theologians, professors from law and the political sciences, and people from the media to explore and explain the issues and/ or current debates around and between Islam and contemporary Muslim communities. The collaboration is based on an agreement which is reviewed every five years.

3.5   Hizmet in the United Kingdom (UK)

The majority of people of Turkish origin in the UK live in England and came from Turkey for employment, with others coming under the 1963 Ankara Agreement, as updated in 1973 and which made permanent residence in the UK more flexible and possible for Turkish businesspeople. In the case of the UK, though, because it was the former colonial power in Cyprus, there is also a long-standing strong Turkish Cypriot presence, especially in London, which especially developed between the 1940s and early 1960s. In relation to Hizmet's development in the UK, Fatih Tedik has an historical web page on "The Gülen Movement's Initiatives in Britain",[69] and the present author has a book chapter on "Hizmet in the United Kingdom" (Weller 2015), although in practice the chapter focuses primarily on England. This, to a large extent, also reflects the geographical concentration of the wider Turkish diaspora which has historically generally provided the core impetus for Hizmet initiatives.

In relation to Hizmet in England, there is a short book by Sanaa El-Banna (2013) that illustrates its overall discussion and argument about Hizmet as a new type of social movement with special reference to both Turkey and England, although in practice the part of the book concerned with England is more narrowly and specifically focused on London. This, again, reflects the geographical concentration of the Turkish-origin population within England itself and is complemented by a more recent journal article from Caroline Tee (2018). From a position hostile to Hizmet and published by SETA, the Ankara, Turkey-based Foundation for Political, Economic and Social Research, there is a report (Bayrakli et al. 2018) that is focused on Hizmet in the UK.

In relation to the province of Northern Ireland, Jonathan Lacey wrote a book chapter on "An Exploration of the Strategic Dimensions of Dialogue in a Gülen Movement Organization in Northern Ireland" (Lacey

2012). Here, the Hizmet-related Northern Ireland Tolerance, Educational and Cultural Association was founded as a limited company in 2016. On the UK Charity Commission's website, the Association's offices were recorded as being in Belfast and the charity's objects were described as being:

> For the advancement of reconciliation or the promotion of religious or racial harmony or equality and diversity for the public benefit by any lawful means but including the following: (1) For the benefit of the public to advance and promote inter-cultural, inter-communal dialogue, understanding and appreciation in NI. (2) For the benefit of the public to encourage, undertake, sponsor and contribute towards academic research, work and publication that relates to inter-cultural, inter-communal dialogue in NI will contribute either directly or indirectly towards advancing appreciation and understanding of cultures, communities in NI. (3) To advance the education of students in NI with a view of providing them with help and support towards their academic studies, helping them forge partnership academic work projects, encouraging them to support ongoing projects of the organisation and overall encouraging them to contribute towards raising interest in inter-cultural dialogue studies.[70]

In 2018, the limited company associated with this initiative was dissolved, but on the island of Ireland, there is now also a new development called Eire Dialogue (see further below under Sect. 3.11). In relation to Wales and Scotland, nothing substantial has so far been published concerning Hizmet activities there and, indeed, until recently, Hizmet has had very little organised activity in these countries. However, in Scotland there is a Glasgow-based initiative called the Nurture Educational and Multicultural Society. This was originally founded in 2004, and, in 2015, it acquired a substantial former listed church building together with a sports hall, offices, manse and grounds which, however, needs substantial refurbishment before it will be possible to run a full range of activities within it.[71]

In relation to the developmental history of Hizmet in the UK, a key interviewee is Özcan Keleş (see Acknowledgements). He explained that "It was 1993 or 1994 or thereabouts, I think when Fethullah Gülen came here twice. At the time, in 1994, we know definitively that Axis Educational Trust was founded, which is a Gülen-inspired educational entity". According to Keleş, one of the first things that Axis[72] did was to purchase a large house in Finchley, North London, that they used as a hostel at which Gülen stayed when he visited the UK in 1994. Inspired by the examples in Turkey, people in London wanted to create an educational initiative. But because developing a school was such a big challenge, they initially took over a lease on Seven Sisters Road to start English language courses, tuition courses and IT classes. This was done in the hope that these educational initiatives would, in due course, transition into a school and, in 1996, the Trust created the London Meridian College Primary and Secondary School. Although a private school, in order that it could maintain access for children whose families were struggling financially, it charged a relatively modest fee. Partly as a by-product of this, the school did not prove financially sustainable and the initiative was therefore put "on hold".

As Keleş explained, in this period, much of Hizmet's developmental work depended on people who came to the UK from Turkey on Turkish Interior Ministry scholarships to do doctorates and they created an Academics' Association. However, unlike the *Fountain Magazine*, which was also an early activity that survived and grew internationally, the Association did not survive and, with this, what could be seen as the first phase of Hizmet development in the UK came to an end.

For much of the time Hizmet has been active in the UK, a key organisation within it has been the Dialogue Society, a registered charity established in London in 1999.[73] The Society currently organises its work around three main fields: the academic, the community and policy outreach. It has the key aims of advancing social cohesion by connecting communities; empowering people to engage; and contributing to the development of ideas on dialogue and community building, all of which it does primarily by bringing people together through discussion forums, courses, capacity-building, publications and outreach.

From its origins, the Society projected its self-understanding as being neither a religious nor an ethnic organisation. It aims to facilitate dialogue on a whole range of social issues, regardless of any particular faith or religion. Unlike in the Netherlands, the Dialogue Society in the UK, despite its name, has not had such a focus on inter-religious dialogue, or even cross-cultural dialogue, though neither was excluded. Of this, Keleş recalls:

> I was much younger then and I was involved in the first meetings and I remember how we were discussing logos, and the name. And then it was

quite interesting actually how when we discussed specifically whether we should call it the Inter-Faith Dialogue Society and immediately there was a consensus that we shouldn't do that because it would be too narrow, and that it may evolve. So, I mean that was interesting to see that we were able to discuss that at the time. So, we had this more expansive idea of the Dialogue Society.

Nevertheless, in Keleş' evaluation, "we went through this period of decline which he put down to there have been "no community-building". In recognition of the need to address that, between 1999 and 2007, the majority of the Society's work focused on community dialogue, a significant part of which was, nevertheless, related to inter-faith activity. This included the organisation of an annual "Essentials of Peace Conference" which focused on the exploration of common themes and characteristics among the Prophets of the Abrahamic religions of Islam, Judaism and Christianity. Between 2004 and 2007, the Society also sponsored a significant number of Whirling Dervishes events as well as fast-breaking dinners, the latter of which included hall-based events by invitation and also marquee events in city centres that were open to the public. Inter-faith picnics were organised and also Noah's Pudding activities that consisted of encouraging people to visit and share Noah's puddings with their neighbours. Although detailed records were not kept at the time about the earliest events, further information about many of these activities can be found in a chronological listing on the Dialogue Society website.[74]

Overall, this early phase of the Dialogue Society's development was characterised by many initiatives that were valued in terms of local engagement, but were limited in terms of broader impact. Thus, Keleş (in Weller 2015) has said that "By 2008 we came to the realization that although we were doing a lot of community work, we needed to diversify our work to achieve greater impact" (pp. 245–246). This growing recognition had already led to the organisation, in 2007, of an international academic conference on the movement, held in the UK Parliament's House of Lords, the London School of Economics and the School of Oriental and African Studies, about which Keleş explained that "it enabled us for the first time to work together in one space as a team for an extended period of time" (in Weller 2015, p. 246). In Keleş' view, this conference was "one of the watershed moments" for the Society's development. As Keleş explains, this was partly motivated by:

by our attempt to tell people who we were, and what we were about. We believed then, and most of us continue to believe now, that this a good thing. Part of it was motivated about transparency. So it was, that was if you like, the 'coming out' of the movement in the UK in the 2000s.

Meanwhile, local Dialogue Society initiatives had been emerging, and between 2010 and 2011 a number of local groups, including those from Leeds and Southampton, began meeting with the London-based Dialogue Society and each other to share ideas and good practice. They were joined by the Midlands Dialogue Forum. Together with groups in Bristol, Durham, Hull, Leicester, Manchester, Northampton and Oxford, and other groups that had been organised in the south of England, they ultimately came together on the basis that many of their activities thematically overlapped and that resource efficiencies could be gained, with the London Society acting as what might be called an "umbrella" for Dialogue Society branches throughout England.

In relation to what by then became the clear transparency of connection between the Dialogue Society in its various manifestations and Gülen (see Sect. 5.4), Keleş notes that such an approach also informed the creation of what eventually became Voices in Britain[75] which was the stage in Hizmet's development to which this author's previously published work on Hizmet had reached by the time of its publication (Weller 2015). However, the initial origin of Voices was earlier with, for example, the organisation's logo having been created in 2011 following the start of consultative meetings that took place in 2010–2011 under the name of Voices. A Voices Twitter account was opened in June 2012. Voices became public in a 2015 letter that was sent to the then Prime Minister, the Home Office and the Department for Communities and Local Government, and which referenced it as having been created in 2013.

As already noted earlier in this chapter, in the UK as in many countries, Hizmet started with trying to meet the educational needs of migrant families of Turkish origin, as with the work of the pioneering Axis Educational Trust (which is also now part of Voices) and which was founded in 1994 in support of the provision of supplementary education. In 2006, the Trust sought to continue its work with the founding of the Wisdom School as an independent and non-denominational mixed sex school in Tottenham, north London, at which Keleş taught for a short period until they found a qualified teacher. In 2010 Axis transferred responsibility for the school to a new and specifically dedicated company limited by guarantee and registered charity. As the school grew, the charity purchased a former police training building in Hendon, North London, which opened in September 2014 as the North London Grammar School.[76]

Among other educational initiatives within Voices is the Lighthouse Education Society,[77] a charity based in south London which, through branches in Welling, Croydon, Peckham and Tooting, is working to enable and empower young people through education, especially via sponsorship of supplementary schools, mentor training, parenting support and educational consultancy. There is also the Amity Educational Foundation,[78] in north London, which is focused on the educational needs of children and young people from disadvantaged backgrounds; and the Spring Educational Society which has branches in Birmingham, Leicester and Northampton.[79]

In support of young people's development is Mentorwise UK,[80] a London-based, UK-wide organisation that aims to support disadvantaged teenagers and young adults in building their confidence and improving their life skills, opening them up to a wider range of opportunities and allowing them to explore different life choices in their education and careers, and their personal lives. Mentorwise focuses not just on young people (mentees) but, in addition, aims to support their parents, carers and educators. Also with a role in support of education but with, in addition, a wider remit to contribute to social integration, is the Fellowship Educational Society.[81]

In contrast to the other educational and dialogical initiatives outlined above, the names of which do not signal either their "Turkishness" or their "Muslimness", the Anatolian Muslims Society[82] clearly articulates its orientation in both its name and its aims. These aims include those of supporting the British Muslim community through cultural and religious work, and the wider society through intercultural events and projects. Its activities include public seminars, vacation camps, trips, weekend schools and relief work. The Society has been a registered charity since 2004 and perhaps unusually for a Hizmet organisation in view of Gülen's original injunction to focus more on the building of schools rather than of mosques, in 2008, it founded the Mevlana Rumi Mosque and Community Centre[83] in Edmonton Green, North London.

The mosque, which was the first mosque in the UK to appoint a female head, was named in honour of the thirteenth-century Anatolian Sufi master Mevlana Rumi. In due course it changed its name to the Mevlana Rumi Mosque (Contemplation and Learning Centre for Community). By making this change, it wanted to place more of a focus on its attempts to reinvigorate and facilitate the implementation of Rumi's Islamic teachings of love, empathy and engagement rather than on Rumi as an historic individual personality. In functioning as a mosque, the building aims to address the urgent need for quality services and education of the British Muslim community in London. However, it also works as a centre for dialogue, proactively seeking to facilitate grassroots social cohesion, and approximately a thousand people use the Centre's facilities each week. It is therefore an example of how, via a division of labour among various Hizmet-related organisations, it is possible also to address the more distinctively Turkish and more specifically Muslim needs, although in this instance even this is done in a way that does not only have a narrow communalist focus.

Perhaps even more unusually than the mosque, Voices in Britain has made more visible and transparent one of the historic basic building blocks of Hizmet, namely the *sohbets*—which are fundamentally concerned with Hizmet religious learning and spiritual activities. In the context of Voices in Britain, the Sohbet Society[84] has been formed to formalise and make transparent this fundamental Hizmet activity alongside the more "outward-facing" initiatives that are better known to the general public. *Sohbet* is a Turkish word which means to talk, converse, discuss and engage with one another in a friendly, caring, warm and informal manner. In the context of Hizmet specifically, the word *sohbet* is used to mean conversing with one another in a study or discussion circle on the big questions of God, purpose, meaning, faith, religion and society. This is pursued through a series of activities including study groups, mentoring, outreach, retreats, excursions and social action. The Sohbet Society's website explained that its *sohbets* are categorised by age (including for adults and for teenagers); by gender (for men and women separately, while under development is one for married couples to attend jointly); by profession (e.g. business people, students and other professionals, perhaps teachers or medical staff); by level (including advanced-level *sohbets* for more studious participants) and by language (currently *sohbets* are provided in Turkish and in English).

Completing the triad of Hizmet concerns with education, dialogue and the relief of poverty is another member organisation of Voices in Britain, Time to Help,[85] which is a registered charity founded in 2013, and which has a current main focus on orphan help, refugee help, homelessness and water. Working in relation to human rights matters, including those of Hizmet people who have had to flee from Turkey, is London Advocacy. Also in the UK is the Centre for Hizmet Studies[86] and the Turkey Institute.[87]

The Centre for Hizmet Studies is, on its website, described as being "founded by a group of individuals who have both researched Hizmet at a Doctoral level and who are personally inspired by Hizmet's teachings and praxis" and that it aims "to facilitate, as well as present, critical analysis of Hizmet for both academic and popular audiences". The Turkey Institute describes its work as being supported by benefactors who "include London based business people with a Turkish background some of whom affiliated with the Hizmet movement". It is based in London and, on its website, describes itself as a "centre of research, analysis and discussion on Turkey" especially for "policy-makers, the media and other relevant stakeholders to enable a more nuanced and thorough understanding" of Turkey.

3.6   HIZMET IN SWITZERLAND

Labour migration of Turks to Switzerland started in the 1960s and Islam in Switzerland is much more ethnically varied than in Germany. However, when the Turkish Muslim Millî Görüş was established in Germany, a number of Turks in the German-speaking parts of Switzerland joined it. At the same time, others adhered to the mosques and initiatives of the Diyanet İşleri Türk İslam Birliği. As in Germany, Suleymancilar and Nurcu communities are also present in Switzerland.

A key interviewee in relation to the development of Hizmet in Switzerland was Ramazan Özgü (see Acknowledgements) who grew up in a working-class neighbourhood, in a family that originated in the labour migration from Turkey. Özgü's father—who was a community worker—was not active in Hizmet beyond going to *sohbets*. However, in common with many parents from Turkey who arrived as *Gastarbeiter* (guest workers) he thought it important to send his children to Hizmet educational initiatives in order for them to improve their life chances. Now a lawyer, Özgü personally benefitted from the *Nachhilfezentrum*—(supplementary school centres) that were a feature of Hizmet's early organisation and activity in Switzerland, as in other European countries. While these *Nachhilfezentrum* originally focused on Turkish children, Özgü notes that "a few years later in the 1990s, there came also many immigrants and many asylum-seekers from the Balkan states, like Albania, Bosnia and the others. And after that, many of these students were also from these countries". As Özgü explained it, "I was the only one student in the community who could study in law", which he did at the University of Zurich before going on to do a master's at the Catholic, Donau-Universität in Krems, close to Vienna, Austria.

In time, Özgü became active in Hizmet and now, as he says, "I am responsible for dialogue activities in Hizmet and I am also responsible for law questions and for asylum-seekers and I am also active in the Swiss media, giving interviews". In addition, and interestingly, with regard to the relationship between the formal and informal aspects of leadership within Hizmet, he explains that "I am also part of this informal network that we call *abis*, and I have a region in the vicinity of Zurich of which I am the co-ordinator. I am part of this community there and I am the so-called *abi* of this region and also active in this informal part of Hizmet". That Özgü has roles in both the formal and the informal parts of Hizmet is important in terms of understanding the development of Hizmet in Switzerland, as in other countries. In relation to the origins of Hizmet in Switzerland, as Özgü explains with regard to the workers who had arrived from Turkey, "The most important thing about Hizmet in Switzerland" is that "It was a movement founded by workers in Switzerland" and that "They had an informal network here, you know these *sobhets*. These were all informal. They didn't have any formal organizations here". Overall, they were "just workers who came together and read the books from Said Nursi and Fethullah Gülen, and they also watched his preaching".

Unlike in Germany and the Netherlands, Gülen himself was never in Switzerland, although as Özgü noted that there were indirect connections: "There were these *abis* connected with him, but I don't think they were directly connected to him". In this early period of Hizmet development in Switzerland, the links to Turkey in many ways went primarily through Germany because Hizmet in Germany had more of a "direct connection to Turkey". According to Özgü, the first formally established Hizmet organisation in Switzerland was set up in 1992 and was called the Hüdavendigar Vakfi Foundation. In 1994 the name was changed to the German name: Stiftung SERA—Stiftung für Erziehung, Ausbildung und Integration (or, Foundation for Education, Training and Integration). This remains active today[88] and according to Özgü "has many projects with the state here in Switzerland", especially in the Canton of Zurich. One of these was the EKOL: Bildungszentrum für Nachhilfeunterricht und Gymnasiumvorbereitung (or, Educational Centre for Tutoring and High School Preparation)[89] that opened in 2003. Another was the private secondary SERA Schule (or, SERA school), opened in 2009. Both of these worked successfully until the impact of July 2016 meant that they had to close because significant numbers of parents, anxious about the potential implications of themselves and/or their children being associated with Hizmet, withdrew their children. As commented on by Tekalan, who had visited Switzerland in 1981–1982, "This is very new: before everyone wanted to send their children to these schools".

Özgü explains that while, in the early days, Hizmet was concentrated in Zurich, SERA was also active in Torgau, in Bern, in Argau and in the other Cantons. Nevertheless, until around 2002–2004 "the people from the other Cantons came to Zurich" for meetings and for inspiration and organisation. Then, "After that, in many other Cantons they also founded their own associations and foundations. In Basel there were two associations, in Bern also two associations, also in Lausanne and in Geneva, there were also two associations". In terms of links between Hizmet initiatives, contact with Zurich became gradually more informal. As Özgü explained it, "just one person came now to this 'main meeting', and all the other people did their stuff in their own Canton". In fact, this development was entirely consistent with the Swiss value of *Kantönligeist* in which each Canton is almost a distinctive nationality. At the same time, Özgü notes that despite their contextual differences, there is a commonality in that they are "all active in inter-religious dialogue".

At present in Switzerland, despite the existence of these informal linkages, there is no formal umbrella organisation. As Özgü noted, "In Switzerland, Swiss law doesn't say that you have to found an association to come together or make anything together. There are other forms to do that. Also, the associations don't have to be in a register in Switzerland. Association law is very free, very liberal". But there is an ongoing connection through the Interessengemeinschaft für Universelle Werte (IGUW), or Consortium for Universal Values, founded in 2017.

3.7 Hizmet in France

The volume of Turkish labour migration to France was not as great as it was in Germany, the Netherlands and Belgium and, overall, the Muslim presence in France has a much more "Arabic" than "Turkic" public profile. Arising from this there have been corresponding differences in relation to the development of Hizmet in France. On this, a key interviewee was Asen Erkinbekov (see Acknowledgements), originally from Kyrgyzstan and who, at the time of the interview in November 2019, had been living in France for around fifteen years, having originally arrived there to undertake his master's and doctoral studies. He has worked in the Plateforme de Paris,[90] founded in 2005, which Erkinbekov described as "an organization which does inter-cultural and inter-faith dialogue programmes in France". These programmes include the Trophée du Vivre Ensemble (or the Living Together Trophy), which was created in 2014 and aims to reward and support initiatives that promote living together, social cohesion, cultural mix and inter-generational mix within four main fields, namely Technology and Media; Human rights, Plural identities, Civil liberties; Education, Democracy, Citizenship; Religion and Society.

With regard to Hizmet's origins in France, Toğuşlu's (2015) book chapter on Hizmet in France explores what it calls "the negotiation of multiple identities in a secular context", while Demir's (2012) book chapter traces what he identifies as "the implementation strategies and competition logics" of Hizmet in France (and, comparatively, in Germany too); and most recently, Bayram Balcı (2018) locates Hizmet in France within its wider European context. According to Erkinbekov, "the approximate start is that it started with the Turkish immigrants who settled in France, who came here for work" which he dated as being "at the end of the 1970s" and "between the 1970s and 1980s". In relation to these workers, he explained that "some of them, they already had a connection with the Hizmet movement in Turkey, so when they came here they wanted to start Hizmet meetings in France", with Erkinbekov dating the start of more organised Hizmet activities in France as being "at the end of the 1980s, I think".

As with Germany and the Netherlands, Gülen visited France and met with Hizmet people there, with Erkinbekov referencing both "a short trip" taking place "at the end of the 80s" that included visits to Strasbourg and Paris, and then a first proper visit "in 1992 or 1991, I think". Initially in Strasbourg and Paris, as in other European countries, there had been what Erkinbekov described as "other associations which were not for the inter-faith and inter-cultural dialogue but they were, as one says in Turkish, *dershane* centres for giving classes for children". According to Erkinbekov, the first association that was created by Hizmet and which included the word dialogue in its name was started in Strasbourg under the name of Center Dialogue. As Erkinbekov stresses, "it was aimed not just for inter-faith dialogue, but it was aimed towards children, giving lessons and so on". In addition, as Erkinbekov explained, Strasbourg was particularly important for the initial development of Hizmet in France "because Strasbourg is very close to Germany, and it was in Germany before in France that Hizmet started". In time, other initiatives similar to those in other countries also emerged such as the business association, Fédérations d'Entrepreneurs et de Dirigeants de France (or Federations of Entrepreneurs and Directors of France),[91] founded in Paris in 2004.

The Platforme de Paris was inspired by, and emerged out of, the Abant Platform conference that took place in Paris in 2005. Given the original Abant Platform's (see Sect. 2.3) focus on wider social issues, this is another example of how, in each European country where Hizmet has developed, there has been a reflection of, and adaptation to, distinctive characteristics of that country in terms, especially, of the relationship between religion, state and society. Toğuşlu, who now lives and works in Belgium, first lived in France when he came to Europe to study for his doctorate. Having also worked in Belgium, he observed in relation to the two countries that "they are very different, especially Belgium is a different country, and France has its own way of doing politics, education, whatever you think of: they have their own unique societal experience or model, especially this laïcité. It's very, very present".

Erkinbekov cites the French notion of laïcité as being "why I think that at the beginning the Platforme de Paris was built as an inter-cultural more than an inter-faith platform. And in most of the actions that Platforme de Paris took, there was inter-cultural dialogue, an inter-cultural platform". In other words, the initial emphasis was more on culture than on religion, again as in contrast to the Netherlands where the early focus was primarily on Islam and dialogue. Nevertheless, Erkinbekov wanted to underline that although it did have a cultural emphasis, "the Platforme de Paris was always in dialogue with the other dialogue organizations based on the faiths—with inter-faith programmes, with dialogues, and the volunteers of Platforme de Paris were in dialogue and organised programmes with other faith-based organizations". Indeed, Toğuşlu's reported experience chimes with this since, at least in contrast to the Turkey from which he had come to study in France, Toğuşlu said that he gained what he called "another picture of the movement", in which "for example, the dialogue and especially the inter-faith dialogue was extended". Indeed, through that he became involved in, and later on began to organise, such dialogues, including especially with a Muslim-Christian group in Paris.

One of the things highlighted by Erkinbekov is that a generational change has more recently been taking place in the Plateforme de Paris. Nihat Sarier had been the President for a decade but "now the others, I would say the young generation of the Hizmet movement in France" are coming through in what Erkinbekov describes as "a transition of the administrative staff". This change in individual leaders was, however, also part of a wider development which, as Erkinbekov explained, "We tried to make very heterogenous". Thus, for example, the bureau of the Platforme de Paris historically had three office-holders—a President, and Treasurer and Secretary. In contrast to that, Erkinbekov explained that, in the future, "So, we want that there will be at least ten persons in the administration staff of the association, and in every association". At the same time, however, while broadening involvements, Erkinbekov noted that although the Platform had some part-time staff which supported the volunteers and that "I think they are looking for recruiting a full-time staff".

In many ways, like London in the UK, Paris is very much a centralised "magnet" for the whole of France. In relation to Hizmet, Erkinbekov explained that the way in which this had historically worked was that "The Platforme de Paris had a partnership with the other Hizmet associations in other cities". Concretely this means that "sometimes the volunteers or administrative staff of the Platforme de Paris have shared in an event or organization with the other Hizmet associations in the other cities" or they were offering what Erkinbekov called "a consulting service" to other associations. This was, therefore, a more informal type of networking than something like the more federal approach like Fedactio in Belgium, being perhaps more akin to the relationship that existed between the Dialogue Society in London and other branches and initiatives of the Dialogue Society in other UK locations prior to the emergence of Voices.

As in Switzerland where the predominantly Cantonal approach to organising was supplemented by an all Swiss Confederation assembly of Hizmet people, it would appear that, also in France, the environment after July 2016 provided an impetus towards the creation of a new all-France association called Cohèsions. This was established, as Erkinbekov explained, through:

> All the Hizmets are sitting together, all the grassroots of Hizmet, all the sympathisers of the Hizmet movement, they came together and they worked on the new Association which will be the umbrella of the Hizmet movement in France. It was a lot of work. We worked two years on this Association and

all the sympathisers of the Hizmet movement participated in a General Assembly of this Association. So, there was four times in two years a General Assembly of all the Hizmet movement participants and they elected an administrative staff of the Association.

Erkinbekov furthermore explained of this that "now we are working on the partnership agreement between all of the Associations" and that in the process of that "We are finding Hizmet sympathisers all over France". As an important difference to Voices in the UK is that Erkinbekov notes that Cohèsions aspires to be "the one and only Association which can take care of and report for the Hizmet movement in France".

3.8   HIZMET IN SPAIN

The history, existence and work of Hizmet in the Iberian Peninsula is something about which there have been virtually no scholarly publications in English or indeed in any other language. It is therefore something about which few people outside the Spanish-speaking world know. This is partly because Spain was not originally a country for any significant Turkish labour migration. Indeed, Islam in Spain has had no particularly dominant religio-ethnic group, which perhaps contributed to the conditions that allowed for the comparatively early foundation in Spain of an organisation that sought to represent the broad range of Muslims in negotiations with the Spanish state. This is the Commission Islamico Espana (Comisión Islámica de España[92] (Spanish Islamic Commission) which brokered one of the earliest European governmental formal recognitions of Islam through an *Acuerdo de Cooperación del Estado Español con las Comisión islamica de España* (or, Co-Operation Agreement of the Spanish State with the Islamic Commission of Spain), signed in 1992, in the context of which certain rights were accorded to Muslims in Spain (Antes 1994).

The interviewee Temirkhon Temirzoda (see Acknowledgements) is a leading Hizmet figure in Spain, who himself originated from the city of Khujand (during the Soviet period known as Leninbad) in northern Tajikistan where he had been a teacher at a high school founded in 1997 by Yusuf Kemal Erimez, a businessman and close friend of Gülen. However, with regard to his name, as interviewee Termijón Termizoda Naziri, from Spain explains it, "here in Spain because of the pronunciation of the names, I just tell Temir Naziri, so this is the short form and I think the easiest form of pronouncing my name so everyone knows me as, like,

Temir Naziri in Spain". Naziri first arrived in Spain in 2007 as one of the first students coming to Europe as part of Erasmus Mundus External Co-operation Window (EMECW) programme, to undertake his master's study, and was interviewed in September 2019.

His initial connections with Hizmet in Spain were with the Spanish-Turkish Association. According to Naziri, this had been founded in 1996 by "Turkish and Spanish citizens. They were businessmen, some of them were academicians" and also by "two or three persons were in Spanish and Turkish and Turkish and Spanish mixed marriages". As Naziri explained it, this Association was formed "to promote Spanish-Turkish cooperation on education, business area, and culture of course, cultural spheres". However, Naziri also noted "there was not so much activity going on, except some journeys and some groups that were coming from Turkey" which contrasts with the development of Hizmet in most other European countries where one of the typically organised activities was that of taking groups of people to Turkey.

While a student in the late 2000s, Naziri began voluntary work with the Asociación Hispano Turca, moving to a professional engagement in 2011. In 2013, he was involved in founding the Arco Forum Association,[93] also a non-profit organisation. He recalls that it had started in around 2010 or 2011, but under the name of Casa Turca[94] (or, Turkish House) because, as Naziri explained:

> In Spain the Ministry of Foreign Affairs, some years ago, started to establish different institutions, public institutions and their names are like, Casa Arabe, Casa Sefarad (for Sephardic Jews), Casa Africa, Casa America, and all these institutions are public Spanish institutions, linked to the Ministry of Foreign Affairs and they wanted to, like, link with all those countries and so it was, like, popular to have "Casa".

In connection with this, Naziri explained that they originally sought a connection with Casa Árabe. However, in Casa Árabe's view Turkey did not fall within its definition, while Casa Asia said that, although Iran was within their association, Turkey was more like Europe, at which point Naziri says, "I said, well, OK, we are founding our Casa Turca. So that was how it emerged and it was, like, a good decision in terms of the mark, in terms of the label and getting to be known very fast in Turkish and Spanish society". On its website Casa Turca shows the activities that it has been working on over the years which include Turkish classes, Turkish cuisine,

Turkish cinema, Turkish art. However, in his 2019 interview Naziri commented that "But now because of all the things that have been happening we have not been so active. Energetic, yes, but because all that has happened, it is economically not possible". In relation to this Naziri went on to explain that until around 2012 they had around a dozen people working there as volunteers, of which "Most of them were Hizmet people, but interestingly enough it was heterogenous: Spanish, I am Tajik, Turkish, some Russian, some even Turkmen. Well, Turks with Kurdish backgrounds, Turkish citizens, like, it was really different".

Regardless of this diversity challenge, Naziri explained that a need was identified also to focus more on Spain itself, not with the idea of being more explicit about Hizmet for the sake of Hizmet's own profile but "Rather to get to know some ideas about, you know, Fethullah Gülen, explaining about the values that he teaches, taking that into the Spanish society, mostly on the inter-religious basis, inter-religious dialogue sphere". As explained by Naziri this led, in 2013, to "me and two other guys founding the Arco Forum", of which Naziri was initially Secretary General and is now President. Naziri explained that a lot of thought and debate went into what to call this new organisation and that he, in particular, had been against giving it a specifically Turkish-related name. Rather, "We wanted to put a name which would be very good and universal, like, familiar to all the people. And so, Arco, you know, it's an arc, and it symbolises a bridge between two different separate things. And it comes from *Armonía* (Harmony), *Arte* (Arte), *Convivencia* (*El Arte de la Convivencia*)".

Naziri recounts that up until around 2016 there were perhaps only around fifty Hizmet people in Spain, so their original plans related to that kind of human resource and capacity. However, although their economic capacities have become even more constricted since July 2016 in Turkey, through the arrival of asylum-seekers, refugees and other migrants from Turkey they number around 300 people. As a result of this, Casa Turka has been changing its focus such that, while it still provides Turkish language and cuisine classes (with, e.g., a Turkish asylum-seeker becoming the teacher for this), the asylum-seekers are also engaging in Ashura, the Noah's pudding, and many inter-faith activities.

In terms of educational initiatives in Spain there is Pangea, which focuses on promoting Mathematics among school children by organising contests or competitions. This was initiated around a decade ago by Hizmet participants from Germany, and since then it has spread through different European countries. Hizmet volunteers coming especially from

Germany have taken a major role in this initiative in which over one hundred thousand students from all the Spanish provinces participated. Indeed, Naziri explained that for over a decade many male and female Hizmet volunteers came from Germany to study in Spain, as "dynamic young people who are Europeans (German Turks), know the language and wishing to contribute professionally and voluntarily in many activities". A minority of these returned to Germany, but a majority are still living and working and studying in Spain, in relation to whom Naziri says, "My pre-occupation is somehow to engage them, if it is possible in our institutions". However, he also comments that is "something very hard for now, even if we have been granted some EU Commission Projects that promise some financial stability for our organization" because "Germany can offer them other great jobs with bigger salary than in Spain". At the same time, although economically there may be better economic opportunities in Germany, Naziri notes that:

> Many Turks no matter whether they are from Hizmet or not, do not like Spain, but love it! They love it. You know, it's a good place to live. But I would say, normally, it is my case, when you know the language, when you learn the language, you don't feel yourself like a stranger or physically the aspect is more or less Mediterranean. And Spain is quite a good country, it's not a racist country, it's an open country. In Spanish classes when you learn there are many phrases: *amable* (friendly, kind, nice). Yeah, you feel it: it is a polite society, you could say. It is a society that embraces you. It is not racist.

3.9   Hizmet in Italy

Relatively little has been published in English or, indeed, in other languages concerning Hizmet in Italy, with the exception of the Luca Ozzano's (2018), "From the 'New Rome' to the Old One: the Gülen Movement in Italy". In Latif Erdoğan's (1995) biography of Gülen known in English as *My Small World*, no date is given for when Fethullah Gülen first visited Europe. However, anonymous Hizmet participant in Italy HE2 (see Acknowledgements) notes that this book included a picture of which he says that "when I moved to Italy, I looked again at this book when I was searching for something and I looked at that picture, and I realised that that picture was taken in Rome, actually. So, it is in front of the Roman Forum" and that "in the early 1990s, I don't know the reason … he just came to Rome".

In sharing his perspective on the development of Hizmet in Italy, this interviewee explained that "there are some different narratives about it", although it is thought that Hizmet people first came to Italy in 1994, supported by scholarships from Turkish foundations, in order to undertake graduate studies in some Italian universities. However, after some months they ran into a number of difficulties, many of which were said to be related to the fact that they did not know Italian, and in the light of which they decided to move to Modena where there was a small pre-existing Turkish diaspora. Between then and 1997 it is not clear what happened, but in 1997 it is documented that Abdhullah Aymaz visited Rome as part of a wider Hizmet-related trip that also included a visit to Austria. This was in a broader context in which Hizmet in Turkey had, via the representative of the Apostolic Nunciature in Istanbul, established some links with the Catholic Church and the Vatican. The Rome visit included both the Pontifical Council for Inter-Religious Dialogue and the Pontifical Institute for Arabic and Islamic Studies, in the context of which discussions took place that led to the initiation of a student exchange.

Nevertheless, as in a number of other European countries, this early initiative did not result in a straight line to later developments, with HE2 explaining that "so far as I understand it, there was a sort of rupture", surmising that this may have been linked to project funding. As again in other European examples, it was sometimes the case that "the benefactors were not able to support any more". But in 2002–2003 it appears that a Hizmet person with good interpersonal skills and good links with other parts of Europe relocated from Austria to Italy; assumed the role there of a Hizmet grassroots facilitator and operated in a way that is illuminating also of other Hizmet developmental contexts in Europe. As explained by HE2:

> This guy was a kind of facilitator, with good contacts, and good skills for fundraising in relationship with businessmen and with others who had better conditions in other parts of Europe. Sometimes things work better through friendships: so, if you live in a country and you are responsible for some Hizmet institutions and in the next country you have a classmate with more resources, your classmate, just being classmates and good friends will find you more contacts.

By the time Pope John Paul II had received Gülen in a "private audience", as HE2 explained it, "this guy came and said, 'Rome is such an important city' " and in the light of that papal audience he raised the question of why there was no organised Hizmet activity in Rome. Therefore, the Istituto Tevere,[95] based in Rome, was founded in 2007. From its beginning, it resolved that it should not be a Turkish cultural centre. Rather, HE2 explains that "It was all focused on inter-religious and inter-cultural dialogue, usually focusing on 'giving voice' to different partners in inter-faith dialogue, like Bahá'ís and Ahmadiyah too, we always invite them to talk and engage". As an example of this, HE2 shared that:

> Last October was an interesting day. It was Eid Al-Adha, it was the Feast of St. Francis, and it was also Yom Kippur. Yom Kippur was challenging because of fasting and being at home all day. But there was a Progressive lady who said I am fasting but I can come. In this case we had some food, so in return I sat with this woman and said I was present, I haven't had any water.

In relation to the opportunities and challenges of inter-faith dialogue HE2 argued that it is important that such dialogue is engaged with "Not just superficially, we love each other, we believe in the same God, yippee, that's nice, but a little bit harder", citing as one example the Istituto Tevere's trailblazing adoption in Rome—via contacts in Cambridge, UK—of scriptural reasoning.[96]

Outside of Rome, prior to the foundation of the Istituto Tevere there had been around seven other Hizmet-related initiatives, including in Milan and Modena. As in many other European countries, these had initially aimed to reach out to the children of Turkish immigrants through after-schooling and similar educational initiatives. At the time of his interview, HE2 reported that, nationally, in Italy, "there are three associations". Among those that emerged after the foundation of the Istituto Tevere was one in Venice. Another is Meridiano, which might be described as a kind of "retreat house", and for which the buildings were purchased cheaply and renovated. This has been a focus for ten Catholic families (especially involving people from the lay Franciscan community) and ten Muslim families who (sometimes in Assisi and sometimes at this place) "do everything together, they cook together, they eat together. Every group reads their own readings, the Qur'an for Muslims etc. and in some common time they share their readings – we learned this or that".

3.10   Hizmet in Denmark

In relation to Hizmet in Denmark, Jacobsen (2012) has a book-length treatment which examines the development of Hizmet in the country, with particular reference to the opportunities that it appears to open up for middle-class people of Turkish background there. There is also a master's dissertation by Ibrahim (2016) which is a case study of a Hizmet school in Denmark.

In the context of Scandinavia as a whole, it was only Denmark where the research project underlying this book and its complementary volume conducted its own primary research. According to interviewee Mustafa Gezen (see Acknowledgements) from Denmark, "The Hizmet history in Denmark began approximately in the late 1980s when a group of first and second generation young and middle-aged people, descending from Turkey, initiated activities inspired from listening to Gülen's audio recordings and video recordings". Gezen notes that, in contrast to a number of other countries, "no-one came from Turkey to Denmark from Hizmet to initiate activities, it was locally initiated" and that "I think that's unique for Denmark. They found Gülen before anyone took the *hijrah*, using the classical term, or decided to move to Denmark". Referring to the oral history tradition of this early period, Gezen went on to explain that:

> Apparently, from what we have heard, one or two people went to Turkey, found those videos and this little group of ten or eleven people were in Denmark and were in search of finding, you could call it, a *cemaat* that they could associate themselves with and help with some of the issues they were experiencing with their kids and with the new country they were in. So, they started listening to Gülen.

As Gezen comments of these pioneers, "Many of these people are great inspiration to many of the people in the Hizmet movement today, because they managed to establish many initiatives while working in different avenues in society". For example, "from the videos they were inspired to establish a school based on science and good manners. They also started looking into finding someone to make contact with in Turkey, because they were aware that people were listening to Gülen and were establishing schools in Turkey". In due course "Someone did come and started living in Denmark, and the idea about opening a school took even more form", with Hayskolen[97] being established in Copenhagen 1993 (Ibrahim 2016), and Gezen himself graduating from this school in 1996 as part of the first class to graduate.

In 2002, the Dialog Forum was founded by a small number of university graduates and students who, as Gezen says, "wanted to engage in purposeful dialogue between people in the Danish society with different cultural and religious backgrounds". Its core values were inspired from the 1997 dialogue initiatives by Gülen in Istanbul, and especially the dialogue dinners organised by the Journalists and Writers' Foundation and, "So, some of the people who established this in Denmark had an initial inspiration from there". As in the Netherlands, explicitly inter-religious dialogue was a big part of Hizmet's activity in Denmark from its beginnings:

> So what Dialog Forum did in 2002 was to establish relations with people of faith, whom with common ideas could be shared. It started with a couple of activities and getting in touch with the religious groups, such as the Jewish community and the Christian community. The Christian community was of course the largest one in Denmark. So, it was an inter-religious start with a Jewish, Christian and Muslim dialogue.

At the same time, today, many of Hizmet's newer projects in Denmark have a much broader, societal focus. Alongside the more traditional kind of business-related associations that one can also find in other countries, such as DATİFED, the Danish Turkish Business Federation[98] founded in 2011, these newer initiatives include Mit Studium which Gezen says is "a university project focusing on helping young students who feel themselves lonely and anxious". There is also Mentor X that Gezen says "is supporting young girls and young boys in getting in touch with the Danish society, like going to the theatre, going to the cinema, going to the opera maybe, and going to museums, and in this way maybe trying to educate them within the Danish context".

3.11   Hizmet in Some Other European Countries

The research project underlying this book and its complementary volume did not conduct its own primary research in the European countries discussed within this section. Further work needs to be done to address both primary research and literature gaps on Hizmet in a number of European countries, especially in relation to the Western Balkans where there is a significant historical Turkish-related heritage, but also in relation to emergent groups in Central and Eastern European countries where there are only very small populations of Turkish origins, but where Hizmet is also present and active.

In Sweden, as in a number of other European countries, in 2011 a business association was founded called SWETURK (Swedish-Turkish Business Network).[99] Today perhaps the highest-profile Hizmet organisation in Sweden, and that has one of the highest profiles in Europe, is the Stockholm Center for Freedom (SCF)[100] which states on its website that it is:

A non-profit organization set up by a group of journalists who have been forced to live in self-exile in Sweden against the background of a massive crackdown on press freedom in Turkey, where almost 300 journalists have been jailed, and close to 200 media outlets have been shuttered by a series of arbitrary decisions taken by the Turkish authorities.

In this regard it is:

An advocacy organization that promotes the rule of law, democracy, fundamental rights and freedoms with a special focus on Turkey, a country with eighty million citizens that is experiencing a dramatic decline in its parliamentary democracy under its autocratic leadership.

Examples of its work include a report on the post-2016 pressures on Hizmet people in Sweden (Stockholm Center for Freedom 2018) as well as a similar report on Norway (Stockholm Center for Freedom 2017).

Although the research project for this book did not conduct interviews in Norway, in the interview held with Alasag from the Netherlands, he noted of Gülen's friend Başaran that he "was also travelling a lot in the whole of Europe" and, as one example of this, Alasag referred to Başaran's visit to see friends in Oslo, while Alasag himself also recalls visiting Oslo in 1992. By that time, Alasag reports that Hizmet people had a very nice mosque and that people from the mosque told him that "they had, in the past, a very small, dirty place for worship, but an imam came from Rotterdam and preached and they got motivated and they bought this place". Similarly, to what has been noted in other countries, there was a business association called NOTURK (Norwegian-Turkish Chamber of

Commerce), founded in 2007. From a position critical to Hizmet in Norway as being engaged in what it calls a "neo-Ottoman conquest" is a master's thesis by Berg (2012). By the time of Berg's thesis, Hizmet had initiatives in Oslo, Drammen, Trondheim and Stavanger.

In relation to the Republic of Ireland, the Turkish-Irish Education and Cultural Society[101] was founded in 2004 by a group of volunteers comprising of businesspeople, academicians and students. A number of publications by Lacey (2009, 2010, 2011) have explored Hizmet's distinctive role in this as well as (see Sect. 3.5) in Northern Ireland. Also as noted in Sect. 3.11, there is now a new Hizmet-related organisation on the island of Ireland, founded in 2021 as a limited company,[102] based in Dublin, and known more widely as Eire Dialogue.[103]

In Austria, Frieda, the Institut für Dialog (or Institute for Dialogue),[104] was founded in 2002 and is based in Vienna. Frieda's activities have included seminars, roundtables, cultural discussion evenings, study trips, excursions, dialogue workshops, concerts and art exhibitions.

With regard to other parts of Central and Eastern Europe, Bekir Çinar's (2015) book chapter has a brief discussion of Romania; in relation to the Czech Republic, the Mozaiky O.S Platform Dialog (or Mosaic Dialogue Platform)[105] was founded in 2005 and is based in Prague; in Hungary, the Dialógus Platform Egyesület (or Dialogue Platform Association)[106] was founded in 2005 and is based in Budapest; in Poland, the Dunaj Instytut Dialogu (or Danube Institute of Dialogue)[107] is based in Warsaw; in Slovakia, Bystra Education is based in Bratislava; while in Slovenia, there is the Društvo Meldkurtuni (or Meldkurtuni Association).

With regard to the Western Balkans, which has a strong Turkic heritage, according to Kerem Öktem (2010), at time of his writing there were "ten such colleges with several thousand students". Focusing on educational institutions alone, in relation to Albania, Agai's (2008) previously mentioned book discusses Hizmet educational initiatives there, as does Bekir Çinar's (2015) later book chapter, while the anti-Hizmet authors Holton and Lopez (2015, pp. 67–68) highlight two universities in Tirana, Albania, as having been linked with Hizmet, namely Beder University College[108] that was opened in 2011, and Epoka University,[109] which was designated as a University in 2012, and which the present author visited in the same year. Bekir Çinar's (2015) book chapter referred to above also briefly discusses Bosnia and Herzegovina, where, based in Sarajevo, there is the International Burç University,[110] founded in 2008. A book chapter by Mehmeti (2012) discusses Hizmet educational initiatives in Kosovo. Finally, in other parts of Europe, in Portugal, the Intercultural Dialogue Platform of Portugal,[111] which is part of the Associação de Amizado Luso-Turca (or Portuguese-Turkish Friendship Association),[112] was founded in 2008 and is based in Lisbon.

NOTES

1. http://www.dialogueplatform.eu, 2021.
2. http://www.epnetwork.eu/, 2021.
3. http://www.unitee.eu/, 2015.
4. https://hogiaf.nl/en/about-us/, 2021.
5. https://platformins.nl/, n.d.
6. https://www.hizmetbeweging.nl/alper-alasag/, n.d.
7. https://ditib.de/, 2021.
8. http://zentralrat.de/, n.d.
9. https://www.igmg.org/, n.d.
10. http://koordinationsrat.de/, 2020.
11. https://www.deutsche-islam-konferenz.de/DE/Startseite/startseite_node.html, 2021.
12. https://www.dmgonline.de/, n.d.
13. http://igs-deutschland.org/, 2021.
14. https://www.gulenmovement.com/gulen-movement-germany-france.html, Emre Demir, n.d.
15. https://buv-ev.de/, n.d.
16. http://bddi.org/, 2013–2021.
17. https://www.forumdialog.org/, 2021.
18. http://fidev.org/forum-fuer-interkulturellen-dialog, 2021.
19. https://www.idizem.de/, n.d.
20. http://ruhrdialog.org/, 2021.
21. https://www.facebook.com/pg/forumdialog/about/?ref=page_internal, n.d.
22. http://intpec.org/, n.d.
23. http://bddi.org/dialog-akademie/, 2013–2021.
24. https://intflc.de/, 2021.
25. http://islam-kompakt.de/, 2021.
26. http://tulpe-essen.de/, n.d.

27. https://diefontaene.de/, 2021.
28. https://www.vhs-leipzig.de/, 2021.
29. https://house-of-one.org/de, 2021.
30. https://www.haus-der-religionen.ch/, n.d.
31. https://www.sdub.de, 2021.
32. https://sdub.de/category/publikationen/dub-zeitschrift/, 2021.
33. https://sdub.de/wp-content/uploads/2019/01/SDuB_ MAG_1-2014_web.pdf, Issue 12,014.
34. https://sdub.de/wp-content/uploads/2019/01/DuB-Heft2-2.pdf, Issue 2, 2015.
35. https://sdub.de/wp-content/uploads/2019/01/SDuB_ MAG-3_2_2015.pdf, Issue 2, 2015.
36. https://sdub.de/wp-content/uploads/2019/01/SDuB_ MAG-4_12_2015_Webversion2.pdf, Issue 4, 2015.
37. https://sdub.de/wp-content/uploads/2019/04/DUB_5_März.pdf, Issue 5, 2019.
38. https://sdub.de/wp-content/uploads/2019/10/DuB-6---Gruppenbezogene-Menschenfeindlichkeit.pdf, Issue 6, 2019.
39. https://vez-nrw.de/, 2018.
40. https://www.lbe-bw.de/, n.d.
41. https://www.lbe-bw.de/mitglieder/, n.d.
42. http://www.vge-ev.de/, 2021.
43. http://www.etoiles.be/, 2017.
44. https://www.facebook.com/betiadfed, 2021 (created 1.2.2105).
45. http://en.fedactio.be/, n.d.
46. https://www.facebook.com/LaTulipeCharleroi/,   2021   (created 21.4.2014).
47. https://www.facebook.com/latulipecentrecommunautaire/, 2021 (created 18.9.2017).
48. https://www.facebook.com/latulipe.centreintercommunautaire/?ref= br_rs, 2021 (created 7.10.2014).
49. https://www.facebook.com/BSPlatformAntwerpen, 2021.
50. https://www.facebook.com/bsplatform.limburg, 2021.
51. http://francolympiades.be/, 2021.
52. http://meridiaanvzw.be/, n.d.
53. www.vuslat.be/, 2021.
54. https://www.facebook.com/betiadlimburg.be/,   2021   (created 16.3.2014).
55. https://ngacademie.be/, n.d.
56. http://asbldialogue.be/, n.d.

57. https://beltudlimburg.weebly.com/, n.d.
58. http://www.goldenroses.be/, 2018.
59. http://inspirationvzw.be/, 2017.
60. http://www.vzwkoza.be/, n.d.
61. http://foryouth.be/, n.d.
62. https://en.fedactio.be/search/label/'Colors%20of%20the%20 World', n.d.
63. http://www.beltud.be/, 2020.
64. http://iftarmee.be/, n.d.
65. https://sowo.be/, n.d.
66. https://wiskundequiz.be/, 2012.
67. https://tekenwedstrijd.be/over/, 2018.
68. https://www.youtube.com/user/fedactio, 2015.
69. http://www.gulenmovement.com/gulen-movements-initiatives-britain. html, Faith Tedik, n.d.
70. http://www.charitycommissionni.org.uk/charity-details/?regid=10112 6&subid=0, 2014.
71. https://www.thenurture.org.uk/, 2020.
72. http://www.axiseducationaltrust.org/, 2020.
73. http://www.dialoguesociety.org, 2021.
74. http://www.dialoguesociety.org/events-by-dates.html, 2021.
75. http://www.voicesinbritain.org/, 2018.
76. https://northlondongrammar.com/, 2018.
77. https://lhedu.org.uk/, n.d.
78. https://www.amityeducation.org.uk/, 2018.
79. https://www.springeducation.org.uk/, n.d.
80. https://mentorwise.org.uk/, 2021.
81. http://fellowshipeducation.org.uk/, 2018.
82. http://www.voicesinbritain.org/?tmlmstf=members&title=anatol ian, 2018.
83. http://www.rumimosque.org.uk/, 2017.
84. https://sohbetsociety.org/how-we-do-it/, 2021.
85. https://www.timetohelp.org.uk/, 2021.
86. https://www.hizmetstudies.org/, n.d.
87. https://www.turkeyinstitute.org.uk/about/, n.d.
88. https://www.stiftung-sera.ch/, 2019.
89. https://www.stiftung-sera.ch/ekol-bildungszentrum/, 2019.
90. http://www.plateformedeparis.fr/, 2021.
91. http://fedif.fr/presentation/, n.d.
92. http://www.hispanomuslim.es/panya/cie.htm, n.d.
93. http://arcoforum.es/, n.d.

94. http://casaturka.org, 2015.
95. www.istevere.org, 2021.
96. http://www.scripturalreasoning.org/, n.d.
97. http://hayskolen.dk/new/, n.d.
98. https://www.facebook.com/pg/Danish-Turkish-Business-Federation-129545357179446/about/?ref=page_internal, 2021 (created 26.4.2012).
99. http://www.sweturk.org/, 2021.
100. https://stockholmcf.org/about-us/, 2017.
101. https://www.facebook.com/Tiecs/about/, 23.1.2012.
102. https://core.cro.ie/e-commerce/company/4755301, 2021.
103. https://eiredialogue.ie/, 2021.
104. https://www.facebook.com/derfriedeORG/, 2021 (created 3.3.2016).
105. http://www.platformdialog.cz/, 2021.
106. http://dialogusplatform.hu/, 2020.
107. http://www.dialoginstytut.pl/, 2020.
108. https://www.beder.edu.al/, 2021
109. http://www.epoka.edu.al/, 2013–2021.
110. http://www.ibu.edu.ba, 2020.
111. https://lusoturca.blogspot.com/, n.d.
112. https://www.facebook.com/AssociacaoLusoTurca/, 2021 (created 28.11.2012).

References

(All web links current at 20.11.2021)

Abadan-Unat, Nermin (2011). *Turks in Europe: From Guest Worker to Transnational Citizen.* Oxford: Berghahn Books.

Agai, Bekim (2008). *Zwischen Netzwerk und Diskurs: Das Bildungsnetztwerk um Fethullah Gülen (geb. 1938): Die Flexible Umsetzung Modernen Islamischen Gedankenguts.* Hamburg: EB-Verlag.

Antes, Peter (1994). Islam in Europe. In Sean Gill, Gavin D'Costa, and Ursula King (Eds.), *Religion in Europe: Contemporary Perspectives* (pp. 49–50). Kampen: Kok Pharos.

Balcı, Bayram (2018). Situating the Gülen Movement in France and in Europe. *Politics, Religion and Ideology, 19* (1), 69–80. https://doi.org/10.1080/21567689.2018.1453262

Bayraklı, Enes; Boyraz, Hacı Mehmet; and Güngörmez, Oğuz (2018). *The Gülenist Terror Organization (FETO) in the United Kingdom.* Ankara: SETA – Foundation for Political, Economic and Social Research. https://www.setav.org/en/report-the-gulenist-terror-organization-feto-in-the-united-kingdom/

Berg, Lara Isabel Tuduri (2012). *The Hizmet Movement: A Neo-Ottoman International Conquest?* Masters Thesis in Middle East and North Africa studies, University of Oslo, at: https://www.duo.uio.no/bitstream/handle/10852/35145/Tuduri-Berg_Master.pdf.

Bruinessen, Martin van (2013). The Netherlands and the Gülen Movement. *Sociology of Islam, 1* (3–4), 165–187. https://doi.org/10.1163/22131418-00104004

Canatan, Kadir (2001). *Turkse Islam: Perspectieven op Organisatievorming en Leiderschap in Nederland* [*Turkish Islam: Perspectives on Organization and Leadership in the Netherlands*]. Unpublished PhD Thesis, Rotterdam: Erasmus Universiteit.

Çelik, Gürkan, Leman, Johann and Steenbrink, Karel. eds. (2015). *Gülen-Inspired Hizmet in Europe: The Western Journey of a Turkish Muslim Movement.* Brussels: Peter Lang.

Çinar, Bekir (2015). Turkish Schools and More. Hizmet Networks in the Balkans. In Gürkan Çelik, Johann Leman and Karel Steenbrink (Eds.), *Gülen-Inspired Hizmet in Europe: The Western Journey of a Turkish Muslim Movement* (pp. 253–265). Brussels: Peter Lang.

Demir, Emre (2012). The Emergence of a Neo-Communitarian Discourse in the Turkish Diaspora in Europe: The Implementation Strategies and Competition Logics of the Gülen Movement in France and Germany. In Paul Weller and İhsan Yılmaz (Eds.), *European Muslims, Civility and Public Life: Perspectives on and From the Gülen Movement* (pp. 101–112). London: Continuum.

Doomernik, Jeroen (1995). The Institutionalization of Turkish Islam in Germany and The Netherlands: A Comparison. *Ethnic and Racial Studies, 18* (1), 46–63. https://doi.org/10.1080/01419870.1995.9993853

El-Banna, Sanaa (2013). *Resource Mobilisation in Gülen-Inspired Hizmet: A New Type of Social Movement.* New York: Blue Dome Press.

Erdoğan, Latif (1995). *Fethullah Gülen Hocaefendi: Küçük dünyam* [*Hojaefendi Fethullah Gülen: My Small World*]. Ankara: AD Yayıncılık.

Fähmel, Anita (2009). *Dossier Fethullah Gülen. Een verkennend onderzoek naar de Fethullah Gülen organisatie en haar invloed in Rotterdam* [*The Fethullah Gülen File: An Exploratory Investigation of the Fethullah Gülen Organization and its Influence in Rotterdam*]. Rotterdam: Leefbaar Rotterdam. Leefbaar Rotterdam. https://www.yumpu.com/nl/document/view/28279547/dossier-fethullah-ga-1-4-lenpdf-leefbaar-rotterdam.

Hazırlyan, Yayına (Ed.) (2012). *Fedactio: Tanitim Albümu/Promotion Album.* Brussels: Musa Soydemir.

Holton, Christopher and Lopez, Claire (2015). *The Gülen Movement. Turkey's Islamic Supremacist Cult and its Contributions to the Civilization Jihad.* Washington DC: The Center for Security Policy. https://centerforsecuritypolicy.org/book-release-the-gulen-movement-turkeys-islamic-supremacist-cult-and-its-contributions-to-the-civilization-jihad/

Ibrahim, Kaya (2016). *Hizmet Educational Philosophy in the Example of a Hizmet-Inspired School; Hayskolen: Could Hizmet Educational Philosophy be an Alternative Solution to Criminality and Radicalism Among Immigrant-Origin Youths?* Master's dissertation: Uppsala University, Theology Faculty. http://uu.diva-portal.org/smash/get/diva2:951144/FULLTEXT01.pdf

Jacobsen, Jens Stensgaard (2012). *Middle Class and Muslim?: Creating New Positions in Danish Society by Engaging in a Turkish Islamic Dialogue Association.* Saarbrücke: Lambert Publishing.

Karakoyun, Ercan and Steenbrink, Karel (2015). The Hizmet Movement and Integration of Muslims in Germany. In Gürkan Çelik, Johann Leman and Karel Steenbrink (Eds.), *Gülen-Inspired Hizmet in Europe: The Western Journey of a Turkish Muslim Movement* (pp. 179–195). Brussels: Peter Lang.

Koçak's, Tayyar (2019). Hizmet und die Flüchtlingsfrage in Deutschland: Initiativen aus dem Raum Mitteldeutschland. *Materialen zu Dialog und Bildung, 5,* 43–51. https://sdub.de/wp-content/uploads/2019/04/DUB_5_M%C3%A4rz.pdf

Lacey, Jonathan (2009). The Gülen Movement in Ireland: Civil Society Engagements of a Turkish Religio-Cultural Movement. *Turkish Studies, 10* (2), 295–315. https://doi.org/10.1080/14683840902864051

Lacey, Jonathan (2010). Investigating the Contribution of Fethullah Gülen Through the Activities of a Gülen-Inspired Religio-Cultural Society Based in Ireland. In John Esposito and İhsan Yılmaz (Eds.), *Islam and Peacebuilding: Gülen Movement Initiatives* (pp. 249–272). New York: Blue Dome Press.

Lacey, Jonathan (2011). Turkish Islam in Ireland. In Olivier Cosgrove, Laurence Cox, Carmen Kuhling and Peter Mulholland et al. (Eds.), *Ireland's New Religious Movements* (pp. 337–356). Newcastle-upon-Tyne: Cambridge Scholars Publishing.

Lacey, Jonathan (2012). An Exploration of the Strategic Dimensions of Dialogue in a Gülen Movement Organization in Northern Ireland. In Paul Weller and İhsan Yılmaz (Eds.), *European Muslims, Civility and Public Life: Perspectives on and From the Gülen Movement,* eds. (pp. 127–139). London: Continuum.

Leman, Johann (2015). Belgium's Gülen-Hizmet Movement Histories, Structures and Initiatives. In Gürkan Çelik, Johann Leman and Karel Steenbrink (Eds.), *Gülen-Inspired Hizmet in Europe: The Western Journey of a Turkish Muslim Movement* (pp. 159–178). Brussels: Peter Lang.

Mehmeti, Jeton (2012). The Role of Education in Kosovo: The Contribution of the Gülen Movement. In Sophia Pandaya and Nancy Gallagher (Eds.), *The Gülen Hizmet Movement and its Transnational Activities: Case Studies of Altruistic Activism in Contemporary Islam* (pp. 212–221). Boca Raton: Brown Water Press.

Öktem, Kerem (2010). *New Islamic Actors after the Wahhabi Intermezzo: Turkey's Return to the Muslim Balkans,* Oxford: European Studies Centre.

Ozzano, Luca (2018). From the 'New Rome' to the Old One: the Gülen Movement in Italy. *Politics, Religion and Ideology, 19* (1), 95–108. https:// doi.org/10.1080/21567689.2018.1453268

Peppinck, Tineke (2012). From 'New Man' to 'World Citizen': The Replication of Fethullah Gülen's Renovation Vision in the Dutch Context. In Paul Weller and İhsan Yılmaz (Eds.), *European Muslims, Civility and Public Life: Perspectives on and From the Gülen Movement* (pp. 91–100). London: Continuum.

Rath, Jan, Thijl Sunier and Astrid Meyer (1997). The Establishment of Islamic Institutions in a De-Pillarizing Society. *Tijdschrift voor Economische en Sociale Geografie, 88* (4), 389–395. https://doi. org/10.1111/j.1467-9663.1997.tb01633.x

Steenbrink, Karel (2015). Gülen in the Netherlands Between Pious Circles and Social Emancipation. In: Gürkan Çelik, Johann Leman and Karel Steenbrink (Eds.), *Gülen-Inspired Hizmet in Europe: The Western Journey of a Turkish Muslim Movement* (pp. 197–223). Brussels: Peter Lang.

Stockholm Center for Freedom (2017). *Erdoğan's Long Arm: The Case of Norway.* Stockholm: Stockholm Center for Freedom. https://stockholmcf.org/wp-content/uploads/2017/12/Erdogans-Long-ArmThe-Case-Of-Norway_15.12.2017pdf.pdf.

Stockholm Center for Freedom (2018). *Erdoğan's Long Arm: The Case of Sweden.* Stockholm: Stockholm Center for Freedom. https://stockholmcf.org/wp-content/uploads/2018/06/Erdogan-Long-Arm-The-Case-of-Sweden_report_june_2018.pdf.

Sunier, Thijl and Landman, Nico (2015). Gülen Movement (Hizmet). In Sunier Thijl and Nico Landman (Eds.), *Transnational Turkish Islam: Shifting Boundaries of Religious Activism and Community Building Turkey and Europe.* (pp. 81–94). Basingstoke: Palgrave Macmillan.

Tee, Caroline (2018). The Gülen Movement in London and the Politics of Public Engagement: Producing 'Good Islam' Before and After 15 July. *Politics, Religion and Ideology, 19*(1), 109–122. https://doi.org/10.1080/21567689. 2018.1453269

Toğuşlu, Erkan (2015). Hizmet in France: Negotiation of Multiple Identities in a Secular Context. In Gürkan Çelik, Johann Leman and Karel Steenbrink (Eds.), *Gülen-Inspired Hizmet in Europe: The Western Journey of a Turkish Muslim Movement* (pp. 225–238). Brussels: Peter Lang.

Weller, Paul (2015). The Gülen Movement in the United Kingdom. In Gurkan Çelik, Johan Leman and Karel Steenbrink (Eds.), *Gülen-Inspired Hizmet in Europe: The Western Journey of a Turkish Muslim Movement* (pp. 239–251). Brussels: Peter Lang.

Weller, Paul and Yılmaz, İhsan (Eds. 2012), *European Muslims, Civility and Public Life: Perspectives On and From the Gülen Movement,* London: Continuum.

Yükleyen, Ahmet (2012). *Localizing Islam in Europe: Turkish Islamic Communities in Germany and the Netherlands*. New York: Syracuse University Press.

Yükleyen, Ahmet and Tunagür, Ferhan (2013). The Gülen Movement in Western Europe and the USA. In Matthias Kortmann and Kerstin Rosenow-Williams (Eds.), *Islamic Organizations in Europe and the USA: A Multi-Disciplinary Perspective* (pp. 224–241). Basingstoke: Palgrave Macmillan.

PART II

Hizmet in Turkish De-centring and European Transitions

CHAPTER 4

Pivotal Issues in Pivotal Times

4.1   The AKP and Hizmet: Walking in Tandem?

The temporal axis around which the pivotal issues with which this chapter is concerned took new shape was that between the May 2013 Gezi Park demonstrations in Istanbul and the events of 15 July 2016 (see Sect. 4.4). Within that period, pre-existing tensions in the relationship between the AKP and Hizmet around a range of issues opened up into clear divergence, culminating in the government's accusations that Hizmet and Fethullah Gülen were behind the 15 July events.

When the AKP first came to power in the Turkish General Election of 2002 there is no doubt that it did so with at least considerable passive support from among the ranks of people associated with Hizmet. This is perhaps not surprising because against the background of an ideologically dominant Kemalism which imposed a radically laicist interpretation of the separation between religion, state and society, the AKP government offered the first opportunity for pious Muslims to be able fully to participate more widely in society and especially in the authoritative branches of the state. At the same time, Keleş says that in relation to the first election in 2001, he does not recall any particular actively organised support for the AKP of the kind that happened later when numbers of Hizmet people were involved in circulating AKP election materials, and indeed:

> In fact, it's an odd one: the movement knew how to work with the secularists because it had been doing so for such a long time, and that was an easier

© The Author(s) 2022
P. Weller, *Hizmet in Transitions*,
https://doi.org/10.1007/978-3-030-93798-0_4

equation to deal with. Somebody that's coming from your own backyard, but actually isn't from your own backyard, but appears to be so; that was more challenging for the movement and the movement wasn't ready to deal with that. But then what happened is that AKP had no people within the state. I mean these are common things that you know – they were being challenged by the military, so what the movement was trying to do, it was not just because the love of the civilian government, but also because in part that was the same military establishment that was going after the movement.

Not only this but, as Keleş points out, it had appeared to many that the Abant meetings had effected a real influence on people in the AKP who were originally from an "Islamist" background, with Keleş noting that "although Tayyip wasn't there, other founding AKP members took part such as Bulent Arinc" and that, because of this:

> The AKP as a project comes out of, it realised the change in discourse, and the change in cultural approach, and the change in political landscape. And part of what helped them to realise that was obviously the parties that kept getting shut down and people were fed up of that, but also the antagonistic politics that had created such a mess at the time, but also the Abant meetings were useful.

Therefore, in Keleş' evaluation, partly due to Abant Platform meetings, "there was a changing political discourse and the AKP changed entirely. It rejected identity politics and political Islam and embraced the accession to the EU; the separation of religion and state; free market economy; and alliance with 'the West' ". Because of this, for a period, there was a commonality of perceived mutual benefit between the values of Hizmet and the declared strategic goals of the AKP to cement democracy in Turkey instead of the previously ever-present threat of military rule and also in the context of aiming for a closer alignment with the European Union. Arising from this, many Hizmet people actively supported the AKP as the party that appeared to be the best opportunity for the kind of society that Hizmet wished to see, while support from Hizmet remained electorally beneficial to the AKP. As Keleş noted in relation to these apparent strategic goals, "This was the position of the movement on these issues all along. The founders of the AKP seemed to adopt them, at least at first".

However, there had also always been some concern within Hizmet about how sincere the AKP's apparent change of strategy had been. In fact, as early as 2005, Erdoğan tried to pass a law that recognised "unarmed terrorism". And this was the first time that *Zaman* newspaper started to publish some negative headlines in relation to the AKP government which, in Keleş' opinion, was "because it saw this as an attempt to go after the movement" given that, with the exception of cyber-terrorism "unarmed non-violent terrorism" is a contradiction in itself, and was clearly not what the proposed law was aiming at. Thus, there were early signs of this mutually of interest changing.

Arising from this and other things, Keleş' evaluation is that "All of this demonstrates that the relationship between Hizmet and the AKP was not rosy at the beginning as some seem to suggest. It was always somewhat challenging". Indeed, as recounted by Keleş (see Sect. 3.4) of the complementary volume, there is a story of a dream that some people in Hizmet had experienced in 2006 about Erdoğan morphing into monstrous form, and concerning which Fethullah Gülen wrote to Erdoğan about as a warning. Keleş himself also notes that "I heard that anti-Hizmet profiling was ongoing in the state in 2008 or 2009. I heard this from colleagues", and as things further developed "Erdoğan heard or suspected that there would be an attempt to split the party, and that Hizmet would open a party, so he apparently pre-emptively tried to say that, but apparently Gülen says that he has no interest in such things". However, Keleş also said that "such is the pressure that he then relents and recommends two people. So, they do become AKP Party members, one whom was the author's former doctoral student, Muhammed Çetin".

In relation to these developments, Keleş noted that "there was a lot of these games going on at the time" which, from his perspective, he evaluated as having been problematic. This is because, as he noted: "we said we are civil society, grassroots movement, focused on education, dialogue, relief work, we are not trying to organise ourselves within the state, we are not about politics, and we are not trying to become politically governing" and that although "by and large, this is correct" through these and other later developments "we've lost the moral high ground".

The opening up of the Turkish state to pious Muslims was especially noticeable in the police and judiciary and, as this occurred, numbers of people associated with Hizmet were in a position, for the first time, to enter the authoritative branches of the state. In doing so, they were inevitably faced with the question of the relationship between their work roles, their personal identities, and their broader identification with Hizmet. Indeed, this became the basis for accusations by Hanefi Avcı, a former chief of police in Turkey, who found himself in prison after publishing a

book, *Haliç'te Yaşayan Simonlar: Dün Devlet Bugün Cemaat*[1] (*'Devotee'
Residents of Haliç: Yesterday State, Today Religious Congregation*). In this,
Avcı (2010) claimed that Hizmet had infiltrated the police and Hizmet
had used this access to secure wire taps useful to it.

When reflecting back more generally on the broader context of these
kinds of issues, Keleş notes that, in comparison with other groups of
Turkish society, which are actually minorities, "The problem with Hizmet
is that it's not a minority" and that it "was more successful". And because
of this, "you had a lot more people within the state structure and the ethical question gets really problematic then. It creates all kinds of conflicts of
interest". Overall Keleş concluded that:

> It's impossible, it's like a casino – the house always wins. And the reason for
> that is that the institutional habitus and culture of these places is more domi-
> neering, both in terms of how it's conveyed to you on a day to day basis,
> than your Gülenial, Hizmet identity. Because, as a police officer, you are in
> the police station, I mean, what am I going to do with Gülen's teaching in
> the police station – it's a police station, I've got a superior telling me to
> interrogate this person; I've got a friend who's doing it a certain way; I am
> inculcated in that culture at that moment, where I am also hiding my
> Hizmet identity, right. So, I am not able to reflect on what it means to be a
> Hizmet-related police officer freely because I am hiding that from everyone,
> including myself sometimes. So, I become more of a Turkish police officer
> than a Hizmet-inspired person, do you see?

4.2   Mutual "Infiltration"?

With regard to the overall relationship between the AKP in power and
Hizmet, Keleş argued that "it's not just that there was these institutional
challenges of being a movement with people in the state"; rather, "it's also
the state culture and mindset" can start to predominate. And it is this
observation that led to Keleş' rather startling way of summarising some of
the issues that arise via the self-critical aphorism that "Hizmet did not
infiltrate the state, the state infiltrated Hizmet". In relation to this Keleş
was not making a specific charge about the presence in Hizmet of under-
cover state security agents, although it would be surprising if such had not
been deployed with an aim of deliberate covert disruption in the classical
sense of infiltration. Rather, he was pointing to the much less dramatic,
but no less real and eventually perhaps at least as problematic an

incorporation of significant numbers of Hizmet people into not only the organs of the state, but also its fundamental mindset. Thus, with regard to the related growth of Hizmet's standing and spheres of influence in Turkish society, Ercan Karakoyun from Germany made the historical reflection that:

> Well, I think everybody liked it. I think because if I talk to people here now, and when I remember journeys to Turkey in these years, I think people enjoyed what they did; they enjoyed being big; they enjoyed working for the state; they enjoyed being diplomats. So, it is somehow human. If your family invests in building an education, if you study, if you work very hard and then the state comes and says, look there is a job, don't you want to apply. OK, I apply. And then when you get it, of course you enjoy being there. It's very human.

Similar issues have, of course, faced many religious and other movements when moving from the social margins into a more central position. If a movement starts small and is to some extent distinctive, and then achieves some success, standing and influence, it becomes more socially "acceptable". After becoming acceptable, it has at least the potential for becoming instrumentalised even while those active within it continue to have the personal intention to work for the benefit of society. However, as Karakoyun notes, one consequence of this trajectory can be that "in the end you become an enemy of the state! – because you are now too powerful, too big, and you are in the end an external influence in the state". In a different European context this is, for example, what happened historically to various Christian religious orders, such as the Jesuits, and concerns about similar dynamics influence how, on the other side of July 2016, many Hizmet asylum-seekers in Europe view their relationship with the state (see Sect. 5.5).

Whatever judgement one reaches on what occurred in Turkey itself, it is arguable that the first signal of at least some people either within Hizmet and/or who associated themselves with it perhaps beginning to overreach themselves was in the so-called Ergenekon affair. With this, in the overall context of Turkish society's tendency towards conspiracy thinking, both imagined and real, and against the background of not unreasonable concerns about a possible coup attempt against the AKP government, the organs of state were deployed against a large number of people who were under suspicion. And at this time, Hizmet-related organisations—for example, *Zaman* newspaper—seemed generally to side with the state's actions.

The point at which this also seemed to blur into Hizmet self-interest was around the publication of the journalist Ahmet Şık's draft book, *İmamın Ordusu* (or, in English, *The Imam's Army*) which claimed to be an exposé of the life and work of Gülen and the Hizmet movement. Şık was detained on 3 March 2011, before its publication. As he was arrested, he shouted (it was thought with reference to Hizmet) that "Whoever touches [them] burns". The draft of the book was seized by the government and banned on the basis of a claim that it was an "illegal organizational document" of the secret organisation Ergenekon. Şık was detained but eventually was released pending trial in March 2012. On 23 March, a court ordered the confiscation of the draft book. In the meantime, and despite the threat of charges to anyone found in possession of a copy, on 1 April 2011, unknown persons made a copy of the book available on the internet. In November 2011, a version of the book edited by 125 journalists, activists and academics was published by Postacı Publishing House under the name *000Kitap: Dokunan Yanar* (000Book). The website of the Democratic Turkey Forum provides some selected English translations,[2] while an English translation of the Epilogue can be found on the anti-Hizmet website tukishinvitations.com.[3]

In *The Imam's Army*, Ahmet Şık argued that "people started to talk more frequently about the existence of a 'Fethullahçı' (Fethullahist) organization in the bureaucracy, especially in the police force". Indeed, it is claimed that "the police organization has almost become the armed unit of the parish (the word 'parish' being a poor English translation of the Turkish word *cemaat*, which is better rendered as 'community')".[4] The Epilogue to the *Imam's Army* argued that "Although there are people suggesting that these communities are religious NGOs, it is a controversial designation for the Gülen Movement". Of course, as was already noted and discussed in some detail in Chap. 1, all the frames of reference that one uses to describe hotly contested phenomena are themselves as much interpretations as descriptions. And while, overall, the author of this book comes down on the side of primarily interpreting Hizmet in terms of its own publicly articulated self-understanding as a religiously inspired movement manifesting itself in a range of civil society ways, in the text of *The Imam's Army*, a very different picture is painted.

Both the overall tone of *The Imam's Army*, and its specific choice of words, convey some very clear negative signalling, as follows: "With the investments that began in the 1970s, especially in the education sector, the Golden Generation that was expected to become the administrator of the future occupied bureaucratic positions now, in the first decade of the 21st century, exactly as scheduled". It then went on to speak of Hizmet educational initiatives in terms of "using their exponentially growing financial power to expand their market share". In this kind of description, the use of words such as "investments" and "market share" already predisposes the reader towards a particular interpretive framework. Such words strongly imply, even while not quite explicitly charging that, regardless of how Hizmet might see and explain itself, that it is *really* "something else". That "something else" is then presented in ways akin to that of a growing business empire having Mafia-like mediations between business, politics and self-interest, with the aim of gaining state control. That, in turn, leads back into the kind of conspiracy theory interpretation of the kinds that so deeply permeate all parts of Turkish society and politics. In the second to last paragraph of the Epilogue to the book, it is argued that "Today, victims of yesterday are getting even with their oppressors" and somewhat disturbingly in view of what did follow July 2016, it concludes that "we are yet to see whether there will be time when some start getting even for what is happening now".[5]

4.3   The MV Mavi Marmara Incident: A Sign of Things to Come

Among commentators who had previously spoken of an "alliance" between the AKP and Hizmet, quite a number cite what is known as either the MV Mavi Marmara or Gaza Flotilla incident as the first big sign of a break in that. An alternative perspective is put forward by İsmail Mesut Sezgin (2014) of the Centre for Hizmet Studies (see Sect. 3.5). He argued that "I don't believe there was ever an alliance between Gülen and Erdoğan of the type imagined by some commentators" and also "far less that this incident was the cause of the split/separation of that alliance". However, regardless of one's evaluation of how far the notion of an "alliance" was an only construction or was more substantive, as Sezgin says, "The flotilla incident can, however, be useful in demonstrating the difference of Gülen's mindset from political Islam" (see also Robinson 2017).

The incident turned around six ships, including one called the MV Mavi Mavi Marmara, that had been organised by the Free Gaza Movement and the Turkish Foundation for Human Rights and Freedoms and Humanitarian Relief, to transport construction materials and other humanitarian aid to the people of Gaza. However, this was organised in the context not only of a humanitarian goal, but also of the specific political intention of breaking the Israeli blockade of Gaza, in the light of which Israel called for the mission to be aborted, seeing it as provocation. On 31 May 2010, Israeli forces carried out a naval commando operation during which, while the ships were still in international waters, they were boarded from helicopters and speedboats. Although activists on five of the ships carried out only passive resistance, on the Turkish ship, the MV Mavi Marmara, a group of passengers began to threaten and use violence. This resulted in nine activists, including eight Turkish citizens and one Turkish American, being killed, with another dying later, and many others being wounded. Ten Israeli soldiers were wounded, including one seriously. It was reported that five of the activists who were killed had previously declared their desire to become *shaheeds* (or martyrs).

The incident caused a major rupture in Turkish-Israeli relations and a number of commissions of enquiry followed until, finally, Israel offered Turkey $20 million compensation. That led, on 22 March 2013, to a telephone conversation in which Israeli Prime Minister Netanyahu apologised on behalf of Israel to Turkish Prime Minister Erdoğan who accepted the apology. This, in turn, led to further discussions and, on 29 June 2019, an agreement that was approved by the Israeli government.

Gülen came under very strong criticism in relation to his public stance on these events because he did not uncritically join in with the strong national outpouring of anti-Israeli feeling which led to the Turkish government recalling its ambassador from Israel and to declaring the Israeli ambassador to Turkey as persona non grata. In this febrile atmosphere, Turkey had also threatened to send another flotilla, this time accompanied by Turkish warships. Therefore, the threat of potential war seemed very real.

In his first comment on the incident, Gülen said that "What I saw was not pretty. It was ugly". However, what especially caused a critical reaction among some sectors of Turkish society was that he went on to criticise the organisers of the Flotilla because they had not sought some kind of agreement with Israel before trying to deliver the aid. Because of this, in Gülen's view, the action was "a sign of defying authority and will not lead to fruitful matters". Some critics have read this as Gülen defending the legitimacy of Israel's Gaza blockade and, as Sezgin notes, this "created a lot of anger and disappointment among nationalists and Millî Görüş". However, as in

Gülen's historical statements in relation to military authorities during periods of military rule, and which some interpreted (see Weller 2022, Sect. 3.4) as being supportive of such coups, it is important to read such statements in the light of Gülen's overall theological and ethical approach in which social stability, even of a problematic kind, is preferable to chaos.

4.4   From Gezi Park to 15 July 2016

In a way similar to that of the Russian Federation's Vladimir Putin, as Recep Tayyip Erdoğan approached the maximum period the Turkish constitution allowed in the office of Prime Minister and that following his third election victory in June 2011 he started to press for what he called a "Turkish style" executive presidency. During this period, authoritarianism grew, and wider social tensions reached a peak around the so-called Gezi Park protests. These began on 28 May 2013 as protests initially undertaken by around fifty environmentalists camping in the park in protest against an urban development plan that threatened this park, and which was forcibly broken up by the police.

Sparked by the outrage about this violent eviction felt by many across Turkey's social and political spectrum, an enormous wave of linked protests began, involving up to around three and a half million people, coalescing around such otherwise diverse issues as freedom of assembly, freedom of the press, freedom of expression, curbs on alcohol and on kissing in public, as well as the war in Syria. As this wave of protests grew, Erdoğan saw this as a trial of strength. On 2 June, he dismissed the protesters as "a few looters", following which many protesters called themselves *çapulcu* (looters), appropriating Erdoğan's insult for themselves, leading to the coining of the new word *chapulling*, meaning of "fighting for your rights".

During the period of these protests more than three thousand arrests were made; twenty-two people were killed; and more than eight thousand were injured, including many with critical injuries. Excessive use of force by police and the overall absence of government dialogue with the protesters were criticised by some foreign countries and international organisations. During the crisis, Gülen refused to take sides with Erdoğan in support of suppressing the protestors, while at this time Erdoğan also moved to shut down all tutorial centres for college admissions in the country, around a quarter of which were linked with Hizmet.

In December 2013, details of a corruption probe were made public involving members of Erdoğan's cabinet; the Iranian-Turkish businessman Reza Zarrab; and the facilitation of payments for oil and gas to Iran. However, Erdoğan charged Hizmet with working with international co-conspirators to effect what he called a "judiciary coup" against his government. The original prosecutors who had been working on the corruption case were first removed, later dismissed and finally arrested, while the new prosecutors closed the case. A more systematic campaign against Hizmet began during which Erdoğan increasingly referred to Hizmet using the terminology of *Paralel Devlet Yapılanması* (or, Parallel State Structure), with Sunier and Landman (2015) noting that accusations of infiltration of state institutions became "the very essence of the conflict between the AKP and Hizmet" (p. 82). In speeches Erdoğan went on also to use ever more extreme, lurid and provocatively inciting rhetoric, including reference to Hizmet people by such epithets as "leeches", "assassins" and "blood sucking vampires".

On 31 January 2014, the author's former doctoral student Muhammed Çetin, who, in 2011, had been elected as an AKP Party Deputy in the Turkish Parliament, resigned from the party stating to a press conference in the Parliament that "Unfortunately the AK Party has of today become blackened. It has become the architect of a process in which corruption is covered up, thieves are protected and the unlawful has become the law".[6] In the wake of the scandal, many thousands of other members of the judiciary were dismissed and replaced with pro-Erdoğan appointees, while a programme of school closures began to be systematically enforced on Hizmet founded schools throughout Turkey. The attribution to Hizmet of the description "terrorist" was first officially deployed in April 2015, while on 28 October 2015, the Turkish Interior Ministry listed Gülen as one of the country's most wanted terrorists. In May 2016, six weeks before July 2016 events, Turkey's National Security Council first described Hizmet as the "Fethullah Terrorist Organization" (FETÖ).

The events of the 15 July and their aftermath became the latest in a long line of disruptions to democracy in Turkey. These had included, on 27 May 1960, the first military coup, in which the Turkish President, Prime Minister and others were arrested and tried for treason and other offences. On 12 March 1971, widespread unrest followed a major economic downturn, and the military intervened to "restore order". On 12 September 1980, following violent clashes between left-wing and right-wing political groups, the military intervened again and, in the following years, thousands of people were arrested and dozens were executed. On 28 February 1997, in what became known as the "postmodern coup", after the rise of the Welfare Party, the military put forward a series of "recommendations" which the government was expected to accept, and the Prime Minister, Necmettin Erbakan, was forced to resign. The Welfare Party was dissolved in 1998, and Erbakan was banned from politics for five years. Recep Tayyip Erdoğan, together with some other former members of the Welfare Party, went on to found the AKP.

On the evening of 15 July 2016, the author was on holiday in the UK, watching TV in a hotel room, when the events of that day began to unfold during which over 300 people were killed and more than 2000 were injured. Those who claimed responsibility for the events at least portrayed themselves as a faction from within the Armed Forces called the Peace at Home Council. As reasons for their actions they cited the erosion of secularism, the elimination of democratic rule, disregard for human rights and Turkey's loss of international credibility. In terms of what actually took place much is not clear, and it is not the purpose of this book to arrive at an ultimate adjudication on this. For diverse perspectives one can consult the Intercultural Dialogue Platform's (2016) report and/or Yavuz and Bayram Balcı's edited collection of 2018, together with Greg Barton's (2017) piece on "What on Earth Has Gone So Wrong in Turkey" which, together with some other sources, are briefly (but more extensively than here) discussed in Weller 2022, Sect. 2.8.

What is clear is that no sooner had the events of 15 July taken place than President Erdoğan very quickly appeared on television and in a way which, given the environment, could not credibly be identified with any kind of evidential certainty, charged Gülen and Hizmet with being behind what had happened. Gülen and those around him denied this[7] and called for an international investigation. Some both within and outside Hizmet have even raised the question of whether the events of 15 July might even have been a "self-coup" initiated by Erdoğan to ensure his grip on power (Alliance for Shared Values 2019). Certainly, in comparison with a classical military coup, the facts of what actually happened inevitably lead to questions about it such as those posed by Norwegian investigative journalist Jørgen Lorentzen (2019) in his documentary film, *A Gift from God?*, picking up in its title on Erdoğan's claim that the events provided him with "a God-given opportunity".

Lorentzen's documentary investigation, among other things, highlights that the troops who appeared on the bridge over the Bosphorus in

Istanbul, and who were at the symbolic heart of what happened that night, were barely trained cadets who did not seem to have any clear idea of what they were doing there, rather than being the kind of elite force one would expect to be in place in any serious military coup attempt. However one might evaluate this, what is clear is that in the wake of this self-proclaimed "God-given opportunity" Erdoğan set about following through on the "cleansing" of society that he had previously threatened—a word with frighteningly inflammatory resonances even if one were to accept there might be any truth in the accusations of Hizmet involvement.

In relation to various international evaluations of what took place, in March 2017 the UK House of Commons' Foreign Affairs Committee (2017), informed by evidence from the Foreign and Commonwealth Office, noted that:

> While some of the individuals involved in the coup may have been Gülenists, given the large number of Gülenist supporters and organizations in Turkey, it does not necessarily follow that the Gülenists were responsible for the coup or that their leadership directed the coup. (p. 38)

The possibility that some individuals, including in the military, may have found Gülen and Hizmet attractive and might also have been involved in the events of 15 July 2016 is one that is acknowledged by some within Hizmet, including among some of the interviewees for the research project underlying this book and its complementary volume (Weller 2022, Sect. 2.8). But this is, of course, not at all the same thing as the event having been masterminded by Gülen, and/or Hizmet acting as a tightly organised subversive movement aiming for political power. The credibility of such a judgement would be dependent on a prior evaluation of Hizmet as being a highly structured cell organisation, rather than a much more diffuse network composed both of highly committed individuals, along with many people who had simply had personal connections with one or more Hizmet institutions and/or had been inspired by what they had read of Gülen's books or heard sermons preached by him either in person and/or through other media.

Indeed, even in relation to the UK Foreign and Commonwealth Office's claim that some Gülenist individuals may have been involved, the House of Commons Foreign Affairs Committee (2017) itself noted that "the FCO seems unable to cite much evidence to prove that it is true". Overall, the Committee summarised that "the Turkish government's account of the Gülenists and of the coup … is not substantiated by hard, publicly available evidence" while, as in the style of Parliamentary reports, also saying it is "as yet uncontradicted by the same standard" (p. 3). In relation to the Turkish government's description of those associated with Hizmet as "terrorists" and the possibility of Hizmet being added to the list of proscribed terrorist organisations in the UK, the Committee noted that "The FCO told us that it did not have evidence to justify the designation of the Gülenists as a terrorist organisation by the UK, and we agree with this assessment" (p. 36).

On the level of the EU, the European Commission publishes a Turkey report in relation to Turkey's accession status, following which the European Parliament also does its own brief report. In relation to the Commission's report HE1 says that "the Hizmet name was mentioned a lot of times objectively" while, in relation to the Parliament's report, although the rapporteurs were open to comments on the draft, the source said that "We asked for some annexes to the report". In response to that HE1 underlines that "All our proposals were accepted by the shadow rapporteurs and the MEPs but there is a negotiation process and the term 'Hizmet movement' was eliminated from the European Parliament report". Thus, in the end, the European Parliament report does not refer specifically to Hizmet but mentions in more general terms the number of victims and of people who lost their jobs. Of course, Turkish government officials such as Permanent Delegation of Turkey to the European Union also play an active role on the negotiation procedure and in relation to the Rapporteur "when we asked why the definition was removed we didn't get any clear answer from her".

In the same month, in an interview with the German magazine *Der Spiegel*, Bruno Kahl (2017), the head of Germany's intelligence service, the Bundesnachrichtungsdienst (BND), expressed the evaluation that "The coup attempt was not initiated by the government. Before July 15 the government had already started a big purge so parts of the military thought they should do a coup quickly before it hit them too" while in relation to Turkey's charge that Fethullah Gülen was behind the coup, "Turkey tried to convince us of that at every level. But so far they have not succeeded". With regard to the Hizmet movement, Kahl described it as "a civilian association that aims to provide further religious and secular education".

In relation to the defining of Hizmet as terrorist, the Council of Europe's Commissioner for Human Rights' (2016) *Memorandum on the*

Human Rights Implications of the Measures Taken Under the State of Emergency in Turkey has questioned the legal validity of the terrorist definition even in Turkey itself: "Furthermore, it ['FETÖ'] has not yet been recognised as a terrorist organization in a final judgment of the Turkish Court of Cassation which, according to the Turkish authorities, is a crucial legal act in the Turkish legal system when it comes to the designation of an organisation as terrorist" (para 20).

However, what ensued was the final turning of the screw in the dismantling of Hizmet in Turkey. In the light of this it could credibly be argued that whatever actually happened in, or was behind July 2016, what might be called a "judicial coup" took place through what happened in the following days, with the introduction of emergency rule that suspended many human rights protections that, even within an imperfect legal system had previously existed, led to abuses such as babies being imprisoned along with their mothers in a way that Turkish law itself, in normal times, would not allow. This state of emergency then became "normalised" as a dehumanising thing, not only in relation to Hizmet, but also in relation to many other groups and people including journalists; people from Kurdish background; Alevis; secularists and many others who have nothing to do with Gülen, including some who have been critical of him and of Hizmet.

In the mass arrests that followed, many thousands of soldiers, judges and teachers—as well as of ordinary people outside of the professions—were detained based on claims about their connections with Gülen and Hizmet. What this in practice meant for many ordinary people is explained in vividly personal terms by some asylum-seekers interviewed for this book (see Sect. 4.5) and in its complementary volume (Weller 2022, Sect. 5.1). In very human stories they explain how, suddenly, they found themselves cut off from their previous lives, either literally in terms of imprisonment, or else through being dismissed from employment and then economically and socially isolated in a kind of Kafkaesque experience in which, at every turn, they were blocked from finding a means of existence independent of reliance on family and/or friends. More recently, aspects of this overall situation were eased for other groups, including in the context of the COVID-19 pandemic when many criminals were released from Turkish prisons because of concerns about the spread of infection, but prisoners associated with Hizmet were generally speaking still kept in jail. More recently, the Turkish government has tried to paint a picture of "normalisation", in relation to which Abdulkerim (known as Kerim) Balcı (see Acknowledgements) says:

To a certain extent there is an attempt of "normalisation" with regards to the left wing opposition; less with regards to the Kurdish opposition; but when it comes to the Gülenists, there is no change in the policy, and in fact only yesterday there was a mass campaign of arrests on duty police officers. So, it is continuing, and it will continue on. I don't see anything changing in the short or long run.

This is, says Balcı, because "Erdoğan managed to demonise members of this movement, not only his supporters, but the opposition groups also believe this". But whatever view is taken of July 2016, what followed has been of massively damaging significance for Hizmet in its original homeland of Turkey. As a consequence, while prior to that Hizmet could already be found in most regions of the world, the events of July 2016 and their aftermath mean that one can truly refer to a pivotal time of what this book calls the "de-centring" of Hizmet from Turkey. A part of that "de-centring" is that its previous presence in Europe has been supplemented by the European destination of many Hizmet asylum-seekers and others who have fled Turkey in search of a more secure environment for themselves and their families.

4.5   Hizmet Trauma in Turkey and Europe

In terms of the inherited base of Hizmet in at least the western part of Europe, Yükleyen and Tunagür noted that, at the time of their writing, what they called Hizmet's "activists" were "a mix of lower and middle-class, composed mainly of working-class, mid-size business owners, and students" (2013, p. 224). As reflected in many of the country summaries in the last chapter, Yükleyen and Tunagür also pointed out that, of the long-standing Hizmet people in Europe, as well as those who made direct connection with Gülen's teaching there were some who came out of Diyanet mosques where they had been frustrated at the lack of opportunity for activism, while others came from nationalist backgrounds where they had become unhappy with internal splits and conflicts (2013, p. 230). The events of July 2016 meant that there was now also another and different grouping layer within Hizmet in Europe, composed of "new arrivals". This, and the effect of it upon Hizmet people and organisations that were already within the various European countries, has brought new challenges and opportunities affecting both the composition and the balance of Hizmet activities and has also done so differentially across various European countries.

The "new arrivals"—whether they took whatever opportunity they could to exit from Turkey as people of independent resources and/or eventually needed to leave as asylum-seekers and refugees—found themselves suddenly uprooted and in a different country where it takes time, both to come to terms with the trauma of what happened in Turkey itself and to orientate oneself to the new environment of the host country. It is therefore hard to over-emphasise the multiple levels of trauma experienced in the wake of July 2016.

This was at its starkest for those coming from Turkey as asylum-seekers. As explained by the female Hizmet asylum-seeker AS4, "Nobody supported us in Turkey. Our neighbours and friends, they know us for years. But they changed their minds in one night". Or, as her husband, AS3 (see Acknowledgements) suggested in partial qualification of that "It might not have been in that one night, but in a period". He went on to describe the distress of this as follows: "We are trying to find the reason about these people, because last week they know us, they like so much, they are coming over to us, we are going there. We are in very good relationships. But sometimes people, they like still, but they don't say, OK you are a good person. They don't call us anything". As added to by his wife: "Some friends of ours, for example, they are all working for the government so they are afraid of this. They can't come to our houses because thought if I come to visit them, I can lose my job again".

Escaping from the country has had a particularly harsh effect on children because, as AS4 says, "Nowadays we can't go back to Turkey because we are 'wanted' together. The police came to our houses to take us – first me and then him. They came to our houses and checked our houses" searching for evidence. Of this time, she explains, "my little child was younger than two years old. So, I ran because I didn't trust law system at this time, because pregnant women and all of us were in jails. So, I ran, and we ultimately ran. So, we can't go back nowadays". At the same time this asylum-seeker couple saw themselves as fortunate to be in Switzerland since, as AS4 put it:

> We were lucky, because our parents supported us. Some of friends they didn't have this support from their parents. We are lucky because of this. For example, when we were coming here and going to Evros River, for example, I thought my Dad would say, "No you can't go, it's very dangerous". But he thought, and he said "No life for you here now, so go" [cries…].

In summary she says that "Turkey is a country of fear now. For example, when we are talking to our parents there, they are afraid still. We can't talk … comfortably … Because we are afraid too". In many ways this was all ironic because, as her husband explained, "In Turkey, even us, we are state loving people – in our background it is so important. But maybe with our history lessons, and in our teaching, that state is so important. The state, the government I mean, doesn't do wrong. People do wrong. That is our background".

Reflecting on all this politically, as AS2 (see Acknowledgements) put it, "It was because of the lack of education and not questioning beyond what is seen. Especially when someone in religion powerful, or in politics powerful, in government very powerful says something, most of the people in Asia, or in Turkey also, believe that and don't examine that". At the same time, those within Hizmet who have suffered such trauma also try to make sense of that not only in relation to socio-political reflection and analysis, but also in the light of faith. Therefore, as another of the Hizmet-related asylum-seekers from Turkey in Switzerland put it, reflecting on it theologically:

> I am a believer and believe in God. And, of course, I believe he is testing us, I believe. And this is not the real life, this is just a place to change into another, eternal life. And I do my best here to please my God and my friends, and the whole humanity, actually. This is what we learned from Mr. Fethullah Gülen. I do my best as a human being and look positively for the future. Of course, some things happen bad in the life, but this is the life, it is not just a straight line. We will see together, all the friends, what will happen in the future.

Nevertheless, not all asylum-seekers are able to interpretively frame and come to terms with their experience in such a way. Summarising what, in practical terms, their trauma can mean for asylum-seekers in the Netherlands, Alasag notes that:

> Some people they are so much traumatised that when they come to Holland and they are in the camp, they don't want to engage with anybody. They don't speak and we don't know what they all went through. So, it's difficult to know these people because they don't contact us, we don't know of their existence. But we know this from other asylum-seekers who say that they saw some people come into the camps and they think they are from Gülen movement, but they don't talk with anyone etc. So, this is our guess – that they are so much traumatised they don't want to engage with anybody for now.

In the UK, based on the numbers of those needing legal aid, Balcı suggests that "It's about one thousand families that managed to come to the UK and apply for asylum". At the time of the interview (7.8.2019), Balcı's own case was still pending as the longest-standing case that had been going on for over two years. It has now been decided in his favour, in relation to which, however, he also said (referring to the attempt made by the Turkish Government to extradite the British-Turkish dual national Özcan Keleş on which see more at the end of this section) that "Most probably, just like Özcan's case, I will have an extradition request waiting out there". At the time of the interview conducted with him, Balcı says, "Up until now we have had about twenty cases of refusals. Half of the cases are not yet answered. So, this doesn't mean nine hundred acceptances – half of them are continuing".

In the UK, most Hizmet asylum-seekers have been based in London, although Balcı also comments that "to a certain extent, the Home Office is helping through dispersing people". Because of this, Hizmet has now developed a presence in Glasgow in Scotland and in Cardiff in Wales, in both of which cities there had never previously been a Hizmet presence. Also within England, Balcı estimates that there are now more than thirty Hizmet families in a place like Ipswich which previously, as he put it, "never existed in our maps, mental maps". Overall, Balcı says that:

> When it comes to the court houses, we have had only two cases of complete failure where we are 100% sure that our friend is a friend, a member of the movement, and is at risk back in Turkey, but still we didn't manage to convince the court. In one case the court didn't believe they are Gülenist. In one case, it was a former army cadet – they didn't believe that the guy was in great danger. They said you are very low profile and so on.

In relation to Spain, Nazari says of asylum-seekers in general, including those from Hizmet, that "Spain is generously accepting them", although "the processes are very slow compared to Belgium, Germany and so on". Therefore, many people have been waiting for over two years for a decision. But at the same time "Spain is like giving them a place to live, money to eat – its OK". Naziri also commented that "Spain's system is good for me because they are not all put in one place in one city". As a by-product, Naziri notes that, whereas prior to 2016 Hizmet people had been concentrated in only three Spanish cities, they can now be found in thirty-three, which he evaluates positively, commenting that "living in different cities is avoiding the natural formation of a ghetto". Of their experience of Spain, Naziri says:

> Yeah, I would argue that it is an open society and many Turks talking about various countries love it, like it, and most of them that I saw, they are very thankful that they are in Spain. There could be other opportunities, like in Germany and other countries where economically they are better. Some of them – you know the Dublin process – came from the Dublin process into Spain and they say, "Well, thank God we are here in Spain, thank God it didn't function" – I heard it from some of them.

At the same time "there are some difficulties: the economic question is important". Nevertheless, in contrast to the situation in a lot of other European countries "I would say that most of them now found some kind of work, because even if you don't get your status you are permitted to work after six months". Thus, Naziri says that "I see that there is like a desire of starting from the beginning and starting a new life" while noting that there also "some cases that are really not happy with the slow process of not giving them the status. So, they don't know whether they will be given or not and some of them are, you know, like small size entrepreneurs, businessmen, so they don't know whether to invest or not". Therefore, Naziri's overall reflection is that "I think it's a process now, a process of learning the language; getting to know the culture of Spain, OK; and the process of loving it".

In Switzerland, the asylum system operates on a Federal basis, but with offices in the Cantons. So, as Özgü explains it, when asking for asylum one goes to one "one of six centres where you can apply". Overall, Özgü comments that since 2019 "within three or four months the immigration office says if you can stay or not" but also that "The asylum-seekers in the French and Italian speaking areas they get recognised faster than the people in the German-speaking areas".

In relation to France, Erkinbekov says that "In France we have the new asylum-seekers who came from Turkey and there are a lot of Hizmet sympathisers in African and in other countries as a teacher". As with those in other European countries "it is a fact that some of them have a very big trauma: some who were in prison for a minimum of one and maximum of two or three years. And they came out of prison and had children who were separated from their parents". However, rather than developing as a separate group, Erkinbekov comments that the newly developed French General Assembly of Hizmet supporters (noted in Sect. 3.7) is:

> Working on a survey to get their opinion and approaches from all over France. And we are trying to make some, I'll say, new organizations listening to their opinions, including the critics of the Hizmet supporters. So, now the newcomers of the Hizmet movement, the asylum-seekers, they are trying to integrate in the French society, they are learning French and also they are supporting actions of Hizmet.

But the trauma of July 2016 also extends to many Hizmet people who had been already living and working in Europe. As an example, interviewee Selma Ablak,[8] from the Netherlands (see Acknowledgements), said of the Hizmet women's organisation in that country that "we had five Board members in Rosarium and they all quit" from such a role although they are "still involved with the movement". As explained by Ablak, this was "Because we had the 'click Turks', Dutch Turks who were texting the Turkish consulate that 'Those people are involved with Hizmet'. Because of this they were frightened of being followed or..." Underlying this "they were frightened about the Turkish Dutch people and the Turkish authorities in Turkey, because of their relatives, because of their belongings in Turkey, they were afraid". As a consequence of this, in terms of Hizmet public representatives, in the Netherlands, they have only "a handful of persons" who are "standing in the front and are trying to represent the movement in the Netherlands". As one of those, Ablak put herself in the firing line, testifying that, especially at the beginning of this period people texted her saying that they had given her name to the Turkish authorities:

> Someone threatened me with killing me and saying that I needed to be raped, awful, awful things. So, I had a time in which I was afraid to go outside. But I was lucky because, until 2015 I lived ... near Rotterdam. And then in May 2015, I got moved to Amsterdam. So, we moved to another city and nobody knew me here. And that was a relief.

Nevertheless, Ablak states that:

> Each time when I went on television or the radio or in the newspapers there were people getting angry and saying awful things, and most of the time because I said clearly I won't go back, this is who I am, and this is what I

stand for, and nothing will change that. And then because they can't reach me they got my mother. So – 'Let your daughter keep silent, otherwise things will happen.'

At that time, Ablak explained that her mother was still living in Rotterdam and that "when I visited her, people were just angry with me and because of me they were also angry to mother and they yelled at her and they hit her. So, she had to move from where she lived in the city from her first moments in the Netherlands for almost forty years". This was, she says, "because of those people who were seeing her as the mother of a terrorist". Two years prior to her interview (which was conducted in August 2019) Ablak's house was broken into and of which she explained that "They didn't steal anything except a beamer and laptops and that kind of thing. They didn't touch the money or any other valuable things. So, it wasn't just a 'normal' break in" with regard to which she commented that "Those are suspicious things. We don't know for sure what it was". In addition, she explained that although "My son had nothing to do with Hizmet", he also experienced "being yelled at and shouted at school" and being called "a terrorist, as the son of a terrorist. So, we are still trying to get over it".

In France, Erkinbekov explained that although "the people who were in dialogue with us, some of them they were very supportive to us" quite a number of long-standing Hizmet people felt threatened by the likely reporting of their names to the Turkish embassy—of which Erkinbekov noted that "we heard that every month they renew the list" and that opponents of Hizmet also "shared the address of Hizmet movement volunteers in the media, saying I know he is in Hizmet, and here is his address". There were also quite widespread incidents of violence against property in which what Erkinbekov identified as being effectively some militia arms of the Turkish government within the diaspora in France "attacked our centres which were known as Hizmet centres in France". For example, in a downtown area in the city of Sens, a Hizmet centre was burned down. In Beziers, in the south of France "they tried to burn down, but the neighbours called the police and the firefighters". In Moulhouse, their centre "was just stoned and hammered, and the person who was trying to break in with a hammer was caught on the camera, so he was in court and sentenced including a certain amount of money to compensate". And there were also incidents in relation to centres in Valence and in Loos, near the German border where there was also "a gunshot".

Overall, concerning the period immediately following July 2016, Erkinbekov summarised that "What we have lived through in France in that period in 2016, I think – the shock that we had – I think our friends in the other countries in Europe didn't have as much pressure as we had in France, I think". And because of what happened, there was a very big pressure on Hizmet volunteers and sympathisers throughout France. Since the majority of them have familial origins in Turkey, as Erkinbekov put it, "They said, so if they do such harm in France, we couldn't imagine what they could do in Turkey". As a result of this "most of them they decided not to show up publicly and they decided to retire from the official lists of our associations" with the impact of this being that "it stopped some of our activities and it was, I think, at that time very difficult". However, by the time of the interview he was saying, "And now we get over this … So, we have started new projects and we started new actions".

By some contrast, in Switzerland, Özgü reported that they had not really had any community-level threats. Rather, "We just had AKP trolls in the internet who were trying to do defamation, but not more than that. We didn't have any blackmailings or things like that".

As well as in relation to Hizmet individuals, the events of July 2016 also had a significant effect on a number of existing Hizmet organisations in Europe. Thus in Italy, the anonymous Hizmet interviewee HE2 explained that, in contrast with the situation in many other European countries, the Istituto Tevere was not physically attacked, although a small centre close to the Retreat Centre in Italy was attacked:

> And the first night of 15-16 July 2016, what happened in Italy could be a very good indication about the truth of the coup d'etat. Nobody knew what was happening, you know, in Italy it was midnight and a gang of young Turkish guys came and tried to set fire to this place. It was shocking. Even the guys within the building, there were some students, they couldn't understand what was going on actually. But it is sure, they knew and he prepared his organization to confront. Because then the Italian security forces found that these guys were motivated by imam of the Turkish mosque, that's it. The General Consul came from Milan. We don't know really what happened. He visited the police and these sort of guys. That happened, although in Italy people got some phone calls, horrible phone call, uneducated guys watching every day and saying, "You are a traitor" and then all sorts of offensive words.

In Spain, many of the European mobility programmes in which Hizmet had participated have finished because the Turkish government determines the conditions for different NGOs and organisations in Turkey in relation to entering into partnerships with various foreign Associations and organisations, including the need for approval by the Turkish embassy in the country concerned, "So this, yeah, it impacts you, yeah".

In Belgium, Toğuşlu explained with regard to the Gülen Chair in Leuven University that:

> When the first rift took place between the Gülen movement and the AKP government in Turkey in 2014 (it had already started before the coup attempt), there were at that time some discussions, discussions especially coming from Turkey to make a pressure to shut down the Chair, especially because the name of the Chair indicates directly, and is supported by the movement. So, within the University also they discussed whether they wanted to continue because in 2015 we started with the Chair again for the second term and they didn't care what the state of Turkey said about the movement or about the Chair. But still with different channels – like the Turkish Embassy, like Diyanet, like the Maarif Foundation (the Foundation directly from the President of the Republic of Turkey).

And especially following the events of July 2016, Toğuşlu said of them that:

> I heard that they wanted also to establish an Islamic Chair at the University. And I heard it said that, not directly, but that they also wanted the closure of the Chair. So, after the coup attempt, they pressed too much and portrayed Leuven University also as a terrorist organization. It was a little bit ridiculous, funny, as a decision coming from Turkey because the Leuven University had a Chair of this kind that they put Leuven University in the list of terrorist organizations. It was funny, but then they removed that.

Then the Turkish authorities threatened that they will not recognise the diplomas of the Turkish students who graduate from the university, in the light of which "there were some discussions between us, the Dean, the Vice-Directors and the Director. But then they removed again the threat and Turkey accepted again Leuven University's Diploma, and they understood that such a kind of intimidation would never work". But Toğuşlu also explained that some of the university's students of Turkish origin became nervous and conflicted about applying to and being interviewed for Gülen Chair awards such that, even if they were offered anonymity (which, of course, can never be completely guaranteed), "I had two or three students who wanted to take my course and they approached me and said, 'Hey Professor, I want to really do this and we don't have such a kind of problem with you, but in many cases we will return back to Turkey and we don't want trouble' ". Also, institutionally he explained that "it created some thoughts also in the University about whether they want to con- tinue … and so they are questioning whether they want this in that sense or not. In that sense, OK, the pressure sometimes coming from Turkey, with different channels, with embassies, with Foreign Affairs, creates a problem within the Leuven community".

Toğuşlu also highlighted the personal and professional cost involved in being associated with Hizmet even when having citizenship of an EU or similar country by explaining that "I cannot go to any academic sympo- sium or conference if it takes place not only in Turkey, but outside Europe. In Africa I also got some invitations, but I am not going because I am not sure what will happen even though I have a Belgian citizenship". As in the earlier briefly mentioned instance of Keleş in the UK, this underlines that, ironically, one's status as a dual national is in many ways more vulnerable than that as an asylum-seeker from Turkey.

4.6   THREE-LAYERED HIZMET: CHALLENGES AND OPPORTUNITIES

From testimonies such as those in the previous section, one can see that in at least a number of European countries, Hizmet needs to be understood as a "three-layered" phenomenon, with the first "layer" composed of orig- inal migrants to Europe; the second "layer" of the second and third gen- erations who grew up and have been educated in Europe; and the third "layer" of asylum-seekers and those who managed to get out of Turkey using such mechanisms as the *Ankara Agreement* for Turkish business- people before they were forced to become asylum-seekers. Where this "three-layered" Hizmet exists, it is both a challenge and an opportunity for all involved.

With regard to Belgium, HE1 gave an example of how issues arising from the events of July 2016 had impacted upon the normal work of the Intercultural Platform in that, the days before HE1 was interviewed, the Platform heard of a couple and four girls who faced being abducted from

Malaysia in relation to which the Platform felt it important to get involved. In this context they "called the Malaysian Department of the European Commission, and also we sent letters to the Malaysian Mission in Brussels". However, on the day of the interview it was learned that the family had been abducted to Turkey and that while the wife and girls had been released, the husband/father remained in prison. The anonymous Hizmet interviewee, HE1, says that:

> So with these things we try to help, but when you see at the end you weren't successful to protect these people, this process has a psychological effect ... We try to do something, but one day later you hear the guy was extradited and we don't know in which prison he is now. It has a big effect ... that's why I think a special team of people dealing with human rights violations, and other people work on their jobs, otherwise there are enough traumatised people in Hizmet right now, and more traumatised people will come from Turkey. So, I think we should try to keep the "normal" ones "normal" or less traumatised, I should say.

In terms of Hizmet asylum-seekers themselves, HE3 (see Acknowledgements) from the Netherlands claimed that "In the Netherlands, the number of people who came from Turkey after the coup is high – let me say if the movement has here, around a thousand people, and a thousand people came after the coup". With regard to these, Alasag explains that the majority of the refugee camps are in rural areas in Holland, but that the concentration of numbers is in that they call the Randstad— meaning Amsterdam, Rotterdam, the Hague and Utrecht. Alasag also notes that "in some places, when there are too many asylum-seekers and just a few people to help them, sometimes the pressure is just too big. Because people want to help them, but it's too much sometimes". This is partly because, as he explained it, "After the coup we became a little smaller, the amount has been decreasing for some time". And there are considerable practical challenges because, as HE3 pointed out, "In Holland there is a policy for asylum-seekers (not only for Turkish, but for all of them): this policy's name is *Versobering*. *Versobering* means making things basic, not cosy, not homely" and what this means in practice is that, for example, "they can put a family with two daughters in a room with two refugees, young boys from Syria, in the same room, basic, answering the basic need of you which is accommodation. But it's not cosy, it's not homely. It's even not friendly". Because of this there are real needs for support and, therefore, as Ablak explains:

The first thing is getting them mentally into a healthy position and then starting to learn the Dutch language, and then in the meantime helping them to integrate, helping them to build a normal life again. So, when they get their status, they get a home – just the main things, having furniture etc. So, we have teams of volunteers helping them with their homes. And then the paperwork. So, we are No. 1 for mailings with the government. That's difficult. Personally, I have some three or four families who I try to mentor with their paperwork. So, if they get a letter they send me a Whatsapp message, so I can help them out with that. And, yeah, so everything is possible to teach them to build a new life.

They also try "to get them out of the camps and to invite them to our homes for a weekend. For example, my family and I went for a vacation in Croatia. So, our house was empty for two to three weeks and we invited a family from a refugee centre – 'here are the keys, just use it as your own house' ". At the same time, Alasag has also highlighted that:

Asylum-seekers are all helping each other. And the refugees founded a foundation to help all these asylum-seekers and they have given them Dutch courses, books, apps. they are helping those who are new in Holland. I think they are helping because they are motivated, because they want to contribute. The connection is thus good here, but not for everybody as I explained.

Alasag's overall evaluation of this is that these developments will therefore ultimately be good for the future of Hizmet in the Netherlands, since "The engagements and contribution and being a part of the Hizmet will be eventually more. The more they learn the Dutch language, the more the chance they'll contribute in some way". At the same time, of course "Just being willing to do this is not enough. These are highly educated people, so when they want to contribute they want to contribute on a good level, just as they did in Turkey, but sometimes the language is a barrier".

In the meantime, there are real tensions. Thus, as HE3 notes in relation to the asylum-seekers, "This is a big dynamic now, and there are some conflicts in the sense that these people from Turkey, the new people, have another orientation, and they are traumatised and they have other priorities, and then there are the people who were born here and they have other ambitions and other things, and they think in another way". Nevertheless, Alasag notes that "The motivation is very big. So, I think in a couple of years, the children will learn Dutch in half a year or a year's time and many will go to universities soon. So, after a couple of years the parents and the children will be integrated, and I think the Hizmet here will grow very fast after that". In addition, HE3 from the Netherlands notes that, alongside asylum-seekers from Turkey, there are also "expats" coming:

> Some of them came to Holland and they found good jobs and they became expats. So, its not only refugees, you know, because the education level is high, some of them – even though they came maybe to seek asylum, they would contact with a company and they would find a good job – so instead of seeking asylum they became expats.

Taken in the round, Ablak's assessment of the "third layer" is that "They are doing better than the people from the Hizmet movement who came before the coup. So, they are getting involved in the society much faster than the people who came via regular migration or who are born here, for example".

In relation to the newcomers to Belgium, in terms of the future Tascioglu sees this as positive in the light of the fact of over the years there always having been a shortage of resources and of people: "So, these newcomers are actually a new energy for the organizations. But, of course, one needs time to get adapted to Belgium". But as helpful to this process, he thought that around 90 per cent of asylum-seekers were granted asylum in Belgium.

With regard to Germany, Karakoyun observed in relation to what he called the "different approaches to Hizmet" as between people in Turkey and people in Germany, in relation to which, "in my opinion, this is the main challenge for Hizmet in Germany at the moment":

> There are three groups that are coming together now. On the one hand, the first people that came to Germany fifteen or twenty years ago with the idea of Hizmet were very much Turkey socialized but slowly becoming something like 'German'. Then, the second group, children being born here, socialized here, and knowing Hizmet here, combining it with what they learned at school, in university, and in the German majority society. And the third group consists of people who are coming to Germany now, during the last three years. So, these three groups come together now, and you can't imagine how different they are. So, there are now three big groups of people that, yeah, now come together and Hizmet has to overcome this challenge.

However, it should also be noted that this more pronounced "three-layering" of Hizmet is not completely uniform across all of Europe. Thus, in some contrast to countries like Belgium, the Netherlands, Germany and the UK, in relation to Italy, HE2 explains:

We don't have any of these clear distinctions, because immigration to Italy, I mean with the whole immigration, Muslim immigration, Turkish immigration, Hizmet immigration, people who were born and raised here are still very young. So, we don't have this category of that many who have grown up here.

In terms of Hizmet refugees, while "people started coming" generally speaking, "usually this was not the destination people from Turkey were opting for. They didn't know Italian, and Italy was seen not as a country for immigrants, maybe". In relation to Spain—which was also not a prior prime focus for Turkish migration—the new arrivals are actually the majority. As in other European countries, these new arrivals come with their own traumas and their own very immediate needs; one can also see that in terms of the medium- to longer-term future trajectories of Hizmet in Europe these new arrivals have brought new potential and, in some contexts, already a new refocusing of old activities. Thus, in Spain, Naziri explains that from among these new asylum-seekers, refugees and migrants, "the majority of them are voluntary members of Casa Turca" and "We have organized some activities already with them, so it's like a good opportunity, like, fresh blood", albeit he then goes on to correct himself to note that "And when I say 'we' are, it's 'they' are organising, because 'they' have become 'we'. They are organising it, like, it's not like we and then they came".

In Switzerland, in contrast to Germany and the Netherlands where, by comparison, Özgü says, "there are thousands of asylum-seekers" from Hizmet. "In Switzerland we have just not more than six hundred or seven hundred asylum-seekers" in relation to which he comments that "that is good for us, as we can handle them and there is not a need for a structure for new asylum-seekers in Switzerland. It's an integrated part of hizmet Switzerland – for us that's very important". Overall, the work with asylum-seekers brings challenges and, from his legal background and professional role, as well as personally and pro bono, Özgü is very involved in this. He is active in Hizmet's own Swiss association for this, but also for people from other countries. Hence, he explains that:

> When I was a student I was also active in other associations like Amnesty International and Sans-Papier Anlaufstelle – that's a law association for people who don't have any permission in the country, and I was also active in an association for the people who get welfare benefits. So that's why my work as a lawyer is not just hizmet, I have also other work. And for most of them I don't do it professionally, I just help the people.

Özgü also comments that, as among those who had previously come from Turkey with the thinking that they could change everything about Hizmet in Switzerland, "among the asylum-seekers are also those people they think they will change everything, they will be very active in hizmet. Now they have time, they have enough time to be active, because they don't have to go to work, but they just go to the German courses for half of the day". At the same time, RO has observed that once these people have begun to work in the Swiss society, "they have no more time for Hizmet and they just come one or two days for Hizmet. And all the people who say we will change all these things just say that because they have enough time now".

As the asylum-seeker, AS1 puts it:

> We just concentrate on what was and what were our principles and what this good man, sir, Gülen, how to you call it, because he gave us as a goal for the life. This is our aim in this life. And we shall remember them and shall continue in our private life in this new society in Switzerland. Otherwise, psychologically, it is also not acceptable for the other people, "Do you know what happened to me in Turkey, blah, blah..." – all the negative things, and no-one wants to hear psychologically the negative things. Explain the good things, and then if they know you, accept you, and see you are a good person, after that they can ask you, "Ok, but why are you here"? – sometimes later when they want to connect with you. Then you can say what has happened.

As well as referencing the pragmatic human psychology in this, AS1 also cites religious exemplars for taking such an approach:

> I don't believe, for example, that our Prophet Muhammad said to the people in Medina "Do you know what happened to me in Mecca?" Or that Jesus Christ said to the people, "Do you know what happened to me or the other Prophets, may God be with them", or others that followed them said, "Do you know what happened to me? Do you know that one?"

From an asylum-seeker's perspective, as AS4 (see Acknowledgements) put it:

> So, we have to use this country. We love this country! It's OK. But it's difficult to come here as a refugee because we were living as normal people in Turkey with good conditions: we had a car, we had houses,

and we could give our children to private schools, for example. We had money. But now, we are refugees. So it's difficult to use this condition. But we have to do it, and we want to learn German and we would like to do this and work again here because we are not used to having money without working ourselves. We want to work and earn our money ourselves. It's better for us. It's normal for us ... We don't like this. But it will take a long time, perhaps, we don't know ... it looks like that. But we have to stand strong.

This is not to say there are not a lot of questions, in relation to which AS1 says: "It is a hard time of life. Economically it is not good; psychologically we are not good; and this, of course, there is a saying, I like it also too: 'sufferings build character'. Now, hopefully it is so for me and for all my friends. Now we are building good characters, hopefully".

Balcı highlights a basic economic difference for the future of Hizmet in countries like the UK and those "like Germany, Netherlands, Denmark to a certain extent, Austria", which "have a sizeable Hizmet diaspora already, and a sizeable Turkish-speaking diaspora who are not antithetical to Hizmet altogether" even though "those countries also do have quite big AKP support bases". Indeed, in relation to the start of his own living in exile, Balcı shares that:

I was looking at Germany, only because of practical reasons and I was saying the new centre of Hizmet is going to be Germany, because they have money. They have support bases, there are schools there already. So, they will be to provide for, you know, creating a middle class of Hizmet that will be able to deal with philosophy, art and so on, whereas here we are largely, you know, lower middle class Hizmet people. But it is changing, as far as I can see, the United Kingdom is becoming a new hub.

In the UK Balcı says that there is only "a small window of opportunity for the newcomers" in which, in Balcı's view, "the newcomers are largely going to be accepted not because of their previous roles in Hizmet, but because of their knowledge of religion, knowledge of Religious Education and so on", some of the potentialities of which are, as articulated by Balcı, developed further in Sect. 6.2.

NOTES

1. The title is often not so elegantly translated into English as *Simon's living in the Golden Horn, Yesterday the State Today the Congregation.* On pp. 13ff of the book it is explained that "Simon" is used as a codename description of a special human type which subordinates individual personality to that of the group.
2. http://www.tuerkeiforum.net//enw/index.php?title=Ahmet_% C5%9E%C4%B1k:_The_Army_of_the_Imam, last edited 6.4.2011.
3. An English translation of the edited version is accessible on the anti-Hizmet website Turkishinvitations.weebly.com at https://turkishinvitations.weebly. com/imams-army-epilogue-by-ahmet-sik.html, n.d.
4. "Parish" here is a poor English translation of *cemaat*, or "community".
5. Turkishinvitations.weebly.com at https://turkishinvitations.weebly.com/ imams-army-epilogue-by-ahmet-sik.html, n.d.
6. *Voanews,* Reuters, "Turkish Ruling Party MP Slams Government in Resignation",31.1.2014.https://www.voanews.com/a/reu-turkish-ruling-party-mp-slams-government-in-resignation-police-purged/1841868.html
7. Fethullah Gülen, *Fethullah Gülen Issued the Following Statement on Events in Turkey,* 15 July 2016. https://afsv.org/wp-content/uploads/2020/08/ Fethullah-Gulen-statement-on-developments-in-Turkey-15-July-2016-LH.pdf
8. https://www.hizmetbeweging.nl/selma-ablak/, 27.12.2013.

REFERENCES

(All web links current at 20.11.2021)

Avcı, Hanefi (2010). *Haliç'te Yaşayan Simonlar: Dün Devlet Bugün Cemaat.* Ankara: Angora Yayıncılık.

Barton, Greg (2017). What on Earth Has Gone so Wrong in Turkey. In The Fountain Special Issue, *What Went Wrong with Turkey? July 15 Coup Attempt. Erdoğan's Rogue State. The Persecution of the Hizmet Movement,* 64–69. https://fountainmagazine.com/special-issue-2017

Council of Europe Commissioner for Human Rights' (2016), *Memorandum on the Human Rights Implications of the Measures Taken under the State of Emergency in Turkey.* Strasbourg: Council of Europe. https://rm.coe.int/ref/ CommDH(2016)35

House of Commons Foreign Affairs Committee (2017). *The UK's Relations with Turkey: Tenth Report of Session, 2016–17. Report together with formal minutes relating to the report. Ordered by the House of Commons to be printed 21 March 2017. HC 615.* London: House of Commons. https://publications.parliament.uk/pa/cm201617/cmselect/cmfaff/615/615.pdf

Kahl, Bruno (2017). Interview with German Intelligence Chief 'Coup in Turkey Was Just a Welcome Pretext'. In Martin Knobbe, Fidelius Schmid und Alfred Weinzierl (2017). *Der Spiegel* (20.3.17) https://www.spiegel.de/international/germany/german-intelligence-chief-bruno-kahl-interview-a-1139602.html.

Lorentzen, Jørgen (2019). *A Gift from God?* Integral Film. https://www.amazon.co.uk/Gift-God-J%C3%B8rgen-Lorentzen/dp/B081ZFS3FV

Robinson, Simon (2017). *The Spirituality of Responsibility: Fethullah Gülen and Islamic Thought.* London: Bloomsbury.

Sezgin, İsmail Mesut (2014). Mavi Marmara and Gülen's Critics: Politics and Principles. *Today's Zaman*, 16 January in *Hizmet Movement News Archive* https://hizmetnews.com/9499/mavi-marmara-gulens-critics-politics-principles/#.Xhmm3m52s2x.

Sunier, Thijl and Landman, Nico (2015). Gülen Movement (Hizmet). In Sunier Thijl and Nico Landman (Eds.), *Transnational Turkish Islam: Shifting Boundaries of Religious Activism and Community Building Turkey and Europe.* (pp. 81–94). Basingstoke: Palgrave Macmillan.

Weller, Paul (2022). *Fethullah Gülen's Teaching and Practice: Inheritance, Context and Interactive Development.* Cham: Palgrave Macmillan.

Yükleyen, Ahmet and Tunagür, Ferhan (2013). The Gülen Movement in Western Europe and the USA. In Matthias Kortmann and Kerstin Rosenow-Williams (Eds.), *Islamic Organizations in Europe and the USA: A Multi-Disciplinary Perspective* (pp. 224–241). Basingstoke: Palgrave Macmillan.

CHAPTER 5

New Foci for Old Questions

5.1 CHANGING CONTEXTS

To understand Hizmet in different parts of the world, including in Europe, one needs to pay attention to the dynamic interplay in the development of expressions of Hizmet between the elements arising from its Turkish origins; the changes and developments in Gülen's understandings and teachings; and the further dynamics in both of these that are related to Hizmet's need for, and practice in terms of, local adaptations. In addition, this takes place in a wider world in which how Muslims are seen; how Muslims are treated by others by others; as well as how Muslims behave and project themselves.

In Europe, Islam is the largest minority religion and, with that, Muslims of Turkish ethnic and national heritage and origin have a very substantial numerical and political importance. Turkey itself is also of great significance as a Eurasian cultural, political and economic bridge that poses important questions for the future of how Europe might in future see itself and its role in the wider world. Therefore, the trajectories being taken by Hizmet in Europe are of significance not only for Hizmet itself, and of wider religious significance, but are also of wider policy importance.

As a part of the de-centring of Hizmet from Turkey that has followed from the post-July 2016 persecution, imprisonment, asset-stripping and civic deprivation of individuals and organisations associated with Hizmet in Turkey as well as the Turkish Government's attempts to curtail Hizmet activities in other parts of the world (including some attempts also within

© The Author(s) 2022
P. Weller, *Hizmet in Transitions*,
https://doi.org/10.1007/978-3-030-93798-0_5

Europe), a greater range of self-questioning and at least some degree of self-criticism have begun to emerge within Hizmet. This is, in turn, feeding into a re-assessment by those associated with Hizmet about the future trajectory or trajectories of Hizmet and the implications for it of its centre of gravity now increasingly operating outside the historical inheritance of the Turkish social, religious and political environment. In the case of Europe, this also relates specifically to the opportunities and challenges posed by European western liberal democratic environments. Many of the issues identified and discussed in this chapter are not themselves new, but after July 2016, they are arguably both intensified and accelerated as pivotal issues in what are also now pivotal times for Hizmet.

5.2   Seen as Terrorists and Challenging Terrorism

Hizmet operates in a European context where underlying Islamophobia has been stoked both since and through 9/11, the 2004 Madrid rail bombings, the 7/72005 attacks on London Transport and later attacks in France, Germany and Austria including by shooting and the weaponised use of vehicles. While similar atrocities have been carried out in the name of Islam in other parts of the world, an aspect of these events that particularly shocked governmental authorities across Europe is that many of the perpetrators did not come externally into Europe but, rather, had either been born in or grown up in European countries, thus giving rise to questions about the presence of violent extremism among European Muslim groups and organisations.

Even prior to the heightening of suspicions arising from the seismic shock of 9/11 and what has followed it, and before the additional impetus given by the concerted efforts of the Turkish authorities to present Hizmet under the guise of an alleged terrorist identity of FETÖ, and as having responsibility for the events of July 2016 in Turkey, in at least some parts of Europe Hizmet has for some time experienced a considerable pressure from those who have portrayed it as being at the least 'extremist'. Both in Turkey itself and in some European countries Hizmet has long faced accusations of having had a double agenda. While Andrews (2011) has argued that, in Germany, overall Hizmet's loose organisational structure has seemed to work in its favour, Sunier and Landman (2015) say that "In the Netherlands and Belgium Hizmet is regularly portrayed in the media as an organization with a double agenda and a strong aura of secrecy" (p. 82). In the Netherlands, in particular, from 2008 onwards, there were a succession of investigations into Hizmet. In relation to the original emer-gence of this, Alasag recalled, "Suddenly there was a TV programme, a news programme, in which some young people, with blacked-out faces, were telling how afraid they were of us etc." This was a NOVA TV pro-gramme with the title *Kamermeerderheid eist onderzoek naar Turkse bewe-ging* (or, "Parliamentary Majority Demands Investigation into Turkish Movement").[1] As a result of this, Alasag said, "We were kind of put down as a terrorist organization, almost". The impact of this led Hizmet in the Netherlands into considerable self-questioning:

> So, we were shocked and we thought what did we do wrong? We didn't know where it came from. As it was on Dutch TV, we thought is it maybe the Dutch Government that wants something? Did we maybe do something wrong? Or is it an initiative of a group and if so which group? So, we were panicked in 2008.

During this period individuals in the Netherlands who were publicly associated as leading various Hizmet organisations and initiatives began to be individually targeted. Thus, Alasag recalls that the *Leefbaar Rotterdam* party (in English, Livable Rotterdam), founded in 2001, and widely seen as the Rotterdam expression of Pim Fortuyn List (after Fortuyn was in 2002 removed from his role as leading candidate of the *Leefbaar Nederlands* party), "put on their website a dossier about Hizmet" (Fähmel 2009) in which "they had written the names of the organizations founded by the Hizmet people, and also the names of the people who were active, accusing us about how dangerous we are etc." On examining this website, Hizmet people noticed that "about half of the information they put on the website was in Turkish". And, because of that, "we understood where it came from: that it wasn't that we had done something wrong in Dutch society, but it was a Turkish leftist, Communist, Kemalist, nationalist, group was initiating this attack" and "almost every year there was a request to make a research about Hizmet".

In relation to these investigations, Alasag said, "The first one was not public. An academician I know shared with me that the government had approached him and asked him to write a report about the Gülen move-ment and he said that he wrote only what he knew and it was really posi-tive". The second was after another NOVA TV news programme, this one entitled *Turkse beweging fundamentale sekte?* (or, in English "Turkish Movement a Fundamentalist Sect?") which was broadcast on 4 July 2008, following which Alasag noted that "the intelligence service AIVD in Holland said they are not a threat for the Netherlands, and they are not busy with any disturbing activities". The third was "the Minister who made a research and said that they are not radical and said further that the Intelligence service didn't think they were not helping the integration". The fourth was "the municipality of Rotterdam, and they also came and they said we researched them and they are OK, we can keep on funding their initiatives". And the fifth, "after a couple of years the new Minister responsible for integration said with all these questions and accusations they have to do something like an open enquiry, open research".

For this research the Dutch Parliament's House of Representatives appointed Professor Martin van Bruinissen, an anthropologist from Utrecht University with expertise in both Turkey and Islamic groups, with a remit to report on the question of whether and, if so, how far, Hizmet in the Netherlands did or did not promote integration. Alasag says of van Bruinissen's work that "in the end he wrote a big research document, after making enquiries on every level and talking to hundreds of people". The outcome of this was that, as summarised by Alasag, van Bruinissen said that "among all the groups, and not only Turkish, this group is the most integrated one and the only issue is that they are not as transparent as you would like".

Despite this thoroughly conducted and positively concluded open research, a sixth enquiry also eventually took place. This happened, says Alasag, because when the Minister responsible for integration presented van Bruinissen's report "the right wing and some leftist Members of Parliament who are originally from Turkey … came with other questions, and then another, and then another". Although the Minister initially responded that those pursuing these matters should not import Turkish ideological issues into the Netherlands "a couple of years later" there was yet another request from a Member of Parliament with Turkish familial origins who had previously been pressing these issues together with some other Members of Parliament, and this led to the sixth enquiry – this time on the question of "if we are forming a parallel society". Two professors specialising in Turkey and Islam undertook this enquiry and again concluded that what was being charged was not, in fact, the case and that, rather, to the contrary, Hizmet people are well integrated in the Netherlands.

When, following the events of July 2016, formal Parliamentary questions were posed to the Dutch Foreign Minister of the time, A.G. Koenders, concerning the government's view of the Turkish Government's position that Hizmet people are terrorists, his answer was: "This is not in line with cabinet policy as the Gülen movement has not been classified as a terrorist organisation by the European Union or the Netherlands. Associated organizations and/or individuals are therefore not considered terrorists".[2] By this time, while there continued to be considerable pressure from within the sections of the Turkish community, Alasag noted that, ironically, even Pim Fortuyn's party argued that Rotterdam and its Mayor should "help people from Hizmet who under pressure of Turkey lost their jobs, had to move to other parts of the cities to flee their own friends and family", and that it should offer support to "people with psychological trauma, with money if they lost their jobs, or with accommodation, in finding houses in other areas of the town". In the end, as concluded by Alasag, "They cared for us! And the reason is that they were following us all these years".

Following July 2016, the charge of having a double agenda and of being an extremist and/or potentially terrorist entity gained new credibility for some, in Europe and beyond, especially through the concerted efforts of the Turkish state, and allied organisations portray it in this way. In some parts of the world this portrayal, when combined either with appeals to solidarity among Muslim majority states, and/or the use of economic leverage, has had significantly negative effects on Hizmet institutions. For example, in Pakistan, with the support and intervention of the Pakistani authorities, the once extensive network of Hizmet schools was taken over by a Turkish-related foundation. In Europe, such discreditation campaigns have been markedly less successful—at least at the level of state authorities. Thus, as noted earlier, the German intelligence service (see Sect. 4.4) is fairly clear on the matter of Hizmet being a religiously inspired civil society movement, stating that while Turkey has continued to try to convince it about Hizmet being a terrorist group, it has not so far done so.

The position in the UK is perhaps not so clear-cut, not least perhaps because the economic upheaval of Brexit means that the UK needs trading friends wherever in the world it can find them. In addition, apart from any other trading relationships, Turkey is an important arms market. Indeed, not only for the UK, but as interviewee HE3 from the Netherlands notes, Turkey is also economically important for the Netherlands too:

Interesting to note that after the coup there is a lot of money that comes from Turkey to Europe. But we see that foreign direct investment – the money Turkey gets from other countries – comes most from the Netherlands in the last three years. Approximately twenty per cent of foreign direct investment in Turkey comes from the Netherlands. There is a good trade relationship between Turkey and the Netherlands. In England, it is not so big, the economic relationship. No country wants to disturb such a mutual economic relationship.

In contrast with these interests, interviewee HE3 notes that "The movement is a small one. It has several thousand supporters in the Netherlands, not members, supporters. It is a small movement. And in the Netherlands, approximately four hundred thousand people with Turkish origin live, and the movement is a small one within that Turkish context" and also that, in the Netherlands as in almost every European country:

> There is a group of 'White Turks', and especially since the coup in the 1980s they came here, and their children were educated people and they have some positions in the society. And in the Dutch Parliament. There are some people who are linked with these persons of Turkish, Kurdish or some other groups originating from such kinds of ideologies as Kemalists. And some ideological groups in the Dutch government and the Dutch state, they listen also to them. And the discussion, the public debate in Turkey, we see similar discussions also here. They transfer the political atmosphere from Turkey to the Dutch context here, want to judge the movement here because of the coup in Turkey.

The importance of Turkish politics has worked itself out on two levels. At the level of popular and economic pressure, as Alasag said:

> Some of the businesspeople lost their business because the Turkish government, asking Turkish people to tell on Hizmet people through a special phone number, and further to boycott the companies run by Hizmet people. People got scared that if they'd engage with Hizmet people they will have issues when they went to Turkey. So, there were lists.

In relation to the question of Gülen and/or Hizmet's responsibility for the coup attempt, HE3 says that whenever he is asked about Gülen he says, "I don't know, ask himself, but as far as I know he said he didn't, but you can interview him". HE3 then went on to say, "But there are some people, I don't know, and the intelligence services – I think they know who the people were in Turkey who did the coup, but I don't think Gülen did it. That would mean tossing the people who followed him to hell. This is in complete contrast to his beliefs". Indeed, overall, in the light of both its own practical initiatives and all the investigations to which it has been subject, HE3 summarises that "The movement is known by the Dutch state, it is OK. It is a movement and its aims and objectives and activities are well known by the intelligence services, and by the governmental agencies, and there is a good relationship", and that this is because:

> The schools are Dutch schools; the people are Dutch citizens and they have Dutch nationality: they think in a Dutch way, with a Dutch mentality, especially the people who participate in the Dutch society, they do not look at Turkey. But we look at the activities which are done – educational activities, dialogue activities, gatherings to bring people together and these are the things we appreciate here.

As Alasag further developed this, in contrast to the initial reaction of the wider society in some other countries, "when there was the so-called coup, in Holland nothing happened. I feel they trust us. The people said, 'we know you'". At the same time, some of the issues faced by Hizmet have nevertheless continued because, as noted by HE3:

> "White Turks" who are mostly anti-religious, they think all Muslims are bad and dangerous. This is their standpoint. They say publicly – and I hear and read it in the last weeks – that the movement is a "sect", and some politicians echo this in the debates about integration in the Dutch Parliament. And then the Parliament members ask the Minister, would you investigate this? And then begins another research for the movement. If a project is successful here, that means that this can also be successful in Germany. In other countries. Furthermore, there are some anti-Muslim groups, who will denounce the movement, it seems that they have job to do that and they use everything, and I can imagine how some such lobby groups and structures work. There are lobby groups, there are ideological structures which are not transparent – not only for the movement, but also for other groups.

One of the consequences of this has been that the latest enquiry in the Netherlands has been focused not on Hizmet alone but the question of how any and all of the Islamic groups – the Diyanet, Millî Görüş and Süleymanli's and Hizmet movement in the Netherlands—might be controlled by the Turkish government. But ironically, because of the coup Alasag noted that:

It was very clear that whatever they thought about the co-operation or the mixing or becoming one, the anxiety was all gone. And it was not merely on the level of the government but also on the level of the society. So they made a big distinction between what is now the Government, what is Turkey and what is AKP and what is the place of Hizmet of the Hizmet movement in this triangle or whatever.

And this was important because until then "The Dutch government etc were very happy with what the Hizmet movement achieved in Holland but they were kind of afraid that the Hizmet was too much involved in the politics in Turkey and the Hizmet movement here was functioning as the long arm of the Turkish government". Alasag explained that until July 2016 and its aftermath "they still had question marks" but "For them the happenings with the coup and after that putting people in jail, arresting etc, it made it very clear and they became convinced".

In relation to the French authorities and media, Erkinbekov commented "That depends on the source they get". In the media "they said that there are some few questions that have to be answered". At the same time, Erkinbekov said that "for the events that happened on 15 July we say we don't have any information about that" and they referred enquirers to the Alliance for Shared Values' statement.[3] By contrast with what over the years happened in the Netherlands, in France there never were such systematic and repeated investigations, which Erkinbekov suggested might be because "We stay very small … that's why, I think". Specifically in connection with the events of July 2016 Erkinbekov explained that in relation to the representatives of the state with whom they were in contact that "we explained our standpoint and version of the events and it was clear that they were supportive to us".

In Denmark, Gezen explained that initially the Dialog Forum received a lot of requests for media interviews to which they responded to the best of their ability. However, "early on in Denmark, already within a year the focus was away". Since then, it has only recurred when something specific has happened in Turkey. Overall, generally speaking, with regard to the Danish media, Gezen commented that:

> Very early in Denmark the majority of media outlets and public knew that there was something wrong in relation to the coup and the Erdoğan government. And now the focus is more and more on the populist, the Islamist agenda, and on the undemocratic developments in Turkey. So, the questions are now more related to what will happen in Turkey with these undemo-

cratic movements. The questions to Hizmet participants in relation to the coup are finished. The media is not covering the coup as much as before because for them the focus is Erdoğan – the Hizmet movement is not being blamed. The case is very clear. I have spoken to many of my friends in Hizmet about this and I believe the coup discussion in Denmark is closed and more people believe the coup attempt has been too favourable for Erdoğan.

With regard to Spain, Naziri commented that "I had to give an interview and two days after the coup it was published in one of the important, let's say, digital newspapers".[4] He was also interviewed on radio and TV programmes, but in terms of the level of attention he acknowledged that "It's not like Germany" in the sense that, because the community of Turkish origins in Spain is not so large, "there is not so much interest about Turkey in general terms in the Spanish media". Indeed, in summary, Naziri commented that "I think, the Spanish society is quite mature". Of course, Spain has its own still relatively recent experience of authoritarian government under Franco and Naziri says that many people in Spain who know him and talked with him about these matters were saying in relation to Erdoğan that "this was like organised by him, 'auto-coup'".

In relation to Belgium the anonymous interviewee, HE1, said that post-July 2016, "There was a lot of interest in that issue. But I think that after one or two years the interest is not there anymore". In Switzerland, Özgü says that "the police and other security staff, they are really open to us, because we are not a security issue in Switzerland". As with France and Spain, Özgü thinks this may also partly be the case because "we don't have so many Turks here, and AKP people are not so evident". As in the UK, the Turkish authorities have made some attempts at extradition, but Özgü says of such attempts that "the Swiss state gave them a strong answer, a strong response" informed by the international law principle of "non-refoulement" which applies when there is torture in a country, and in relation to Turkey, Özgü states that "Switzerland says there is torture in your country which is why we don't send them to you".

Overall, Hizmet has had to position itself not only in relation to specific charges from the Turkish government, but also in relation to an overall context in which a number of European governments have, since 9/11, as a policy goal, tried to support and promote a "moderate Islam" in order to marginalise by association with terrorism what can be seen as "radical", "fundamentalist" or "extremist" Islam. Such an approach on the part of the European "powers that be" runs the risk of eliding the condemnation of terror crimes against humanity conducted on religious grounds into the criminalisation, or at least social marginalisation, of religious conservatism and/or radicalism by legitimating simplistic distinctions between "good" (understood as "liberal" or "modernist") and "bad" or "suspect" (understood as "traditionalist", "radical" or "fundamentalist") Muslims and forms of Islam. But because Hizmet has been actively concerned to project a different face of Islam and Muslims in Europe than the one which dominates Western media headlines and much public perception, it can fit into what Caroline Tee calls the construction of a "good Islam" (2018).

In the UK, perhaps surprisingly, Keleş says of 9/11 that it did "not really impact" the Dialogue Society's work. However, the 7/7 London Transport bombings were different. At that time policy-makers had experienced what the present author (Weller 2009) elsewhere calls the "social policy shock" (pp. 146–207) of suicide bombings having been carried out by young Muslim men who had been brought up in British society and to all intents and purposes appeared to be integrated members of it. Therefore, in the period immediately following that, government and policy-makers were looking for partners from within the Muslim community who would clearly reject not only the bombings themselves but would also offer an alternative to the Jihadist ideology that had inspired them. In this environment, the Dialogue Society questioned itself about whether it was doing enough in relation to these issues, with Keleş commenting that "since no policy-maker really knew we existed, it made us think that in addition to doing all the grassroot work we were at the time, we needed to communicate that to the people responsible for shaping social policy". One important product of this development was the publication of the Dialogue Society's (2009) booklet *Deradicalization by Default: The 'Dialogue' Approach to Rooting out Violent Extremism*.

As its name suggests, this was an attempt to engage with policy concerns about "radicalisation" by arguing that, instead of attempting to tackle Jihadist and similar ideologies on grounds external to the Islamic tradition, it was important to do so by reference to an alternative logic and grammar from within Islam itself and in relation to which the teaching and practice of Gülen offered a creative and helpful resource. With regard to these ongoing issues, perhaps not surprisingly as an academic, Toğuşlu from Belgium, stated that "My perspective is let's start with the term 'radicalization'! – it's a kind of concept where you can get everything!" But in reality:

It's a very complex issue, it's a multi-layered problem. It's not only directly related to theological issues, but there are theological issues in it; it's an economic issue, but we cannot reduce it to only economic disadvantage. It's not a matter of age, from fourteen years old to fifty or sixty years old are being involved. It's not either a matter of education because it goes from a Diploma to early drop out students. It's not only about the converts. It's not only about the migration because these converts take part. So, from this multi-layered perspective, in that sense the governments, the NGOs, the theologians, the intellectuals should all come together to work together. You can't have a unique perspective to solve in one day. It's a generational matter, I think. You have to tackle this issue for another fifteen or twenty years again, because it doesn't pop up in one day, this problem.

As Toğuşlu expressed Hizmet's approach in his own words:

By the way, it's not directly part of it to deradicalize people, but with its activities, aims, principles – especially with its Islamic interpretation, I think it provides some elements to "prevent", not deradicalize I think. Some alternative narratives, some alternative discourses, some alternative experiences, models, OK, for this young generation who are frustrated; who have lost their moderation; who cannot follow, for example, a kind of Islamic process since if you go the website you may find everything there, from the radical, the modernist and the progressive sides, but most of the time these are the Salafi teachings who are not contextualised. So, these are some things you have to look at.

The UK Dialogue Society's publication *Violent Extremism: Naming, Framing and Challenging* (Harris et al. 2015) points out that extremism is not always or only a by-product of those who respond reactively to disadvantage and discrimination, but also attracts people who have, in principle, positive ideals; who want to create a new world and for whom an ideal of (re)creating the Caliphate can seem to offer a way to do that. Options for channelling such a positive motivation are not straightforward when many young people identify the great suffering and injustice in the world that Muslims and others are experiencing, and the only alternative option to "radicalisation" seems to be acceptance of the global status quo alongside the practice of a traditionalist form of Islam that is concerned with just performing the rituals.

Informed by a more complex analysis of this kind and the question of what Hizmet should do, Toğuşlu suggests that Hizmet should "maybe continue all its activities"—in other words, that there is perhaps no need for Hizmet to take special initiatives, but simply to carry on with its alternative way of being Muslim. This is not least because, in terms of a clear Muslim differentiation of Islam from terrorism, Hizmet has been able to cite and deploy Gülen's clear condemnation of terror and suicide attacks in the name of religion to the effect that: "No one can be a suicide bomber. No one can rush into crowds with bombs tied to his or her body. Regardless of the religion of these crowds this is not religiously permissible" (Gülen in Çapan ed. 2016: 1).

Of course, Hizmet and Gülen have, of course, not been alone among Muslim voices in such condemnation. What has arguably been more less straightforward for Muslims to tackle has been the challenge of questioning and confronting the legitimacy of the kind of Qur'anic hermeneutics that undergird not only the specific organisational forms of Al-Qeda and ISIS, but also the general trends of "radicalisation" and "Islamism" that have been of special attraction to numbers of young Muslims towards understanding the world in highly dichotomised ways. In this context what Hizmet has, arguably, been able to bring is a more sophisticated and grounded understanding of the tendencies present among Muslims that goes beyond the ephemera of political rhetoric and media reportage. And this is that it has been able to promote a form of Islamic teaching and, even more so of an embodied practice, that challenges terror in the name of Islam and promotes Muslim engagement with civil society within which it offers an alternative and positive vision of a struggle, informed by Islam, that can offer a resource for civility and also a challenge to the powers for Muslims and the wider society alike in terms of overcoming the challenges of ignorance, conflict and poverty.

Prior to July 2016 in Turkey, a considerable amount of this kind of "indirect" work was done by many Hizmet organisations across Europe focusing on radicalisation, extremism and similar topics. For example, Tascioglu explained in relation to Hizmet schools in Europe that:

> So, with these problems of radicalisation, extremism and terrorism in Europe, specifically for people with Muslim backgrounds, they try to educate these role models for the new generation in order not to get involved in these activities: radicalism, extremism and terrorism. So, they don't try to tackle the problems directly, but to work through the education system of the country. So, the people who graduate from these schools have generally very tolerant mind-sets and are open to different ideas and ideologies.

On a broad European level, there was also a lot of contact and dialogue with relevant European institutions, with these efforts culminating in a big International Symposium on *Countering Violent Extremism: Mujahada and Muslims' Responsibility*, held on 15–16 March 2016 in Brussels.[5] By 2019, much of the work of the Intercultural Dialogue Platform was focusing on "countering extremism"; "countering discrimination, antisemitism and Islamophobia"; and "working in Inter-cultural dialogue". Whereas previously a lot of such work had been financially supported by Turkish businessmen, after July 2016 it was necessary to apply to the European Commission calls for various projects in these areas because, as Tascioglu said, "You cannot, for example, add more people to your team because some people might start to complain about people in Turkey who need financial assistance and is this the right time to employ more people, and to have that much of a budget at this time". Therefore, overall this fed into the reflection by HE1 that:

> So, I think these things allow us to face the reality. I saw this: that all the other societies, all the other associations are writing projects, applying for them and organizing activities according to their budgets. For us it was always the other way around: we always made our activities and then asked for support from our volunteers and, of course, it was unsustainable.
>
> All these things showed us that we are not exactly facing the reality of Europe. I think for my organization we faced the reality and for us it is that the only through for more sustainable and professional work is writing European projects with local partners, with European partners. And in that we are creating more concrete outputs in our interests in terms of dialogue, countering extremism and countering discrimination in the society, like promoting social cohesion.

An important part of all these approaches is that they are consistent with Hizmet's self-understanding as an educative movement within its internal logics rather than it becoming externally instrumentalised by the state. Bearing all this in mind, what Toğuşlu proposed was that:

> What the movement should bring out within the European context is a new kind of interpretation, based not only the rituals. Rituals are maybe important, but what is the sense of Islam in terms of its teachings in the European context. For example, what should it be? – climate crisis? Globalisation and global issues? These are, to some extent what, to some extent we have to renew our work about Islam, not only for the radicalization issue, but also

for the next generation coming now who want to learn something about Islam, about the Muslim faith.

This also connects with Keleş, Sezgin and Yılmaz's (2019) argument that, of course, "The Hizmet Movement did not generate and grow to address the perils of Islamophobia or Puritanical Islamic Extremism" (p. 278). Rather it had its own much more directly religious inspiration in what they called "the practice-focused teachings of Fethullah Gülen which sought to articulate an authentic expression of faith and religion in the light of contemporary challenges predicated on the notion of service to God and humanity". Nevertheless, it is clear that "the underlying teachings and practice of that self-declared aim have direct and indirect implications for the ground upon which Puritanical Islamic Extremist ideology and Islamophobia flourishes and connects with potential recruits". At the same time, this kind of thinking and the kind of initiatives following from it represent an evolution and adaptation of Hizmet's more traditional role because, in interaction with the wider societies of which they have become a part, Hizmet organisations (as distinct from Gülen himself and his teaching) have not been so much—if at all—on educating about religion.

Where this has taken place, it has been primarily in the arena of extra-curricular activity supplementary to the main formal education system. As Tascioglu explained, "We do have cultural centres where, during the holiday periods, families voluntarily send their children to them and they have Qur'an lessons. It is completely voluntary and it is for kids: kind of summer schools". And as Toğuşlu notes, "I think this is one of the aspects in which the movement is maybe still related to the Turkish identity – why, because Turkey has a hard line secular Kemalist ideology exists there, and this has prevented showing this Muslim identity in a clear way".

However, in Europe now, particularly because of Hizmet's asylum and refugee situation but also, as argued by Balcı, in relation to its overall minority context, Hizmet is becoming concerned with the meeting of educational needs a fresh way (see Sect. 6.2). This entails seeing oneself and one's world in terms of Islam, but also in a way that is not closed either to the constraints of a minority sub-culture or trapped within a potentially inter-generational trauma relating to Turkey, but can open up Muslims working within such a vision to make the maximum possible contribution to European societies in a way fully informed by, and not apologetic about, their Islam. As AS2, says of radicals:

So, in Europe, the Hizmet movement will be better, and it will be a chance to live peacefully because, as you know, now in the world when you call "terrorist" most of the youth, or Christians or Jewish people think "Muslim" terrorists. We have to make something for this. We have to show that a Muslim can't be a terrorist. We have to show all the world the real Islam, so they think, the Muslims are not terrorists, but good guys and in their inner life, they are good. But radicalism is always bad, even if it is in Christianity or Judaism, it is always bad. So, in Europe, the Hizmet movement will be better, I think so.

5.3   Turkishness and Beyond

It is arguable that a phenomenon such as *Hizmet* could only have emerged and developed in the special conditions of Turkey's geopolitical situation and history (see Weller 2022, Sect. 3.1). The rich Islamic heritage of the country combined with its emergence as an independent modern state embracing aspects of secularism contrasts with the experience of nearly all other Muslim majority societies where secularism was externally imposed as part of a package including colonialism and imperialism. However, a consequence of that specificity is also the question of how far, in practice, might Hizmet have become "ghettoised" within its inherited Turkishness. In relation to this, Keleş poses the issues involved quite starkly:

I always said that the Turks were for Hizmet like the "oil curse" for Saudi Arabia. When Hizmet encounters a Turkish enclave of people in 'foreign land', it simply ploughs into them, serving them. This helps Hizmet to take root among and within the immigrant Turkish community quickly but it also "curses" them in a way in that, like the Saudi oil, it inhibits them from branching out to other cultures and communities.

This position was also reflected in that HE2, who said with regard to Italy that, in contrast to the situation in Germany and Austria, "thank God, we didn't have any type of big Turkish community, so people have been forced to engage". Such matters are very much under internal, including inter-generational debate and, indeed, were already so before July 2016. But, despite the relatively long history of some awareness and review of these issues, Toğuşlu reflected that "We are still somehow organising in a Turkish way" and that as a consequence "we cannot adopt or integrate fully into a local identity where we are". As a result, in relation to non-Turkish people in Hizmet while, "They are present in our community here in Belgium" nevertheless, in reality "they are not representing Fedactio, for example" and that therefore "in the leadership I never really see an Albanian, a Senegalese, a Turkmen – most of the people are coming from Turkey: ninety to ninety-nine per cent". And therefore while "it's not a long history I know, but for almost fifty years now, it is still a little bit surprising that in the decision-making process we see only the people coming from Turkey, if we have only the Turkish experience". So, the challenge is that "We are always working together, but the problem is integrating these people as fully members". Drawing on his comparative experience in France and in Belgium, Toğuşlu notes that:

> In the beginning I did not understand, OK – I am from the movement and they are from the movement, but we sometimes cannot communicate very well! We cannot understand each other very well. But when I stayed about eight years in France and now I am eight years in Belgium, now I understand more correctly what they mean, what they want, what kind of pedagogical preference we have to use in the movement. In the beginning we just used what we brought from Turkey with us and in the early eighties imagine. So, I think it never worked.

Toğuşlu says this is an ongoing debate among Hizmet people: "should they keep this Turkish identity or not?" and "What is the relationship between this Turkish descent and a Muslim identity?" In relation to this question he says, "Especially the younger generation coming from different European countries – from France, from Germany, from Denmark – the younger generation who were raised and schooled here, they don't want to carry this Turkish identity as far as I can see".

At the same time, there are significant differences in terms of the presence of Hizmet in various European countries. Thus, as Keleş puts it, those of Turkish background in Germany "are the 'majority minority' whereas in the UK, they are the 'minority minority' ". Related to this Keleş argues that, generally speaking:

> Most of the Hizmet workforce in any geography that has a sufficient Turkish presence, ninety per cent of it will focus on the Turks which is a minority in the country, and the ten per cent Hizmet workforce (if that at all) will focus on the majority of the country. And that's a problem, whereas if there are no, or a small number of Turks there, then all of Hizmet participants and supporters in that locality will focus their energies on activities that are inclusive of all communities.

As illustrative of this, interviewee Sadik Çinar (see Acknowledgements), from the UK, notes that initially almost all Hizmet activities were focused in London and that even after he moved to the UK's second city of Birmingham in October 2013, "Again, we started by doing community-building activities among the Turkish community in Birmingham, but numbers were so limited … The Turkish numbers were only a couple of hundred". And in that context Cinar noted that "Because we have limited Turkish people in numbers, actually: the less Turkish people, the more we have to reach out to the wider community". In the UK, in order to mark out its identity as a British organisation, in due course the Dialogue Society developed a Green Paper on *Towards a British Hizmet*.

In the Netherlands, Alasag explained that in order to move beyond the kind of cultural misunderstandings or assumptions he and others were making, they needed several years to learn the quite different Dutch majority cultural codes. As interviewee HE3 notes, there was a cultural tension:

> The problem we experienced was sometimes that people grew up here who had Dutch roots and were focusing on the Dutch society, they had a clear vision of how Hizmet could engage with the society, with the government, whatever Hizmet is doing in the Dutch society. But it was sometimes clashing with the people who came from Turkey and were involved here and who had a Turkish mindset and worked in a Turkish way.

Of course, part of the reason for the initial close alignment between Hizmet and Turkishness was also due to the continuing and important channels of communication and support within Hizmet between Turkey and the relevant European countries, with HE3 noting that, of course, Turkey still had influence "because people were coming from Turkey and going to Turkey. I was going to Turkey and visiting Turkey and we were talking with the Journalists and Writers Foundation and following their initiatives". Historically, "we were not always able to develop something very Dutch" and when visitors from Turkey asked why we did things in a certain way "we were hesitating – is it correct what we are doing?" and this "caused sometimes tensions within the Hizmet". But he said at the time this was:

> Because Hizmet in Turkey was so well organized, and Hizmet in Holland was so small when we went to Turkey, we looked up to the Hizmet initia-

tives in Turkey. There were many schools, universities, dialogue centres and when they organized dialogue activities everybody came. It was so big.

Taking the example of a Turkish Hizmet visitor to the UK who organised the Rumi programmes with the whirling dervishes in London, interviewee HE3 said that "So, we organised them here as well. It was kind of, we didn't know what to do to reach out and he was our kind of guru, or whatever. We had visited him and in time we had regular meetings. He developed something and we put it into practice". Overall, HE3 evaluated this in terms of "So, it was kind of copying a lot", although "he was also copying from us. So, if one country had developed a concept, other countries were trying to put it into practice in their own countries". Similarly, in relation to the example of the people who first started Hizmet in the UK, Keleş said of them that:

> They depended on Turkish people that had come from Turkey that were temporary and they would go back. So, these were people who did not have any roots. But they were able to support the movement, I mean, they knew the ideas; they knew the Hizmet modus operandi, if you like. So, they didn't need to be recruited into Hizmet, so to speak. And as a result, they were ready to support the movement here.

However, in the longer term, Keleş identified this as detrimental "because it meant that the movement didn't develop its roots, it didn't do enough community-building here". And Keleş noted that when these people left "we didn't have sufficient base for other people to carry the movement forward and we overestimated our capacity to do things because it was based on temporary resources". In addition, in relation to the substance of what they were doing, Keleş said:

> It didn't reflect the needs of the people, of the Turkish people, or the needs of British Muslim communities here. It was more about replicating what we had seen Hizmet do in Turkey here, without necessarily refining it and changing it, and asking the question as to whether or not the same methodology needed to be applied, or the same products needed to be produced. So, because Hizmet opened schools in Turkey, so we should open schools here rather than, well, why do we open schools here and what is the nature of those schools going to be?

In 2001 and 2002, Keleş claimed that "things started to pick up again", which he attributed to the fact that "Hizmet went back to doing what it should have been doing which was about building community support and not relying on people from abroad. Sadly, that created a second problem. Community support meant *Turkish* community support". Nevertheless "you had the flourishing of various organizations. Education and dialogue were, if you like, the main two Hizmet-related activities in the UK, and the creation of various charities". But in the light of the impact of July 2016, Keleş underlines that "we've also seen now how that can be temporary – when they pull back their support, then Hizmet again gets left in the open".

Of course, even before July 2016 there were key Hizmet people in Europe who already had a different understanding of, and approach to, the relationship between Turkishness and Hizmet stemming, at least in part, from their own different ethnic and national origins. As Erkinbekov put it: "Me, personally, I am from Krygstan. I got to know Hizmet in University when I was a University student. So, I have a different perspective on Hizmet compared with others". And the question of the relationship between Turkishness and Hizmet has also always at the least been differently inflected in different European countries. In some countries, what had been a previous awareness and already a matter of some debate for some time was brought into sharper focus through July 2016. HE3, from the Netherlands, noted in relation to Turkey itself that:

> Since the coup, I haven't been there. I had some emotional relationship with my country of origin. I am a first generation migrant here, according to the definition in the academic literature. I was born in Turkey. But I think now at this moment, when I listen to people, they come from Turkey, their emotional relationship with Turkey is almost over. It is a country which is Turkey, I was born there. But this is the only relationship I have with it, it is over for myself.

Or, as HE1 from Belgium put it, "I think that, as an identity, I already lost the Turkish identity. I don't attach myself to Turkey anymore" while going on to explain that:

> All these events after the coup bring a test emotionally, and don't reinforce any positive things between the Turkish identity and what we are doing right now. Of course, all the Turkish culture, all the background is used a lot

of the time, and we should all give thanks and use them in our action. But it is more important to be a main element in our own countries. So, I don't see any value to be Turkish again. Maybe it's more emotional, because I feel I have already emotionally detached myself from Turkey so when a form asks me nationality, I just write "Belgian".

In the light of this, HE1 concludes that, for those who have been in Europe already, "I think it is a bigger advantage for us to improve the cultural integration in the European culture, because we are not attached to Turkey anymore". At the same time, HE1 recognised the greater complexity of this for those who had more recently arrived in Europe as asylum-seekers when he said that, in comparison with himself:

I mean, I am someone who was working and being in Belgium since 2010. So, I am not affected this much, so I cannot imagine someone who lost their job, who sometimes lost their family members, or their families are in prison and they had to come here. I think they are in deep trauma, and that trauma is not a small thing. I think it will continue for a while.

Karakoyun also highlights the contrast between the understanding of Hizmet that has been developing in Europe that which newcomers from Turkey were bringing with them:

I think Hizmet in Germany is quite different from Hizmet in Turkey ... it has to do with the political system in Turkey and also has to do with the mentality of the people in Turkey; of the education system; of the patriarchal system; of the way of living; of experiencing; the Ottoman Empire; and all these things that you see everywhere – the statues of Atatürk, the flags. So Hizmet in Turkey was very much Turkey-oriented, not to say nationalistic, but patriotic maybe, and very much oriented on bringing to the world the Turkish culture, the benefits of Turkish language.

However, because of its history Germany has basically "another approach to nationalism, to nation state, to what makes Germany 'German', what makes the Germans 'German'. So, you have a very different discussion here and we found ourselves here rather in a country that is also very self-critical of their past". The question of what might be called "operational style" has also historically affected the relationship between Hizmet in Turkey and Hizmet in Europe and elsewhere with Karakoyun noting that, historically, because something has been done in Turkey "yes you do it now as well, there is nothing to question about it. It's perfect, this is what they have told us". However, in Germany the culture (as informed by the education system) is based on democratic consensus-building through the contribution of open opinions and that, therefore, "In Germany all circles, institutions, groups, initiatives, on the one hand are democratic and they are based on building a consensus. And in Turkey it is, rather, 'obedience' – you have to obey".

As an example, Karakoyun suggested to imagine someone coming from Turkey and saying, "On Wednesday we have the children's feast of Atatürk here and we should also bring flowers to the children", but that the response of Hizmet in Germany is that "No, we won't because in Germany we don't have this day, but we can give flowers to the people on the day the two Germanies were united, but not on Atatürk's children's festival!" In summary, Karakoyun argues that:

> Of course, two mentalities are confronted: because, on the one hand, the mentality in which everyone is critical and should always speak openly, never hiding his opinion (German mentality) and on the other hand, the patriarchy, the strong man, the obedience and the "I say what you have to do", from the Turkish context. And, of course, this was not always easy.

Unlike in Germany and Belgium, however, in Switzerland (as in the UK), the Turkish community is neither the biggest "foreign" community nor the biggest Muslim community. This is because in Switzerland there are roughly as many Bosniaks as Turks and Albanian Muslims are the biggest Muslim group. Nevertheless, initially in Switzerland, SERA (see Sect. 3.6), for example, was very much a Turkish association, having in its statutes that it would do things like assisting Turkish students. However, with the emergence of the second generation of Hizmet in Switzerland came the realisation that, as Özgü put it, "we are not just Turks … but we are also Albanian and Bosniaks, and also connected them. We also had many members in the Advisory Boards and Board members in the associations who were not Turks, who were Albanians or were Bosniaks". Therefore "in the early 2000s we began also to talk about our *sohbets* and the meetings being Turkish" and the question of "is this topic Turkey important for us?" and by "the early 2010s we decided that Turkey is not the most important country because we were no longer only Turkish associations".

Despite this, as Özgü says, about ten years prior to when he was interviewed in August 2019, he cited the example of a group of "people from

Turkey who came to Switzerland, about forty people. They were well educated and they were very active, and they thought they could change
Switzerland, but Switzerland changed them". However, as Özgü puts it,
"now when you look globally, most of the Hizmet authorities are from
Turkey. They were socialised in Turkey. And they also have this Turkish
understanding and thinking of things". But, overall, now, as Özgü suc-
cinctly summarises it "we try to emancipate from Turkey", which relates
to what this book calls the process of the "de-centring" of Hizmet from
Turkey and which process is still ongoing.

In Denmark, Gezen says that, the majority of Hizmet youth in Denmark
"want the language to become Danish and this is, I think, a natural sociological development. It's difficult and it's challenging. But it is inevitable".
Over the past five years, discussions and developments in both the Dialog
Forum and in the wider Hizmet have centred more on contributing
towards solutions for local problems rather than using energy on problems
that are outside Denmark. Nevertheless, Gezen notes of Hizmet that due
to "the origins of the people" and "until the association receives more
members with backgrounds who are not from Turkey" it is inevitably the
case that "It will still have an attachment to Turkey". In relation to this
Gezen notes that "Right now, in Europe, the Turkish Kurdish communities are those who are moving the movement. So, you don't find many
Moroccan people, Pakistani people. You won't find many Arab people as
such in Hizmet". But Gezen's opinion is that this will change more and
more in future "especially through marriages. There are more mixed marriages". This is also a theme which HE3 from the Netherlands picked up
and commented on as follows: "From my ideas that I shared with young
people here – that when they are not married, I say marry with a Dutch
girl or a Dutch man, and you will see that this will change your life within
ten or twenty years" and further:

> And people have babies here and they sometimes ask my opinion and ask,
> "Do you have some good names"? And I tell them, and I will continue over
> the next years if they ask me, say: don't take the Turkish name which is
> problematic in the Dutch pronunciation here – not Ayesha, not Davut, or
> Abdullah – no, give them a name, another name, which sounds good within
> the Dutch language. And one of them is Ferdi – Ferdi is Fedinand and Ferdi
> is also a Turkish name. And one of them gave this name to his son. And Sara
> is also a Turkish-Arabic name, the wife of Abraham – and that people think
> in that way which is also a process. And I think I have heard it, but not

properly from Gülen, that he thinks also in that way. But he can't say this. If he says this, it will be a problem, especially in Turkish politics and Turkish people will think that he is a person who promotes assimilation. The recent years, Gülen increasingly and publicly resonates more and more: NO for assimilation and YES for integration.

At the same time, as Keleş from the UK notes:

There are some people who believe that Hizmet will return to Turkey; believe that the Erdoğan government will be toppled; people will realise the mistake and will call Hizmet back, and will ask for forgiveness. And Gülen refers to this as well, and he says that when they ask for forgiveness you need to prepare yourself to be ready to forgive. And that's fine, I guess, but there is the idea that Hizmet has now come to a realisation that Turkey is no longer viable, I'm not sure it has come to that. There are some people that still look at well, we will return.

From the Netherlands, interviewee HE3 sees a contrast with previous Hizmet migrants in terms of the "newcomers", that:

They came sometimes with their children, ten years, fifteen years old, and twenty years old, and they all have a better self-confidence when I compare them to the children who were born here in the Netherlands, with Turkish origin. So, if these groups from Turkey, the parents, if they will not be a barrier or an obstacle for their children, I think that in about ten years, twenty years, in about one generation, their children is a great asset to the movement and will generate a lot of ideas for the movement, for Hizmet here in the Netherlands.

Indeed, noting that there is already a new generation of leadership in the Netherlands, this interviewee argues that:

I think if their children and a new generation here can find a way to come together, this will also create a big dynamism for the movement, and a rebirth of the movement, maybe, with new ideas, the old generation leaders, you can't change them much. But if they make place for these new generations then I think the movement with these ideas can contribute to the Dutch society more.

The one matter that quite a number of interviewees noted could have a further and potentially unpredictable impact on these processes is that of the question of any possible return to Turkey consequent upon any change in the political situation there. In relation to this from the UK, Sadik Çinar reports that "The idea of returning to Turkey is diminishing day by day, but still people predominantly believe they will return to Turkey, but that is diminishing". Of the asylum-seekers in the Netherlands, Alasag says that, as compared to the past when Hizmet people from Turkey and those from the Netherlands had quite different ideas: "So the difference now is that we are all – even the asylum-seekers, even the refugees, even the expats who came last year and all these people who came from Turkey five years ago, for them Turkey is finished. They only see their future here in Holland". In terms of the "dream of return", he says that there are "maybe a few". However, he also said that in relation to "ninety-nine per cent" that "They came here to live here forever. So, the focus is also that they opened themselves up one hundred per cent for the Dutch society", which he attributed to the fact that:

> They left the country under very difficult circumstances, escaping without friends or family etc. and in the end they came here and it was a struggle and it was very difficult. And it was a long process of two years or three years, of hiding in Turkey, then coming into Greece, and then coming here. It took for some of them, it took three years. So, when they are here, all these things that they lived through on their way, it made it very clear for them.

And he contrasts this with the previous situation of five years or so previously, of which he says, "when they came they brought Turkey with them" and "it took them ten years to learn Dutch and some of them never learned Dutch". However, under the present conditions for, and circumstances of, arrival "now everybody learns Dutch" and "It is also the psychological difference" in that:

> Now, they left Turkey behind one hundred per cent. And they talk about, for example, what shall we do; with whom we will do; and if we do this, what will change in the society; is it good; are we then helping something or supporting something; or being a part of something? The focus is only that they are looking and trying to orientate themselves in this society and trying to be helpful.

In Switzerland, Özgü says:

I talk about this issue with many people, and most of them say, no, we don't want to go back, but in a few years when they will work here – you must understand people who were in Turkey professionals or academicians, or teachers – Turkish teachers or religion teachers – they will not find good work in Europe. They will work in a factory in a Doner Kebab shop and things like that and they might want to go back because they might want to get all this teacher and academician stuff back. But the people who will be well integrated in the professional world, I think they will stay in Switzerland.

From Germany, Karakoyun says:

Well, of course, people hope that things will change in Turkey. But, well, I am – many people say in Germany say it like that "I'm a pessimist optimist". Well, the people are hoping, of course. But I think when looking to Turkey that it is difficult to say things will change, I think it will take years, because there is a deep mentality that exists there now, a deep hatred, and it will not change from today to tomorrow, I think. It will take years.

As a result of this, he says that:

So, people that are now living here and that are fleeing to Germany, they should realise, I think, that they have to become part of the German society, that they have to integrate. Nothing else will work. It won't be possible to return to Turkey within the next few years, I think. And it is also important that they realise that they can't change Turkey from Germany. Because no matter what you do and however intensely you do it, things won't change, because Turkey has its own dynamics.

At the same time, Karakoyun notes that, for some "it is a situation in which people can find themselves again, in the idea of Gülen, of the movement, they know each other" but also that "it is a big dynamic at the moment and I do not know how this will develop. And the future depends on the developments around Gülen himself, and the young generations".

Summarising the issues involved around Turkey having been what might be called the "centre of gravity" of the movement, Keleş says: "For me it's finished", but he also asks "Has the movement come to that realisation?" to which he himself gives the answer, "No, it hasn't", which for Keleş this links with the issue of transparency and his whole argument for self-criticism in the movement (see Sect. 6.6) because:

If we can question the centrality of Turkey to Hizmet's project and the possible return of Hizmet to Turkey, if that is something we can question and doubt, then we can start questioning and doubting a lot more. So, even the fact of questioning this, and disagreeing with Hizmet's and Gülen's views on this, is actually more significant than just disagreeing on that particular point. But it is a bit of a litmus test in that sense. It's more indicative of wider issues.

5.4   Charisma, Structures and Transparency

A number of authors writing on Hizmet pick up on the issue that, whether or not it is seen as being potentially terrorist in nature as charged by the current Turkish authorities, Hizmet nevertheless faces charges of a lack of transparency. In relation to this, Sunier and Landman (2015) accurately note that "The loose organizational structure of the movement causes different reactions in different political contexts" (p. 82). Some degree of organisation is, of course, necessary in any movement however informally it operates because, in order to achieve a reach beyond that of individuals acting alone, structure is needed and structure entails the transfer of resources. At least within modern societies such transfer of resources also entails a readiness to accept quite a lot of transparency and with it a considerable degree of external accountability.

When addressing issues in relation to which Hizmet needed to improve, interviewee HE3 from the Netherlands highlighted "more transparency, about financial issues" as a key example of this, the reason for which being that "Money is a big issue here. If you can't explain how you use that money and how you get that money, that will be a big problem not only for the movement, but also for the big companies here. Thus, the movement can be more transparent in such a kind of things".

It is also, of course, the case that organisational forms can become constraining upon an inspiration as a source of action and should therefore be carefully evolved. In broad terms, organisational transparency is necessary to give confidence to the wider society that it is possible to work co-operatively with groups that do not necessarily do everything in a bureaucratised way, but which can make an enormous contribution to the common good, partly because their mode of operating sometimes allows them to do things which more formalised bodies are not able to do.

In some contexts, including those which originally pertained to Hizmet in Turkey, it is entirely understandable that certain expressions of religious life have felt it necessary to be less visible. In connection with this, the illegality of Sufi Orders within Kemalist Turkey, and the direct experience of many of those inspired by Gülen's teaching, play a continuing role as can be seen when Alasag explained from his own biography that:

> Before I came to Holland in 1989, I was put into prison in Turkey a couple of times. First time was when I was fifteen, just because I was reading the books of Said Nursi at the time, and listening to the sermons of Gülen and that was then enough to put you in prison. And it was not a problem of Gülen people, many other groups had the same problem. Because of this some Alevites for example were also kind of reluctant to be open in the Turkish society about their identity. Some leftist groups in the past also had the same fear. So, the more open you are, the bigger is the chance that maybe not now, but in the future, you may pay the price. So, it was for us also this fear.

When initially faced with the kind of investigations outlined in Sect. 5.2 of this chapter, Alasag says that Hizmet in the Netherlands consulted with their advisory groups which included many people from the wider society: "We asked all of them what is this about what should we do?" Their advice was "To tell about Hizmet and to be more, how you call it, transparent". In the first instance, they thought that meant "to tell more about Gülen". As a result, part of their response to this was to organise conferences focused around Gülen and his teaching. In addition, they published in Dutch a fairly substantial book called *What Is Hizmet?*, of which Alasag says: "We also put in that book everything, including also all the accusations, and all the positive things people in say in Turkey, outside Turkey. So, we tried to give a really neutral, objective information". However, somewhat ironically:

> When we organised a conference and also published this book, and also tried to give this information to people, some people reacted like "why so much effort"?! – they interpreted this as if we were trying to hide something by giving all the answers to all those accusations etc. They said if you are not guilty, you would just laugh about this and get on with your life. That you are trying too much it means that it is all true – that was the interpretation! We did it because people advised us to do it. For us it was very puzzling.

On reflection, Alasag sees this as all having been part of a necessary learning process that Hizmet in the Netherlands underwent in connection with the process of becoming more fully integrated into Dutch society and cultural ways of doing things. In relation to this he explained that "Although we were so long in dialogue, although we built so big a network, although we had so many friends, it took many years to understand what's the dynamic and how to engage in this dynamic with the society, with the media" and of this he said that, in the end they arrived at the understanding that "It's kind of, in Holland, the dynamic, the society pushes, and then looks at the reaction. And the way of Dutch to engage and trying to communicate their fears, their questions, their hopes. It's the way Dutch people deal with things".

As a consequence of this, in due course they also came to understand about the issue of transparency that "It wasn't a kind of transparency in the sense of just telling everything, but trusting the society, not defending, but being open about yourself". In addition, and very importantly, it meant "being critical to your own position, accepting all these questions as a critique and trying to not 'answer' it, or kind of defend yourself, but try to understand and try to do something about it". Alasag said, "we were very relieved when we understood this", in the light of which they set about trying to establish an overall "platform" for the organisations founded by Hizmet people.

Referring to the Voices initiative in the UK (see Sect. 3.5), Alasag explained that, from around 2012, "We had a kind of a similar platform with fifty-three different organizations in Holland". But again somewhat puzzlingly for them at the time "some of our Dutch friends (although we had asked some of them beforehand) reacted very negatively". The explanation their friends gave for this was that some individuals from the wider Dutch society who had been supportive explained that they could justify that supportiveness to others on the basis that through engaging with Hizmet on a local level they were able to have a significant influence. However, the formation of the national initiative meant that "it was suddenly a very big platform with a very strong identity. So, they said if you continue with this, I stop, I quit. So, they said they told us they will quit our boards; they will quit our advisory boards; they will quit whatever and however they were engaged with Hizmet". Alasag also confided that there were people from the government who had, in the informal terms, also urged caution about this wider development, citing the right-wing reaction there had previously been to the otherwise small initiative of opening a school for a couple of hundred students and therefore warned that "if you open such a platform which is so huge, so big, those groups will see it as a threat, so they will engage with you on another level".

In many ways what is recounted here as having happened in the Netherlands underscores how seriously Hizmet organisations take the advice they are given by these external people whom they trust, because Alasag explained that, as a result of this advice "we stopped this initiative before even we were able to send a newsletter. So, it was opened and within a couple of months, we stopped". Instead, they decided to approach the challenge of transparency by being more transparent on their website:

> So we translated *Istishare* (in Dutch translated as *overleg*), we said we had *overleg*, and we put every information about our Hizmet, how we are active, what is our position, and the names of the Istishare group, all this information on the website. And we said you are welcome if you have questions, if you want to engage or contact with Hizmet, just send us an email or call this number.

In the UK, according to Keleş the 2007 international conference organised on the movement and held in London under the title of *Muslim World in Transition: Contributions of the Gülen Movement*[6] also generated internal discussions "about what we were and how we were" which fed into a small follow-up event (in which the author participated) held in Istanbul in 2008, and which included more in-depth panel discussions to which the current author contributed a number of critical questions (for the detail of this, see Weller 2022, Sect. 6.1). On the other side of that, in 2009, the 'About Us' page of the Dialogue Society's website for the first time acknowledged in written ways what the Society has previously started acknowledging verbally—namely that it was an organisation founded by people inspired by Gülen's teachings and example on dialogue. Earlier this was not explicitly stated because of concerns that the nature of such inspiration could either be misunderstood, or any reference to it misused, by those who wish to assert a "conspiratorial" view of the Hizmet. Therefore, Keleş claims that, for the UK, this website acknowledgement:

> Begins the process of a wider transparency around Hizmet – not just the Dialogue Society, but also all the other Hizmet organizations. And we were sort of leading that conversation because of the type of activity that we were doing because the question of transparency kept coming to us as the Dialogue Society because we were doing things that brought us into contact with people who had very little knowledge about who we were, and also we

were doing this on a basis that required an understanding of where we came from, you know. So, we were talking about, doing events around dialogue, and part of dialogue is, well, who are you?

And Keleş went on to say that eventually "we were pushing all the Hizmet-related organizations and *activities* in the UK to become transparent and to make that open. We were doing that in discussion with our Advisors".[7] However, Keleş also acknowledged that "while everyone agreed in theory that this is what we should do, when it came to doing it in practice, habits kicked in, cultural mindsets, if you like, and ways of thinking about this kicked in, and it was a challenge". When the scholar Caroline Tee talks about "hidden hierarchies", and the *ablas* of the various houses of the movement, Keleş explained that she was referring to *bölge-cilik*. In providing their religious mentoring, *bolgecis*, however, work more closely with adults, professionals, workers and businesspeople. But another less visible aspect of Hizmet has been what David Tittensor has talked about when referring to religious mentoring in Hizmet schools and in other contexts which is *rehberlik* which, in general Turkish means "counselling" or "mentoring". In the Hizmet lexicon it more specifically refers to the religious mentoring of younger people undertaken by *rehbers* who operate within these particular parts of Hizmet. While such *rehbers* work closely with the *bolgecis*, they are themselves not *bolgecis*.

In the UK, this is now all much more transparent in organisational terms: thus the Sobhet Society and Mentor Wise are limited by guarantee companies and within Voices all the organisations active within it also now have on their websites an acknowledgement of their Gülen inspiration and, when talking about Hizmet structure, organisation and activity in the UK. But Keleş explained that there were, historically, two elements of Hizmet activity that have not been so transparent, in relation to which he claimed, "We've now convinced the people engaged in this part of Hizmet that what they are doing is not something to be upset about or worried about. I mean it's a great thing they are doing – it's just that the way they are doing it in this cannot be sustained, so we've asked them to 'come out' ".

The first of these relates to the *sohbets* in which Hizmet people gather to study, learn, mutually encourage and challenge. In relation to this now, in the UK, the Sohbet Society's website's section "How we do it" transparently explains to "outsiders" some of what it calls "pre-existing and well-established practices and roles" that are known to insiders by their Turkish names, such as *abi*, *abla*, *bölgecilik* and *istishare* which, to outsiders without a knowledge of the Turkish language, can sometimes seem opaque and/or mysterious. Furthermore, the "Sohbet Plus" section of the website also gives access to some of the religious resources, in both Turkish and in English, with which people in Hizmet work in their *sohbets*.

The second area that had historically not been so transparent concerns what is covered by the Turkish word *bölgecilik*, and which Keleş explains as being "constituency-based grass roots religious activity". Indeed, it is this informal network that is precisely what makes it possible to speak about Hizmet as a social movement. Thus, although there are lots of organisations, *bölgecilik* is what Keleş describes as the "bit that you can't see" which, as in his evidence to the UK Parliament Foreign Affairs Committee, Keleş was transparent about in terms of its activities in organising *sohbets* (religious circles), "camps" (religious retreats), *mutevelis* (meetings with donors).

Before these developments, whereas in the Turkic countries of Central Asia, Hizmet had very largely developed around schools and teachers, in western Europe the *bolgecis* had acted more as community organisers to build up a community base within which they collected *Qurbani* donations for slaughtering animals for Eid celebrations; opened and ran *dershanes* or student houses; collected subscriptions for the *Zaman* newspaper and facilitated the religious *sohhets*, doing all of this within what Keleş calls "a very clear structure of hierarchy".

Keleş claims of the UK approach to this that "As far as I know, no other Hizmet in the world has done this", although he does acknowledge that in other parts of Europe what are perhaps similar attempts are underway even if in a more "indirect" manner. For example, in Belgium, Fedactio is now choosing its regional co-ordinators from the people that are *bölgecis*, although Keleş has questions about this on that basis that "that's not really transparent because you are not really making this line of work clear and obvious … not making it transparent in itself: we are trying to make it transparent by reference to something else and that doesn't really help".

In Denmark, however, in contrast with the history of this in the UK, Gezen says that right from its beginning, the Forum has been "proud to say that we are inspired by Gülen, but we have a couple of members and friends, like ethnic Danes, who want to support us, and are not inspired by Gülen. But we are openly inspired by Gülen and that is how people know us". In Switzerland, in the immediate aftermath of the events of 2016, when only a few journalists asked about Turkey, according to Özgü, the way in which July 2016 had an impact was that "we began to talk in

Hizmet about the transparency thing". While prior to this they did already have a small working group founded in 2015 and had also "talked about things like that" after 2016 "all the people in Hizmet started to talk about this transparency and we began to ask ourselves, how can we make ourselves more transparent, how can we be in the media". In pursuit of this they held three big assemblies in Switzerland to which all Hizmet active people in the country (described by Özgü in terms of "hundreds of people") were invited "to discuss what can we change, what do we need" and among the questions with which they were concerned, "We asked the question about gender in Hizmet and dialogue in Hizmet".

Reflecting overall on the transparency issue, as Kerakoyun from Germany explained it, "In Turkey nobody said, 'Look, I am from Hizmet'. There was a big lack of transparency in all institutions", and not only in Turkey, "It was a problem everywhere in the world". As an example Kerakoyun explained that, if one visited a school in Turkey founded by Hizmet people and asked the head of the school, the head would say something like, "No we are not a Hizmet school, we are a school of the Turkish people for the world". In contrast to this, the attitude of Kerakoyun and his generation of Hizmet leaders in Germany has always been that of "we are German Turks. We are born here. We are socialized here. There is nothing wrong with Hizmet. There is nothing that is wrong with the teachings of Fethullah Gülen, Hojaefendi. So why should we hide something? We spoke very openly".

What Kerakoyun describes perhaps to some degree reflects the more "direct" nature of German culture. But Kerakoyun also states this as a matter of principle on the basis that "If the state funds our school and if we have German parents sending their children to us, we have to be honest – not only because we are Hizmet, but even as human beings, we have to be honest". As a consequence we need to explain about our schools that:

> We don't have Islamic or Qur'an lessons; we don't teach or read the books of Gülen in the class, but we are schools whose founding has been motivated by the teachings of this Turkish Islamic preacher, and we are doing very good education with (a), (b), (c), (d), (e) criteria, and this is our education. So not hiding and then catching the children should be the strategy, but showing the qualities and benefits and being open and saying, yes, we are Muslims, but we don't teach Islam.

Therefore, "If you feel that your child is being missionized, or that we are trying to put on him Islamic values, then you can protest against us". In Germany there is partial state funding of religious-based schools and, although in the UK, this has also been the case in relation to the voluntary aided sector, that has only relatively recently in practice extended to include Muslim-based schools. Hizmet's Wisdom School initiative in the UK has already been noted, and Keleş explained that when the new Academies initiative came in they also tried to take advantage of the new forms of publicly funded schools "but you had to put £2 million down" and then "when the Free Schools came in, we tried that again. Six applications were put in".

Keleş cited these examples self-critically as "One of the battles where we lost the transparency battle within ourselves". This was because the applications were put in under such titles as North London, South London, West London and East London, but without acknowledging the connections between them: "For some reason they did not disclose, and did not realise that titling in that way would actually disclose, the co-ordination between these applications". In relation to this, Keleş recounts that a few years later when he was speaking at a seminar on religious movements and education and he made the broad point that, on the one hand the British state apparatus seemed to be saying to Hizmet that it welcomed Hizmet's form of religious interpretation and practice and wanted to see it influencing the wider Muslim community, but on the other hand "when we attempted to open a free school in Walthamstow, with a large Muslim presence, we were rejected, even when we were open about our links to Gülen's views". In relation to this, Keleş recounts that:

> During the lunch break two people in civilian clothes approached me, and they said, "We are the due diligence people" (AKA MI5) who rejected your applications. And the reason we rejected your applications was because the people you have put their names on the applications, we do not actually believe they are the decision-makers; we believe that there is second layer of decision-makers.

Within Hizmet itself, then, there has been an ongoing debate and there have been what Keleş called "competing interests". As he explained: "So, the people within the education side would say to us, 'Look, we've got Gülen's name on our website, but we've got prospective teachers and parents who don't know anything about anything and they're coming up to us and saying what's all this Gülen thing, it's just muddying the waters' ".[8] And, indeed, as Keleş noted from their perspective it is factually the case that, in operational terms, "Gülen's philosophy in practice makes no difference at least in the UK context, and actually in many other places, in relation to the type of curriculum that is being presented – there isn't that type of religious mentoring, there isn't any underlying religious ethos". Thus, many of those in Hizmet whose primary involvement has been with education had a stance along the lines that, since there is no direct translation from Gülen's philosophy into the day-to-day running of the school, "all that we are telling them is something at the beginning of our story, of how it came about, and the cost of doing that is, well, it upsets people, it puts some people off, and is it worth it? So, they were looking at it from that point of view".

However, Keleş and other colleagues associated with him in the Dialogue Society refer also to wider debates on this as they have developed, especially in the USA, where both Hizmet and Gülen himself have come under criticism for erstwhile supporters such as in Pervez Ahmed's *Open Letter to Fethullah Gülen, Founder of Hizmet Movement,*[9] of 31 July 2019 concerning the effects that arise when charter schools that are clearly Hizmet-founded schools and are founded by Hizmet-related people are not acknowledged to be such. And in relation to this Keleş has been arguing that "But we, I think, had a broader perspective to consider because clearly these schools and institutions were considered, and were, and are a part of the movement".

As things currently stand, whereas the Wisdom School did not mention Gülen or Hizmet, once it had transitioned into the North London Grammar School, the FAQs[10] on its website, while not mentioning the name of Gülen, do nevertheless acknowledge that the school's founders (who are described as business people and educators of Turkish background) were "personally inspired by the teachings of Hizmet". This is explained as "a Turkish word which means 'service' ", and it is described as "a civil society education movement" which "emphasises the importance of inclusive and nondenominational education to help children achieve their true potential". In relation to "the nature and character of the school" among other things, it is stated that it is an "independent school" run by its Board of Governors and School Management Team; that it "follows the national curriculum"; and that it is "registered with and inspected by Oftsed and all other relevant stakeholder bodies"; and finally that it is "nondenominational and inclusive in terms of student background, ethnicity and religion" and "does not promote or teach a particular religion or philosophy including that of Hizmet".

Post-2016 new challenges have emerged in relation to transparency, both for those who have been in Europe already for a long time and for those who have suddenly found themselves in Europe as asylum-seekers. Thus, in relation to the new 'three-layeredness' of Hizmet in Europe, Keleş notes, "we've also now got a new influx of people that are coming with this mindset that they were used to in Turkey", and this creates a significant challenge for Hizmet in Europe in terms of its efforts over the past twenty years or so to integrate Hizmet into more European ways of doing things. And there are, of course, also great challenges for the asylum-seekers themselves among whom many were one day normal civil servants and the next day found themselves being treated as fugitives. And for them Keleş understands how challenging these matters are "Because the moment they concede that, actually, it's over – their whole purpose then, and the meaning that they have attached to their very careers and lives and work is gone". On the other hand, alongside these understandable reactions Keleş also argues that:

> There are some people that want to continue that because they also want to continue other practices in relation to the movement – such as not being very open about your identity; such as not being very critical about certain things; such as continuing a certain form of decision-making that is closed. Because of the way they have worked they have a vested interest in continuing the package.

And it is in relation to these that Keleş says that "When we question the decision-making processes; when we ask for greater transparency; when we question why certain types of activities are not being put into the open, these certain types of people feel threatened because it then exposes them". He goes on to explain that, of course, "None of this is to suggest that what they are doing is illegal or criminal. But it goes against the grain of what they have got used to doing, and a certain culture in which that was embedded". And in addition, Keleş acknowledges of such Hizmet people that "in some ways, they feel vindicated" since, for example, the Hizmet transparency of having in Turkey created a Trade Union for teachers unwittingly became one of the mechanisms through which people could be rounded up, "So, there you go, they say".

This irony was also acknowledged by Alasag when he explained that "in the end we became in the Netherlands very transparent as I explained, and we put the names and other information about the movement on a website". But having reached this point a year or two prior to the events of July 2016, one of the consequences of that transparency became that "Now we are paying the price as we cannot go to Turkey. Our names are known and if we go to Turkey we know what awaits us". Despite this, and in the context also of the quite unique level of scrutiny experienced by Hizmet in the Netherlands, and their continuing frustrations, Alasag's overall evaluation was that "it cleansed our name".

In relation to the overall European future, Keleş says, "I think that if the movement can be transparent and open about its identity and what it wants to do, then it can do that more comfortably in the public and private sector because it will be clear as to where its limits are". As part of this, and as will be discussed further in some detail in the next two sections, Karakoyun argues for "a transparent approach towards our Islamic identity". He explains why he thinks this important by saying:

> I think that by saying that we are a social movement and by sometimes even neglecting that we are Islamic, we lose a lot of potential. Because I think the Hizmet movement with its Islamic values and ideas is important for countries like Germany because it is an Islam that is democratic; it is based on human rights; it brings people together; it is open to dialogue; it is tolerant. And now we have a lot of people coming to Germany we different understandings of Islam. And so, we as the Hizmet movement that is not part of a state like Diyanet can serve as a partner in terms of Islam for the state and for local bodies, and so we have to take more responsibility with this and not to hide our identity. I don't know if it means to open mosques, or it means to open Islamic academies, but we have to do something in this direction.

5.5   Relating to Civil Society, Politics and the State

As noted at the beginning of the previous section, in Turkey the impact of the "secular" did not, as in so many other Muslim majority countries, come hand in hand with the external imposition of imperial and colonial power but through social and political developments adopted internally, even if primarily by elites, in support of the country's independence. This also had an impact on the forms that political Islamism has taken in Turkey.

Thus, as Sunier and Landman (2015) put it, in Turkish history, "Erbakan pursued the transformation of the secular state through democratic political empowerment", while by contrast "Gülen argued that a strong civil society and an open public sphere were much more important" (p. 85).

Through the inheritance of Kemal Mustafa Atatürk and Kemalism, Hizmet has always had to engage with the interplay between the religious and secular. In principle this has given it some advantages compared with other Islamically inspired movements which found themselves, through migration, in what they often experienced as a "secular" Europe, in relation to which they did not have the historic preparation of the Turkish of history of engaging with secularism. In addition, Hizmet has always had a concern to be integrated with the wider society, even though as discussed in the previous section this has sometimes been in tension with transparency in relation to its origins as Islamically inspired and also its relationship between its organisational forms and the person and teaching of Gülen.

In terms of its activities in Europe, Hizmet has very strongly projected an image of itself as being "apolitical". Yükleyan and Tunagür (2013) argue bluntly that "The goal of the Gülen movement in Europe is to raise well-educated and observant Turkish Muslims who can reconcile their religious identity with their lives in Europe" (p. 229). In fact, in the very strength of its orientation towards "integration", there is a question of how far Hizmet organisations in Europe might have adopted political concepts such as "social cohesion" in a relatively uncritical way to the possible extent of what Yükleyen and Tunagür (2013) identify as the potential for "unintended consequences" such as "inner secularization" (p. 226).

With regard to Belgium Tascioglu explained that "We are always making good contacts with Belgian politicians. Because of elections and electoral reasons, politicians do not participate as much as they would do in our projects and activities. But personal contacts are still maintained. So, they understand the situation". Citing what has happened with Hizmet asylum-seekers in the country, Tascioglu stated that "And there are hundreds of families that migrated from Belgium to Turkey because of problems in Turkey, and almost one hundred percent of those people got asylum. So, this means that the contacts with the Belgian government are good".

In relation to political engagements, the majority of those associated with Hizmet in Europe seek positive engagement with political authorities. In Switzerland, where most of the Ministry of Interior staff are based at Cantonal rather than Federal level, Özgü says that "for them it is very important to talk with the people who are behind these associations". So Özgü also underlines that, broadly speaking, "Turks in Switzerland, they are not really like in the other countries: the foreigners in Switzerland are very well integrated – they don't really live in, like, a parallel society, which was also very important in this context". With regard to Hizmet specifically Özgü says that "at Cantonal level the relationships with the authorities are very positive" and that "We have had many projects which many Cantons help us to fund. They are open to us, and when we want to talk to them they are well connected with us. We don't have any problems to get in touch with them". In relation to Turkey, "We say Erdoğan is a dictator" but "We are also not active against AKP in Switzerland" and that "we have to talk about the problems in Switzerland, and that's why we don't really have any problems with the state, and the state in Switzerland is also very open to us".

However, the overall idea of being a-political may be more complex than at first sight portrayed. Traditionally, as argued by Turam (2007), Hizmet had in Turkey been involved in a "politics of engagement" (p. 10) or what Hendrick (2013) called "the conservative democratic turn" (p. 52), or what some of the Hizmet people themselves refer to a "civil Islam". Thus, in relation to Hizmet's history (including in Turkey) and stance with regard to political participation, Keleş argues that "the movement's position, the discourse on this is misleading". Indeed, on this point Keleş goes so far as to criticise what he says is Gülen's articulation that "we are of equal distance to all political parties", saying of this that "That's not true". However, the reason that he gives for this is not what some might expect in relation to what has been identified by some critics as a general tendency of Hizmet people and of Gülen himself as having been towards the right of the political spectrum. Indeed, as Alasag said reflecting on Hizmet in the Netherlands:

> There were many people who had a history in other groups and became involved in Hizmet. For example, some people from leftists, for example, my parents are from the leftist, Communist side. Others for example from Millî Görüş etc. So there are many different ideas within the Hizmet because of the variety of different backgrounds.

In relation to these issues and how they worked out in the Netherlands, Alasag says:

As far as Holland is concerned, the impact of this 2016 coup was that they see the difference between the AKP and Hizmet. This had started in 2013 and it was growing, but they didn't see the difference between AKP and Hizmet. For many, it was a kind of a co-operation, and for many it was a kind of the same type of Islamic groups working together for the same aim: to bring Islam to the country, or whatever. And because of that there were also anxieties: they had question marks about Hizmet in Holland. They didn't know where Hizmet was ending and where the AKP was starting. They saw two different beings coming into one in a mixed whatever.

With regard to those who came from the background of Millî Görüş or political Islam, Alasag says that from 2013 onwards as difficult things started to happen, "So as long as Gülen was supporting the democratisation of the country, they didn't see any distinction between Hizmet and the AKP and when the Government turned against Hizmet, they left" and this was "because they couldn't understand that we are a different entity and that we have our own agenda of helping people, dialogue etc. It wasn't about AKP but about democracy". In relation to this Alasag says: "If there is a government that is working for democratising Turkey, Hizmet in Turkey tries to help when positive things are happening on that level. Turkey is so far from democracy that anything going in a good direction, you have to support". In the end, overall, Alasag thought this differentiation within Hizmet in the Netherlands was a good thing because "Dutch government, the Dutch society know that this is Hizmet, pro-education, pro-dialogue and pro-helping people to overcome some problems in a societal setting" and this had to do with organisational maturity in the Netherlands.

Thus, in contrast to Hakan Yavuz (2018) who frames the tension and conflict that emerged between the AKP and Hizmet as an "Intra-Islamist Conflict", Keleş argues that "the movement has always been antagonistic to political Islam and parties that represent political Islam from the very beginning" and that has been a consistent position. Therefore, Keleş says that it is clear that one point the movement rejected supporting the Welfare Party and, because of that "it can say, if it wants to, that it wasn't supportive of political parties as an entity, and I can see how that is true". However, "that doesn't mean that the movement has no political implications, or that the work of the movement doesn't have political implications, or the movement doesn't have political positions". Because of this "To say we are equal distance would suggest that we are of equal affinity or proximity to the left, the right, the ultra-nationalists and political Islam" whereas "Gülen has a clear rejection of political Islam". There is also the matter of the multiple-layered meaning of "politics" in relation to which Keleş says that "I think, in Turkish the word *siyaset* was conflated with being 'political partisan'. So, to be politically partisan is one thing; to be politically involved or to have a political position is another". This is, of course, also an issue in the English language where the same word is used for party political activity and for other forms of organising to effect change in the public sphere, although Keleş adds the footnote that "it's clearer in Europe". Nevertheless, and also in Turkey, Keleş recognises that the movement's wish to open schools has been connected with particular political opportunity structures:

> We can see where the schools do better, right: where there is the Charter school and the state allows for private entities to take part in public education, that is a political position. So, if we had it our way, we would prefer to have a political position that allowed – not everyone, you know, with certain checks and balances – but we would to be able to have the ability to contribute to education if, indeed, the educational contribution was needed in the country. That's a political position.

As other examples of at least being advantaged within particular political frameworks, Keleş cites:

> Supporting the EU, as Gülen did against Erbakan, that's a political position; a small state; a civilian constitution – a political position; non-discrimination, all of these are actually political positions. But I think it's not because the movement was being disingenuous about this, genuinely, in Turkey there's big distinctions being created about this, so it wasn't clear about that. But as it came out into Europe and the United States, it's actually clearer that we have political positions. So, at that level, the movement does.

At the same time, how Hizmet people who have been used to dealing with the Turkish system now engage with politics and civil society in Europe is not straightforward. For example, Karakoyun highlighted that "especially the experience of what happened in Turkey makes them also afraid of consequences in Germany, because once you experience the state as an enemy, you think every state is an enemy. So, the people are also very afraid of co-operating and working together with Germany". And especially in the post-July 2016 context, when looking back at the "mutual infiltration" discussed in Sect. 4.2 of this book, Karakoyun says that many Hizmet newcomers are particularly nervous of entanglement with the state: "Many people say, don't do that, we did this mistake". These issues are not, of course, unique to Germany and, reflecting on the relationship between Hizmet and political participation from an asylum-seeker's perspective in broad terms similarly expressed by others who were interviewed, AS2 put it in the following way:

> I am not interested in politics, because I have a lot of troubles in Turkey because of politicians. So I hate politics. From now on, I believe that, I know that I will never be interested in politics. You know, politics means to be the fan of something. If you are the fan of something you put your logic here, always supporting something. So it is not the true. And I will never look at parties or politics as a "fan". For example, I don't think I am a 'fan' of the Hizmet movement. This is something different. So, politically, Hizmet will do something in Europe, I don't believe so. I think they will never go into politics. They will be, I think they will try to be close to all the people and all the parties. They are equal, all the parties. They have to be like that.

As AS2 put it, "I don't think they will be in politics", at the same time going on to say that "But they will always help to be connected with politics of course". And this is the difference between "politics" in the narrow sense, and public life in relation to which AS2 stated: "It's very important for me". And therefore as AS2 says:

> No problem if it is right wing or left wing. We have to be equal with them. We have to see them as people, as human beings. Because, for example, it was my fault: I was in Turkey ten years ago. I supported the right wing of politics, and yes I voted for Recep Tayyip Erdoğan, also, but I regret it now. But, at first he was always talking about the integration to European Union, democracy and human rights and so I supported accordingly. But right wing or left wing is not very important – the human is the main point I think.

And indeed these kinds of responses highlight one of the further risks for at least sections of Hizmet in Europe—which is that of potentially over-reacting to the experience of Hizmet in Turkey. In Turkey the seduction by the possibilities of social and institutional influence led in directions that were to become problematic. But in Europe this could result in a wish to avoid that by adopting what might be called "pietistic" withdrawal from social and political engagement, and especially from involvement in any form of governance, on the basis that the wisest course of action is to concentrate on the religious life of the individual, the family and among like-minded religious people. From Karakoyun's perspective, though "what they don't understand is that the Turkish experience is not ordinary – it is extraordinary, and this is not something that can happen to people twice in their life I think" and "Well, we live in Germany but of course we have to go to the German state, and bodies and governments, and somehow have to co-operate" and to, "keep on keeping up the dialogue especially with the politicians".

Finally, not all who came from Turkey bring with them the reactions previously highlighted among asylum-seekers. Engagement with civil society and the wider political system is clearly something from which at least some Hizmet asylum-seekers are open to learning and to making a connection with Islam. Thus, as AS1 put it in relation to experience of their new Swiss context:

> What I am seeing in Switzerland it was very surprising for me, this Confederation. It was like the first state ruled by our Prophet: in Medina they declare an agreement that we are all together, Muslims, Christians, Jewish. They said if someone attacks us, we are always together to defend. And everyone accepted this. At those times, if I remember truly, maybe only fifteen per cent is Muslim.

Similarly, despite the fact that many people of Turkish origin, including also Gülen, sometimes evoke the Ottoman heritage in relation to positive diversity, there is also a recognition, shared by many in Hizmet, that there is much to learn from western societies as also expressed by AS1:

> They also have this tolerance. And for instance, this lady who opens her restaurant and gives a chance for that little society in her region to live together, to understand each other, to try to be a mosaic. These things, actually, they are our little worlds. And what I am seeing is that we were very, very – I can't find the exact word – "primitive", the Europeans are so advanced ... They saw these things many, many years ago, and they succeed to be a good country together with their neighbour countries, they could build a not micro but a macro climate. But we are so at the beginning of this kind of life.

Speaking on behalf of himself and his wife, AS3 said that "We came here thanks to the Swiss people and support from the government and we will learn many things from them by talking with them and speaking with them. That's the main thing that we can do here maybe" and so "We will learn many things from them, because they are ahead of us on the road and we are behind them".

Overall, in discussing the relationship between Hizmet, the state, politics and civil society it is, however, important to keep in mind the experience of those countries where Hizmet is present but where the wider community of Turkish background is neither the largest ethnic/national minority nor the largest component of Hizmet itself. More common in Europe so far has been the kind of political engagement that Gezen explains, in Denmark, took place over a number of years in relation to the wider authorities:

> Already from the beginning there was an interest, having contact with the officials, politicians, ministers and mayors. But that grew bigger, I think, after a couple of years. And then, you know, we started arranging European Union election panels where we would invite candidates for the European Union elections; candidates were invited for national election panels that we arranged. So, there were those kind of contexts. We wanted to get in touch with the politicians and bring some awareness of being active in elections and also, of course, through these events to be in touch with politicians and hence try to engage them and so on in engaging them in the kinds of activities we were doing. Being in touch with politicians, of course, led to other things.

In relation to such social and political engagement and participation, Gezen explained that the Dialog Forum went on "to arrange role model events where we invited politicians, journalists, artists and so on to talk with university students about how their journey was to success". In 2012 it established the Dialogue Awards. Many politicians engaged with this and came to the ceremony every year, with the award being made by a committee of which one of the members was a former Danish Foreign Minister. In fact, although Denmark has at times proved to be a quite hostile environment for Muslim organisations—as during the so-called Cartoon Controversy (Kublitz 2010)—relationships with the Danish authorities have not been anything like Hizmet in the Netherlands experienced in terms of investigations, Parliamentary enquiries and the like, including also not following July 2016. Therefore in Denmark, in contrast to the Netherlands, Hizmet has not had to "push back" on the political level. On the contrary, Gezen says: "We have no issues getting in touch with the officials. There is no sense that they don't want to meet with us. So, that's why I can say that everyone who knows the Dialog Forum as an association would know that we are inspired by Gülen". However, at the same time, Gezen explains that the Dialog Forum and others are now not so focused as they once might have been on "getting in touch with politicians, making big events, getting keynote speakers, and so on, that's not the aim. Maybe it wasn't the aim from the beginning. But that's not our focus today" which is now moving in a more "grassroots" direction.

Taking the example of Spain, Naziri says that, even after July 2016, in relation to Casa Tura and the Arco Forum that, even though their work (including their resource base) has been impacted, fundamentally speaking "our projection is that nothing changed and we have our objectives and goals in our constitution and we are working towards it". And in terms of the future, Naziri's evaluation is that "I think it is going ahead quite good, with many, many partnerships in the local, here in Spain, with many, many NGOs, both with religious backgrounds, academic backgrounds and, like, state organizations etc etc of all kinds".

In terms of overall learning about how to engage with social and political life, when reflecting on the political opportunities Hizmet had in Turkey, Balcı thinks that in the future there is likely to be a real question to answer about why at a certain point in political developments in Turkey Hizmet did not seize the democratic opportunity through the deployment of a more campaigning mode of activity. But in doing so he noted that "the very first protests that took place in Turkey were also alien to us" and that it required what he called a "retraining of our characters" to participate in them. Furthermore Balcı acknowledged that "I still believe in the motto of Bediüzzaman Said Nursi, '*Şeytandan ve siyasetten Allah'a sığınırım*' ('I seek refuge with Allah from Satan and from politics')", thus making it clear that this orientation was not only a guide for him in the more divided society and politics of Turkey but, rather, that "even in countries like the UK – I am a member of the Labour Party, I always felt myself a Fabian – but, I am not interested in making politics, or appealing to power positions. I'm a student, I'm learning, and I want to contribute to my society, to my new home, yes, but not as being a leader".

But as Balcı explained it, "the level of persecution back in Turkey had pushed us to something that we not only didn't know how to do, but also we were unsympathetic about". Therefore, because of the extremity of what was happening there "we had to go to the streets, to the squares, in front of court houses, to raise our voices". A concrete example of this was when the newspaper *Zaman* was taken over (see Sect. 2.6) and "the police did not make any distinction between who is protesting and why they were protesting, and whether they have a right or not. So, people were beaten there, ladies had their heads wounded and bleeding and so on".

So this development of a more campaigning mode of expressing Hizmet is, in itself, an interesting and unusual development relative to the historic pattern of Hizmet activities up to more recently with which Balcı was also involved in Chicago and New York in the USA (see Weller 2022, Sect. 6.5). After his arrival in the UK, as an example activity in Europe, Balcı reports that he worked with others to "set up a prison cell, made out of pipes in the Trafalgar Square", concerning which he noted that "And of course, the Dialogue Society was completely alien to the idea of protesting. So, it became something new to them". And in relation to this protest, he explains that:

> We, of course, brought all kinds of Turkish cultural reflexes with us. So, when the police came, to ask us questions I thought I had to guarantee them that we wouldn't be making nonsense, noise and so on. So, I tried to explain to the police officers that we are good guys, we are not going to shout, we are not going to make a noise. We are just going to make the installation and tell people that there are children, babies, back in Turkey in jail with their incarcerated mothers. But the police said, look, you have the right to shout. Shout! Make all kinds of noises! It's obvious that you have to shout, there is a problem. But I am here only because of health and safety. Normally the police in Turkey or in many parts of the 'Muslim world' wouldn't come caring about health and safety, particularly not my health and safety!

Therefore despite his experiences with these kinds of activism now in Turkey, the USA and most recently in the UK, Balcı still said of himself that "I never was able to shout still, but this was a learning experience". This was, as he explained, because "As Hizmet people we usually prefer a low profile 'passive activism', passive in the sense of non-confrontational activism. As Hojefendi would say, 'active patience' ". So more "activist" modes of activity still remain a relatively new departure, including in Europe, and to develop further will likely need the development of new thinking in the light of both Hizmet's inheritance and the actions themselves, some of which thinking Balcı is beginning to do and is set out and discussed in Weller 2022, Sects. 6.5 and 6.6.

5.6   RELATING TO OTHER MUSLIMS

The question of the relationship between Hizmet and Muslims from other identifiable groups has always been a complicated one not only in Turkey itself, or only because of the extension of tensions from the Turkish Muslim scene into Europe, but also in terms of the ethnically and religiously diverse composition of Muslim groups across Europe. In relation to this, HE3 from the Netherlands notes that:

> The movement is weak, is not strong, in connection with other migrant groups in the Netherlands, or in Belgium, and in Germany also. So, the movement has focused on the Turkish people. But within the Turkish society here, also in Turkey, there are other groups, Kemalists, Millî Görüş and Süleymanli movement, Alevis, and other groups and this is something that the people of the movement have to pay more attention to, to make it open to other Turkish/Islamic groups.

On the other hand, to engage more with other Muslim inspired groups can be challenging "because of a strong ideological stance that they all on their own think that they have the best ideology". And while, as discussed in Sect. 5.3 of this chapter, the question of the Turkishness or otherwise of Hizmet is pertinent to this issue, so also is the question among Hizmet people in Europe of how far one should or should not emphasise an Islamic identity for Hizmet. And Toğuşlu from Belgium summarised some of these key questions as follows:

> What should be our identity? – Muslim, Turkishness, Belgian, what should be our identity? Or European identity? We came to the conclusion that, OK, the Turkish identity is somehow a part of our identity but we should also pay attention to the Belgian and European side, but mostly the Islamic side, that the Muslim identity is the most important identity, that we have to change and we have to make this is a little bit more visible. Because most of the people when we discussed this – and we did not discuss only with people from the movement but also with people from outside, OK. And they said, "OK, we know that you are a Muslim, but we need some 'good Muslims', so please make it visible. When we went to your website, your activities, we cannot see that they are, unless we know that."

Since July 2016, especially in European countries where organisational forms of Islam strongly linked with Turkishness and Turkey are strong, the marginalisation of Hizmet by the Turkish government authorities and by the Diyanet has made some wider Muslim relations even more difficult. Thus, while noting the strength of Dutch Hizmet's engagement in both inter-religious and inter-cultural dialogue, Selma Ablak acknowledged "the problem is that since 2016 we don't anymore have contact with Dutch Turkish Muslim society". Indeed, more recently, there has been the additional difficulty of the Turkish authorities being actively involved in cultivating Muslim groups in Europe positively to view the form of Muslimness associated with Erdoğan and the AKP party in Turkey through the activities of bodies such as the Maarif Foundation[11] which, among other things, is engaged in replacing Hizmet schools with Turkish government–approved governing bodies.

The kind of challenge this poses for organisations such as London Advocacy is that while such Hizmet people as Balcı want to affirm that "Hizmet is not only a Turkish movement", and that, as he says, in relation to its future in the UK "the Pakistani population in this country is a natural expansion zone for us" it was necessary for Balcı to add the cautionary note that "We don't want them to have that stigma already in their minds about Hizmet". Over the years in the UK a number of the members of the Dialogue Society's Board of Advisors have challenged it to work more closely with other Muslim groups. Generally speaking, on balance, the Society originally felt it potentially more problematic than beneficial to undertake such collaboration. This was because, on the one hand, it ran counter to the Society's historic wish to avoid conveying an organisational profile defined by having a Muslim membership and ethos and, on the other, it could raise questions for others about Hizmet's alignment in relation to some of the tensions and fissures within the Muslim scene, both globally and in the UK.

While asylum-seeker AS2 acknowledged that "There are a lot of good groups, kind groups, of course", just as Toğuşlu acknowledged that, within the overall Muslim scene "there are some good institutions run by other Muslim communities". But AS2 also expressed a nervousness about entanglement in association with potentially problematic other Muslim groups when commenting that "These kind of groups, I don't want to integrate with them or touch that kind of group. I couldn't tell anything to them of course. They are very, very radicalised, so you couldn't teach or tell anything to them".

Despite all these challenges, there are positive examples of Hizmet organisations working in a broader way within the Muslim scene, including in the UK where, for example, the Dialogue Society published the important book *Dialogue in Islam* (Kurucan and Erol 2012). This, on the one hand, sets out what aspires to be an Islamic and Qur'anic rationale for engaging in dialogue, including inter-religious dialogue. On the other hand, it attempted a serious exegetical and hermeneutical engagement with texts in the Qur'an which, through either aspects of their traditional or more recent interpretation, have presented difficulties and stumbling blocks to dialogue, both for Muslims and for other than Muslims. In more directly practical terms, three of the Society's ten *Community Dialogue Manuals* (Dialogue Society, The 2011a, b, c) series specifically address Muslims in relation to dialogue, while beyond publications, in 2012, the Dialogue Society convened a sensitive and significant "roundtable" discussion between the Royal Air Force Marshall and Muslim communities while in 2013, all the Society's Connecting Communities Circle activities were with non-Turkish Muslim community groups (from the Somali, Pakistani, Bangladeshi and Arab communities).

In some countries, the issues posed in terms of working with broader Muslim groups were never so acute as they were in countries with a stronger Turkish community and/or overall Muslim community presence. Thus, in relation to Spain, Naziri noted that:

> This may be partly because in Spain, unlike in some other European countries, there is no single strong alignment between an ethnic group (for example Turks or Moroccans) and a Muslim population in the way that might be in some other countries and which then leads, in the perception of the general public and/or perhaps in the thinking of these organizations themselves into thinking: "We are the Muslims" of whichever country.

As result, with regard to other Muslim groups, Naziri's summary evaluation was that "we have quite a good relations" and that "There is a good, I think, atmosphere and sometimes they sponsor our activities, and sometimes they are sponsoring institutionally, giving the institutional support". Indeed, as already noted in Sect. 3.8 the lack of dominance on the part of one religio-ethnic Muslim group in Spain was probably a significant factor in creating the conditions that allowed the relatively early formation of the Comisión Islámica de España (Spanish Islamic Commission). At the same time, in relation to this Commission Naziri explains with regard to Turca Casa and the Arco Forum that "We don't join, because our Association is a cultural one, not a religious one". However, he went on to comment that "if it were a religious one, we would have an option to be part of this system too. But it's not the case, so we are like, knowing them, getting into contact with them, their programmes, co-operation etc." Here too, Naziri says that "You have to have some kind of caution, be a little bit cautious with some of them", giving as the reason for this being that "there are some Islamist-minded ones and so mostly probably they are like pro-Erdoğan by default", although as Naziri also said, "I think it's not the case here, at least I hope not, but I can't know it".

In Denmark, however, which is another country in which the Turkish presence and/or wider Muslim presence are not so dominant as in Belgium, the Netherlands and Germany, as early as in 2008, Hizmet was, specifically on the basis of its Islamic identity, involved in an intra-Muslim dialogue initiated at an individual level with a Muslim convert and Imam, Abdulwahid Petersen[12] about whom Gezen said, "We had good relations with him from the beginning because he was already doing dialogue activities". In its early years, Petersen became Vice President of Muslims in Dialogue and Gezen said that "we came to know him through our dialogue". In 2008, following the so-called Cartoon Controversy in Denmark when "some Muslim organizations and some Muslim personalities got in touch with the Chairman at that time", the Dialog Forum became one of the founding members of the Muslim Council of Denmark (of which Abdulwahid Petersen later became Vice Chair).

In fact, the membership of such a Council makes Denmark fairly distinctive among Hizmet organisations across Europe because, as noted by Sunier and Landman (2015) in Germany, "Hizmet did not take part in national advisory boards" but "Also in other countries Hizmet operates a low profile in this respect" (p. 88). Gezen's comment on Danish distinctiveness in this regard is that it was perhaps having been very much connected with the above noted Danish context of the time, in that:

> The context triggered a necessity I think to take this action at that time. If the context hadn't been there, maybe it wouldn't have, it's difficult to measure that – whether it would have happened or not. But in the context, the association's Chairman and the Board decided that it was a good idea. We do dialogue already so why not?

In relation to Muslim diversity and inclusion more broadly the anonymous Hizmet participant in Italy, HE2, argues that the challenge of relating to wider groups which identify themselves as Muslims is one that should also extend to include also engagement with "Ahmadiyyas and other Muslims whatever within the community" citing Gülen as saying that "You should have a chair for everyone else in your heart". In summary, Balcı identifies this area of relations with the wider Muslim scene as one of the key challenges for Hizmet in the future:

> I believe that Hizmet has to come out of its own shelter, and become relevant for the general Muslim world, well general humanity, yes, but I feel myself more at ease speaking to you, or to a pastor, or speaking to a monk, rather than in speaking to an Imam because you look at me and say you are a different religion and you respect my religious understanding. But when an Imam, a Salafi imam for example, when he or she looks at me he says you are wrong, I have to fix you! So, it's not easy and there's a legitimate criticism about Hizmet which is that we are not in intra-faith dialogue, because it's harder.

5.7   GENDER IN TRANSITION

In the Introduction to this book it was acknowledged that the primary research behind this volume will, in future, need at least complementing and potentially correcting due to a gender deficit in the interviews conducted. Across most European societies, issues around gender, Muslims and Islam have become a big central focus of public debate especially, but not only, in France and Belgium and in relation to question of head covering in public jobs and in public spaces. Some aspects of gender-related debates, such as that of gender violence, tend to get focused on Muslims alone when in reality that issue is far from being restricted to community or group however constructed.

Generally speaking, though, Hizmet has historically reflected the gender balance and profile of traditional Turkish society. There is also evidence that aspects of Gülen's teaching both reflected and reinforced that reality in terms of general male-female relationships, but especially with regard to public role holders in Hizmet. Indeed, in English translations of some of Gülen's teachings, gender-related matters are sometimes referred to as "details" which makes it sound as if these issues are not given the kind of centrality of importance that feminists would accord to them, although the English of this translation can sound more dismissive than the Turkish that it translates is intended to be.

Nevertheless, arguably, the area of gender and gender relations is one of those areas where it is possible to identify the effects of the contextual interaction between Hizmet in other (especially non-Turkish and non-Turkic contexts) and the development of Gülen's own teaching and practice. Indeed, in relation to this, close associate of Fethullah Gülen and interviewee Ahmet Kurucan (see Acknowledgements) specifically suggests that Gülen's encounter with the Netherlands had a "reverse engineering" effect on the emerging Hizmet engagement with education in Turkey and beyond (Weller 2022, Sect. 2.7). As Kurucan put it, in Gülen's visits to Europe:

> He saw how there was this hugely reliable system in the West where there is huge communitarian work, independent with each other, where there are also ladies and different people from different walks of life involved in that, and that I think Hojaefendi was deeply impressed by that.

And growing out of that, especially in relation to the opportunities for women and girls within Hizmet-related initiatives, Kurucan says:

> Especially our schools for girls actually started and expanded after 1992 because of his trip in the Netherlands when he saw our sisters, our ladies, the second generation there, that they had already started their own tuition centres, perhaps schools, their dialogue facilities, and Hojaefendi was deeply impressed and influenced by that. He also said we have not been fair to our girls, to our women. So, you see from that point onwards schools starting to open for girls and women. That's a huge change in his discourse from that year also, because he visited them so frequently that he could see that progress in first-hand experience.

However, this remains an area in which a lot of debate is still under way. As HE3 from the Netherlands, puts it, "We have also a lot of discussions with Dutch politicians here and government organizations, that the women's groups, the women's participation in the society is an issue. It is a cultural issue in the Dutch society". The question of how quickly or slowly these changes are taking place and how far they are likely to go can be illustrated by the trajectory of Selma Ablak notes that she became involved with the Hizmet movement in 2002 when she married her husband. From this, she recalls that she moved from general helping, through women's organising, and then into overall Hizmet leadership noting that "At the beginning I volunteered with just paperwork or things like this".

Then, in a new stage, Ablak says that "From 2013 onwards I got a major role as being the head of a woman's organization, based in Rotterdam". This was Rosarium, that in 2007 had been "the first women's organization set up by Hizmet volunteers". Ablak recounts that when Rosarium was set up "we had Pim Fortuyn and all the right-wing extremists telling that migrants don't belong to Holland, especially Muslims", in which context she explained about the founders of Rosarium that "they wanted to make a difference". This was a context in which "You could stand on the border and say 'They are talking that about us' – but that can be a case of with one hand one finger is pointing to the other and three are pointing to yourself. So, with that in mind they started the women's organization".

At the beginning they started with modest steps and "celebrated Mother's Day, organized Tea Tables, Breakfast Mornings and those kind of basic activities in order to get women outside their homes. And it wasn't especially meant to get Hizmet women involved with Hizmet, but it was for all women in Rotterdam". When Ablak and her friends first became involved, while affirming this they also thought: "We could do more than that, because there were highly educated women there. Some of them were highly educated but still not working and not having any contacts in society: they were just at home" and in the light of that "We tried to get them out of their comfort zone to do volunteering jobs, to be in the middle of the society, but we needed to be trustworthy to get those women outside their homes". Therefore:

> we organized political evenings because there was a huge gap between politicians and just people. And then we organized language conversation lessons to learn the Dutch language for the women who weren't educated and were just housewives. And then we also organized some projects in which we tried to solve problems in the society.

However, Ablak explained that many of the women who were coming to the organisation had a low self-esteem and self-perception which they wanted to challenge: "So, we just brainstormed and then said, 'We could cook', and then thought there's a home there so, 'What if we go to there and ask if we could arrange a meal for them, just once a month' ". As a result of that a "project called 'Generations at the Table' started in 2011. And so we involved socially isolated women with elderly people who were also isolated, and we solved two problems!"

In 2013 this project received a prize from the King of the Netherlands. Importantly, through these activities the women learned that there are people who were in as bad or worse situation than they were, and therefore to look out for even the smallest things that they might be able to contribute to the society and with that also to contribute to their own development. Of this initiative, Ablak said that "it was the first organization and then we saw that women can make the difference. And then it spread out, like all over. So, there was another new organization founded in the Hague and in other cities in the Netherlands. And then women got involved in the society".

After Rosarium "I made a switch to Platform INS, first in the Hague and then in Amsterdam. And now from 2015 until now I am the General Representative of all the women's organizations in the Netherlands. We have nine regions in Holland and most them have or had women's organizations". Since 2015, Ablak has been working as General Representative of all Hizmet women's organisations in the Netherlands with new "umbrella" organization for women called ZijN (meaning 'To be') which she says works across nine regions:

> Some with formal organizations and some not. My main job is to help them go on with new activities – with how to get into contact with politicians and get your voice heard. So the activities themselves, they are responsible for themselves, but we come together in order to think about in what way we can, as women, contribute to this society.

Commenting on this she says that "So, to bring those organizations to a higher level has been the main aim" but "you have to work with persons who only know Hizmet and nothing outside Hizmet. That's very hard to do". As she then went on to put it:

> And you have got a bunch of *Abis* – because they fund some of the activities, because they have the money, then you want to do a certain activity, and then there is no money, so … you have to find ways to raise money to do your activities. Well, most of the women's organizations achieved to be independent from the *abis* and we didn't need their money, and we saw that the activities flourished – but not the same in all regions and some of the *abis* said "We don't need women's organizations." So, in those regions it was difficult to keep the organizations going.

Some kinds of organisation don't need much or any money, but as analysed by Ablak, "you need the support of the locals to be successful. If you don't have the support, if most people don't believe in why gender equality is important and why we need more women at that the table, then that is a struggle which you are not going to win". As a result of this "I tried, I tried to find new people, young people, who have the same outlook on the world in relation to gender equality. But they weren't there". In addition, others who in principle might have been ready and interested to participate had other initiatives which they judged it as being more important to get involved with. Therefore, because of this, Ablak made an explanation which is worth quoting from at length, that:

> So, then I found another way to be the voice of those local women – in particular women of colour, to be politicians. We have the stigma here in the Netherlands that Muslim women are just housewives, just cooking and caring. And about coloured women that they aren't able to work in high positions, that they are not highly educated. But I am the living example that isn't true. So when I attend conferences, Dutch feminists in their fifties and sixties come to me and say "Do you speak Dutch?" and "You must be isolated and you must be a housewife" and I said "No, I have a job at the University and, in the meantime, I am the chairwoman of a women's organization" and they are then like, "Oh, so you aren't a Muslim woman who is beaten by your husband and not allowed to get outside?!" and I am, like, "No I am not." Those conversations I still have them. So, to show the politicians who are making laws about Muslim women, about coloured women, giving them input about the struggles that we have. Because they are just sitting on their chairs and they are just implementing laws and regulations which affect us. And no-one comes to us and asks "What are your problems in real life? What do you need from us?" So, I am trying to be that between that key role between women of colour, Muslim women, and the local and national governments. You can call it lobbying, although I don't see it as lobbying because it isn't to gain a personal interest.
>
> Since a couple of years ago we have joined the CSW– the Commission on the Status of Women, including a two weeks programme with the United Nations in New York. So, we have been organizing two or three meetings and have been trying to get involved. The first year we joined and attended there were only white women from a particular age – above fifty – who were representing Dutch women. But Dutch women are not all white and not all old. So, we ask "How can you represent Dutch women?" So that was a huge step for us, and we had good contact with the politicians, and with the Dutch minister of education. So, then, by little steps we have been trying to change the mindset about our kind of women. That's my main goal right now. One the one side I am still trying to achieve a better position for women in the Netherlands and also to advocate for those women and that is successful.

More generally in relation to Hizmet in Europe, taking the example of Fedactio in Belgium, Tascioglu noted that "It's throughout the years that it has gradually changed" and that "The situation is changing more and more in the way that women become more flexible. For example, in Fedactio we have six co-ordinators and another six co-co-ordinators which are all couples of men and women. And also the platforms have female platform representatives". In the UK, for a number of years the co-Director of the Hizmet-related organisation, the Dialogue Society, was a woman, and—even more innovatively—a female organiser was appointed to the north London Rumi mosque associated with Hizmet. At the same time, neither of these initiatives was undertaken without challenges being involved. Indeed, as Tascioglu more broadly underlined, "you have to understand that we come from an oriental tradition where it is not that easy to change things very quickly. It will take time before this equality between men and women will be achieved".

Thus, HE3 from the Netherlands, while speaking with more general reference than to the Netherlands alone, said very clearly of Hizmet that "It is still a male dominated movement" and that "in leadership especially they are the decision makers and they decide about the activities and projects", although "the female group in the movement they do the job – they are the hard workers, dedicated persons! They spend a lot of time on the movement activities". In order to action this, HE3 noted that "Just before the coup we had decided, we had advised here, that we have to change – and the Netherlands is actually one of the first countries in Europe that did that change, and two women here that participated also from that time in the gatherings, meetings, talks at a national level".

Even so, reflecting on this from her own experience, Ablak noted that when she first got involved in the "monthly meetings where we discuss the Dutch Hizmet" the fact is that "I got involved as the second woman in a group of thirty males!" And indeed, HE3 also went on to note that note of Hizmet women that "in such kinds of workshops and meetings that I have moderated, they are taking their places after the males in the meeting rooms. I said to them, you have to come here and invited them to come and sit next to the real persons who have a position". He also adds that "there is something from their religious belief or their cultural orientation that it is not accepted that I sit there", although of "Especially the generation who have been educated here, they sit next to the men, they talk straight, they say what they want to say". Of the younger generation, HE3 says, "They are almost feminist, they think differently, they act differently, and they will change the movement in that way if they gain that position in the movement". However, ultimately he thinks that "it depends on the women themselves that they have to take this responsibility. Some of them will do this well and some of them not. And the women will learn here that they can have a role as change agents in that process. I am hopeful. I think it will change".

With regard to Hizmet and gender issues in Germany, Kerakoyun's summary comment was, "Well, it is starting" although he believes that it still has a long way to go primarily because, since Hizmet was originally developed in Turkey "everything was very patriarchally oriented, male and *abi*-based. So, this has to change, otherwise we can't cope with the future because the reality in Germany is gendered and so we also have to be gendered or else it won't work".

With regard to Switzerland, as Özgü notes, "Swiss people are very conservative", to the extent that it must be borne in mind that it is only after a long struggle that, since 1971, Swiss women were able to vote in federal elections. So, as Özgü puts it in relation to Hizmet, "We need also women who fight for their rights". Historically, in Switzerland, there was an association called Rosarium and another called Lotus, which were specifically women's organisations. But as Özgü observed:

These are flower names and reflected women just as flowers and mothers and things like that and I was not sure that was correct as I didn't want to be thinking of women just as flowers, or family mothers, or things like that, but that they should be part of the overall hizmet associations and that it would be better to have them in the associations as Board members rather than them just talking about their children and their family because that is not all that we think about women participating in the community.

Unlike in the Netherlands, in Switzerland there are no longer any specific formal women's organisations, but instead there are "platforms for women" within broader organisations and, overall, Özgü summarises the situation as being, "The second generation in Switzerland they want that women should be very active and participate in Hizmet structures, but I think there is now a fight between conservatives and progressives in Hizmet about that". In analysing the current situation in Hizmet, Özgü contrasts the formal and the informal dimensions by saying that in many associations "we find women who are active or are in the Board, but when we look at the informal networks of Hizmet, there are two worlds: on the one side, you have the men – they have their own meetings; and on the other side there are the women who have their own meetings". Complicating this, however, is that of the recent "third layer" of Hizmet in Switzerland, "especially people from Turkey they are not really open-minded, and there is also this Anatolian thinking about women".

In relation to Belgium, Toğuşlu says in echo of what was also reported by Ablak in relation to the Netherlands that "There was a period in which there were some developments, really especially in France and Belgium, for example, in which the women created their own associations in which they not only wanted to be visible, but they wanted to take some decisions for themselves". However, he acknowledged that "on the decision-making process, the decision-making side, almost only men are taking the decisions". And Toğuşlu acknowledged that this applied to both the visible and structured organisations and also beyond that because "in the visible and formal organizations and institutions, there are very few female members there and even if their names are there they don't very often participate in the discussions and in the meetings. So, it is very male dominated, what I see in the movement. So, we have to tackle it".

Nevertheless, recognising the issue in principle and developing concrete strategies and steps to tackle it in practice can be two different, although related, things. Therefore, along with HE3 from the Netherlands, Toğuşlu noted of the Hizmet women in Belgium that, overall, "maybe, they don't always want to take the positions from us". But notwithstanding this, in locating the primary responsibility for the difference between men and women in Hizmet leadership positions, Toğuşlu did not hesitate, as a male, to engage in sharp self-criticism to the effect that "I think we failed". And in reaching for an explanation for this he suggested that "Maybe as male participants in the movement, as male followers in the movement, we did not create a suitable environment for these ladies and we maybe dominated the discussions as men". Even though post-2016 there are the very real added external pressures arising, such as those experienced by Ablak, when one moves into a public Hizmet role, Toğuşlu says that one should not accept that as an excuse and that referring to Hizmet more broadly that "I think problem is not visibility – the problem is they have not really changed the rules. This is the problem".

Asked about what "concrete steps" might be taken to address such an issue, Toğuşlu stated: "Quota, I think. I am in a favour of a quota in the Hizmet meetings etc." This is being actively discussed in Belgium, with one of the proposals being, for example, that if less than 20 or 25 per cent of women were involved then a decision should not be taken forward. Although this was not yet the practice, Toğuşlu said, "I think there should be strong decision saying that without the quota, we cannot do. So just encourage not only women, but also the men to share their position".

NOTES

1. See https://www.youtube.com/watch?v=yPMsCeGm4Sg, 22.12.2014.
2. See the Foreign Minister's response to question 4 in the record of the House of Representatives of the States General, part year 2016–2017, 7 October 2016, reference 2016D34594 https://www.tweedekamer.nl/zoeken?search_str=Hizmet, 2016–17.
3. Alliance for Shared Values, *Statement by Alliance for Shared Values on Developments in Turkey*, 15.7.2016. https://afsv.org/wp-content/uploads/2020/08/Statement-by-Alliance-for-Shared-Values-on-Developments-in-Turkey.pdf
4. El Confidencial, Por Á. Villarino, "Hablan los seguidores de Gülen en España: 'Erdogan es un maestro del islam emocional'," 19.7.2016. https://www.elconfidencial.com/mundo/2016-07-18/turquia-gulen-espana-golpe-de-estado_1234513/
5. https://counteringviolentextremism.dialogueplatform.eu/, 2016.
6. http://www.gulenconference.org.uk/, 2007.
7. This is something that the present author, as one of the Advisors concerned, can independently confirm was indeed the case.
8. Again this is something that the present author has witnessed at first hand since he was invited to speak about Fethullah Gülen with teachers and students at the school concerned.
9. Parvez Ahmed, "Open Letter to Fethullah Gülen, Founder of Hizmet Movement," 31.7.2019. https://medium.com/@drparvezahmed/open-letter-to-fethullah-g%C3%BClen founder-of-hizmet-movement-2257031 34cc8, 2019.
10. https://northlondongrammar.com/our-school-london/faq-about-our-school/, 2018.
11. https://turkiyemaarif.org/, 2021.
12. https://en.wikipedia.org/wiki/Abdul_Wahid_Pedersen, last edited, 16.9. 2021.

REFERENCES

(All web links current at 20.11.2021)

Alliance for Shared Values (2019). *July 15, 2016, Turkey: A Genuine Attempt, or a "Synthetic Coup" for Media Consumption?* New York: Alliance for Shared Values. https://afsv.org/wp-content/uploads/2020/04/July-15-A-Genuine-Attempt-for-a-Synthetic-Coup.pdf

Andrews, Mathew (2011). Building Institutional Trust in Germany: Relative Success of the Gülen and Millî Görüş. *Turkish Studies*, 12 (3), 511–524. https://doi.org/10.1080/14683849.2011.604206

Çapan, Ergun (2016). *A Perspective: Muslims' Responsibility in Countering Violence*. Leuven: KU Leuven Gülen Chair for Intercultural Studies. https://afsv.org/muslims-responsibility-in-countering-violence/

Dialogue Society, The (2009). *Deradicalization by Default: The 'Dialogue' Approach to Rooting out Violent Extremism*. The Dialogue Society, London. http://www.dialoguesociety.org/publications/Deradicalisation-Policy-Paper.pdf.

Dialogue Society, The (2011a), *Community Dialogue Manuals Series: Noah's Puddings*. London: The Dialogue Society. http://www.dialoguesociety.org/publications/community/Noahs-Pudding.pdf

Dialogue Society, The (2011b), *Community Dialogue Manuals Series: Open Mosque Day*. London: The Dialogue Society. http://www.dialoguesociety.org/publications/community/Open-Mosque-Day.pdf

Dialogue Society, The (2011c), *Community Dialogue Manuals Series: Fast-Breaking Dinners*. London: The Dialogue Society. http://www.dialoguesociety.org/publications/community/Fast-Breaking-Dinners.pdf

Harris, Emma Jane; Bisset, Victoria; Weller, Paul (2015). *Violent Extremism: Naming, Faming and Challenging*. London: Dialogue Society. http://www.dialoguesociety.org/publications/Violent-Extremism.pdf.

Hendrick, Joshua (2013). *Gülen: The Ambiguous Politics of Market Islam in Turkey and the World*. New York: New York University Press.

Keleş, Özcan; Sezgin, Ismail Mesut and Yılmaz, İhsan (2019). Tackling the Twin Threats of Islamophobia and Puritanical Islamic Extremism: Case Study of the Hizmet Movement. In John Esposito and Derya Iner (Eds.), *Islamophobia and Radicalization: Breeding Intolerance and Violence* (pp. 265–283). Cham: Switzerland.

Kublitz, Anja (2010). The Cartoon Controversy: Creating Muslims in a Danish Setting. *Social Analysis. 54* (3) pp. 107–125. https://doi.org/10.3167/sa.2010.540307

Kurucan, Ahmet and Erol, Mustafa Qasım (2012), *Dialogue in Islam: Qur'an, Sunnah, History*. London: The Dialogue Society. https://www.dialoguesociety.org/publications/dialogue-in-islam.pdf

Sunier, Thijl and Landman, Nico (2015). Gülen Movement (Hizmet). In Thijl Sunier and Nico Landman (Eds.), *Transnational Turkish Islam: Shifting Boundaries of Religious Activism and Community Building Turkey and Europe* (pp. 81–94). Basingstoke: Palgrave Macmillan.

Turam, Berna (2007). *Between Islam and the State: The Politics of Engagement*. Stanford: Stanford University Press.

Weller, Paul (2022). *Fethullah Gülen's Teaching and Practice: Inheritance, Context and Interactive Development*. Cham: Palgrave Macmillan.

Yavuz, Hakan (2018). A Framework for Understanding the Intra-Islamist Conflict Between the AK Party and the Gülen Movement. *Politics, Religion and Ideology*, *19* (1), 11–32. https://doi.org/10.1080/21567689.2018.1453247

Yükleyen, Ahmet and Tunagür, Ferhan (2013). The Gülen Movement in Western Europe and the USA. In Matthias Kortmann and Kerstin Rosenow-Williams (Eds.), *Islamic Organizations in Europe and the USA: A Multi-Disciplinary Perspective* (pp. 224–241). Basingstoke: Palgrave Macmillan.

CHAPTER 6

Continuing Values, Different Expressions and Future Trajectories

6.1 Contextual Transitions

At a 2010 international conference held at Felix Meritis, in Amsterdam, the Netherlands, and organised by the Dialog Academie and VISOR (Institute for the Study of Religion, Culture and Society) on the topic of "Mapping the Gülen Movement: A Multidimensional Approach", an opening keynote presentation by Doğu Ergil (2010) summarised the overall emergence and development of Hizmet in what this author judges to be a succinct and insightful evaluation of the movement's trajectory. Beginning in Turkey and then spreading out through the world including Europe, Ergil identified the main trajectory as having been that of what he called "a group of listeners" who:

> Have become followers; have transformed into being a local congregation; a congregation growing into a national community; a community expanding to be a comprehensive international organisation of volunteers and stakeholders, that can neither be defined as a religious sect, or denomination, although it is religiously informed. (p. 19)

The above quotation does not explicitly name Fethullah Gülen as the one whose teachings have shaped this "group of listeners" who "have become followers". But it is a central argument of this book that any evaluation of Hizmet's future trajectory or trajectories in Europe (as elsewhere in the world) needs to be undertaken in profound interaction with

© The Author(s) 2022
P. Weller, *Hizmet in Transitions*,
https://doi.org/10.1007/978-3-030-93798-0_6

reflection on and issues around the preservation, interpretation, reinterpretation of Gülen's teaching and practice inheritance (as discussed also Weller 2022, Sects. 6.3 and 6.4).

At this pivotal time for both Hizmet and for Gülen, it remains clear that the movement originated in Turkey and in many ways (see Sect. 5.3) has continued to have a quite strongly Turkish flavour. In Turkey itself, of course, Hizmet's previous profile and ways of operating have effectively been strangulated. Globally, it has experienced wider political and economic pressures from the agencies of the Turkish state. At the same time, because of Hizmet people's voluntary migration especially, but not only, to teach, Hizmet has become present across all continents. In each continent, it found itself in interaction with different national, regional and local cultures and diverse religion and belief groups and communities. Therefore, even if July 2016 had not occurred, it is arguably the case that Hizmet was already and increasingly needing to address an increasingly insistent set of questions that arise for any religiously inspired movement that starts in one place, one time and one culture and then attempts to translate itself into other places, times and cultures.

Writing in broad terms, but also with specific regard to Hizmet in the USA and in Europe, Yükleyen and Tunagür (2013) argue that "localization is not a one-time occurrence, but, rather, an ongoing process which goes through multiple changes and shifts in action and in the way individuals reflect upon them" (p. 227) and also that such a process is not mere one-way "adaptation". In discussing Hizmet, they speak about what they call the "malleability" of Hizmet's principles that needs to be understood in terms of transitions that manifest themselves in an "ever-shifting and processual fashion", in which as well as engaging with their contexts, they are also in turn "shaped and transformed as a result of these interactions" (p. 240). Nevertheless, as AS1 put it from the perspective of an asylum-seeker:

> Because of this coup d'etat that happened in 2016, accelerates something in Europe also too. And they understand what is our country. Previously we were thinking so emotionally about our country. But what I am thinking, so I am sure the Turkish diaspora in Europe also they saw it, we had too much of a nationalistic feel. And this was a barrier to us to come together for the other part of the world, actually.

And, as Ablak formulated it from the perspective of one already fully located within Europe:

So, way before that we ourselves had a wrong view about the society. Of course, it is a warm burrow, it is your comfort zone to be with Turkish people, to be with people with whom you can talk the same language. I understand that fully, but that isn't the main purpose about Gülen and the Hizmet movement. So, 2016 was a shake up – OK look at yourselves, look at the mirror and learn from your mistakes. So, it was an important moment and since then volunteers who didn't speak the Dutch language started with Dutch courses and people who said that they were a part of Hizmet movement are starting to get involved with their non-Turkish neighbours, and started organising activities with them and getting into volunteering jobs outside of Hizmet too. So, the coup attempt is negative. It brought horrible things. But if you look at the positive side, it also brought something in terms of opportunities because we become more critical about ourselves about how it could change, how we could do it better. So, we lost our comfort zone.

As discussed in more scholarly terms, aspects of this process have been explored in Watmough and (Ahmet) Öztürk's (2018) journal article on "The Future of the Gülen Movement in Transnational Political Exile: Introduction to the Special Issue", and their article in the same special issue on "From 'Diaspora by Design' to Transnational Political Exile: the Gülen Movement in Transition". Concerning Europe in particular, it is the argument of this book that, within the overall context of an acceleration of what this book calls a "de-centring" of the Hizmet from Turkey, including in the most recent and traumatic ways following July 2016, two main things have occurred. On the one hand, as Toğuşlu has put it, the profound shock of what happened in Turkey had a substantial impact resulting in his challenging observation that "I think we are now a little bit stuck". But in addition to this, there is also evidence that a more open self-criticism has emerged within at least parts of Hizmet relative to its recent experiences particularly in Turkey and that has, in turn, been starting to feed into a growing re-assessment by those associated with Hizmet about its overall future trajectory or trajectories. Of course, as Toğuşlu says: "It's not unique for Hizmet" because for all "transnational, faith-based communities or other non-believer communities as well, this transnational in terms of being global but also being local at the same time is always a challenge. It brings some questions that you have to face and maybe you don't have some solutions".

What does, however, seem to be the case in relation to Hizmet in particular, and especially in Europe, is that a number of questions, issues and challenges which have in principle always been present have been both accelerated and underlined by the impact of July 2016 in what are ways that are now unavoidable. As Ablak articulated it arising out of reflection on what had happened in the Netherlands:

> It gave another view on what Hizmet should be. I mentioned the problem that mostly Hizmet was focused on Turkish people and that was their comfort zone. But I said, "We are in Holland, and why are we focusing mainly on Turkish people?" And if you talk about dialogue activities and so on, most of the Hizmet people saw that activities done by Platform INS or the women's organizations wasn't important for the volunteers. But with the failed coup attempt we got another view on society – because all the Turkish people who had eagerly helped all those previous years, they closed the doors and told us we were terrorists. So, we had no other choice. But if we had better listened to Hocaefendi to Fethullah Gülen, if we had seen it from his view about what Hizmet should be, we didn't need a coup to change those views.

Arising from this, Ablak argued that "the main thing is that we need within Europe and the main thing we need in Europe is the European Islam. And I can't say that Hizmet is the role model for European Islam. But we should try, and we should give more effort in contributing to that. So that's a point of attention". Similarly, HE1 says, "I think it should be first step in the countries and having a consensus maybe at the European level. Maybe this will be the way for it to go through". However, it is not obvious that this can be done structurally, or at least not necessarily through the existing Intercultural Dialogue Platform based in Brussels. This is because, as also noted by interviewee HE1:

> The Inter-Cultural Dialogue Platform normally claims that it should represent the other eight European countries, and at times it also included the UK ... So it brought another challenge. We are all the same. We all reject hierarchy among the institutions. So there is no hierarchy and I think more than six countries – like Italy, Spain, Poland, France, Belgium. So, we get together every month and try to co-ordinate with each other. So there is no, like, "Big Brother".

Therefore, in terms of a European-level development of Hizmet, while up to a certain point this is possible, there is also arguably also a potentially prior task to undertake at an individual national level. This is because, for example, in France, the impact of the country's model of laïcité means that how one goes about being active as a religiously inspired (even if not con-fined to religion) group will necessarily be reflective of that national con-text. As HE2 from Italy expressed this more broadly:

> The international system (based on the nation state system of course) is very much affecting how Hizmet people are operating, because that is depending on the church and state relations; issues about citizenship; how institutions see the presence of people from different cultures and backgrounds etc etc. And that's why I don't know what will really happen in general, because it's very complicated. But for each case, I will say, of course, that should be the general principles, whatever we can call them, list them, will be the main, I will say, platform or background for Hizmet activities, that seems more con-vincing to me because in each case, in each country, you have a different activity, different connections.

In the Netherlands, a process of localising Hizmet is continuing, at local, regional and national levels, as set out on the website on the nation-wide consultation,[1] in which both Ablak and Alasag have been involved. As Ablak explains:

> We started to work in that way before the coup attempt. And then with the coup attempt it got accelerated. We needed to publish the documents on which we were working. And we got all kinds of Hizmet people involved – including the young ones, the housewives, and everyone who wanted to say something were invited in groups. And we got a document – we called it a Vision Document, and we had a press release, and we accelerated that pro-cess of change and of more transparency about what is the Dutch Hizmet, how we work, and how our decisions are made and so on. And we published that much more quickly than we originally wanted to. But then we have the document, but it is important to implement that. In terms of fully imple-menting that, we aren't there yet. We still try, each day, to get a step further in implementing that document, but it is a beginning.

According to the document *de Nederlandse Hizmet: een beweging in beweging. Visiedocument* (in English, *The Dutch Hizmet: a Movement in Motion. Vision Document*), overall "Our mission is to stimulate personal, spiritual and professional development. In cooperation with others, we want to contribute to an inclusive and peaceful society". It states that the "Dutch Hizmet movement" has values that are focused on "freedom, jus-tice, equality, commitment and respect" and that it is committed to achiev-ing the following four goals: "1. Self-development; 2. Connection; 3.

Contributing to solutions to social issues; 4. Develop and share knowledge about Hizmet".[2] Ablak goes on to explain:

> So, when we developed our Vision document, it was seen as "best practice", and copied by Belgium. And we went to Germany to talk about how we coped with the aftermath of the coup attempt and how we got into that transition with more transparency. So, we had, yeah, lots of meetings about how we copy the "best practices" from other countries within Europe.
>
> So, we try to learn from each other, but the main thing is, within the context of the country we live in. So, the Dutch context is very different from the German context and the Belgian context. And then we see that it isn't possible that Gülen says, "Do this, and do that" and we copy it to our activities in the Netherlands. It is impossible. The whole story of a cult or sect ... we don't work that professionally!

According to Toğuşlu, Fedactio in Belgium had always kept under review the question of "what should be our aims in this society, but always with connection to the Hizmet ideas and principles and how these principles can be translated and adapted in our context". Therefore even "two years after the establishment of the Federation, then we started again" and this was done by means of "some workshops with different people from different groups in the movement, including students; from movement women. We made some quotas, so we had some women". In due course, Fedactio also began work on a "principles statement", although Toğuşlu acknowledges that "we did not focus our energy on these principles, why? – because we wanted to do something especially in a practical way to open eyes and to bring people together". At the same time, reflecting on his own country of Belgium, and against the background of a strong relationship Toğuşlu also argued that many of the transitional developments flagged in this book were, in fact, already in process in terms of having "identified as what the next steps should be, but then came the Turkish coup attempt". Tascioglu spoke of post-July 2016 as follows:

> Hizmet always held universal values and worked on global projects and didn't mean to only work within the Turkish community. Nowadays, there is no connection with the Turkish communities more broadly because, unfortunately, most of the people here in Belgium are politically oriented towards Erdoğan politics, therefore if the politics in Turkey do not change I don't see how we could form a community with the Turkish community here in Belgium? Because of these politics of Erdoğan there is a very strong

polarisation within the Turkish communities in Belgium, and it has become worse.

In relation to different national contexts one can see differential developments within Hizmet in Europe. Thus, while the UK Dialogue Society was founded in 1999 with the name The Dialogue Society, it did not specifically link that name with religion, whereas what was called in the Netherlands Islam and Dialogue was founded in 1998. At the same time, Keleş says that:

> And then they changed it, and then they changed it again, I don't know why. So they have gone through – I don't know why it is – it might be to do with the pressure they have been under as part of being a significant majority there, I mean when people say Muslim in the Netherlands, they think of Turks and Algerians. And they have been investigated by Parliamentary commissions there, and so on. So, they have felt that kind of pressure and you certainly have that there.

From Keleş' perspective, "I mean it definitely has something to do with the kind of socio-cultural context in which these kinds of organizations are created. So we didn't feel under pressure one way or another". But, as Keleş put it: "religion doesn't 'do it' for the Brits, as far as we can tell. It's not a great conversation opener", although it is also the case that "There's definitely need for religiously-based conversations and we thought we could do that in the Dialogue Society, and we can be open. And we spent the first ten years doing inter-faith. But we always thought that it's going to evolve beyond this". Indeed, Keleş set this within a wider view of the movement's evolution:

> So, it began as a religious congregation in the 1970s/1980s, it turned into an education movement, and it turned into dialogue. And we were watching this from the UK, especially the last few years, and so we could see the transition. So, we felt that even though we are here now, if we do the whole inter-faith thing, its going to move on from there, so let's do something sufficiently expansive. And I remember having that conversation – it's maybe to do with the people who were involved at the very beginning. But I also think that if we were in Rome, we may have been a bit more selective in that.

At the same time, Keleş notes that interplay between structure and agency is more complex than the context being simply determinative, when he notes that:

I also think it's the geography that attracts a certain kind of individual. So, my colleague, my counterpart in Rome, he is all about inter-faith, and I love him for it, and it's great. But I can't see how he would have been here and I would have been there, being how I am – either I would have changed or moved on.

That there is debate between emergent national models for Hizmet is clear. Thus, Keleş from the Dialogue Society in the UK has a critique of the German "federation" model of which he said, "I have issues with their operational model, because Federations create pyramids", even though "In the sense that they've understood it, Federation has a representational value". But, of course, German society has very particular ways of doing things, of acknowledging or making space for organisational initiatives in which, overall, it can tend to be more bureaucratic and pyramidical. And there is always a strong push from government and the public to ask: What is your representation? What is your legitimacy? Where, in terms of structure? While there are echoes of this also in the UK, in Germany it is very strong. Keleş also has a critique of Fedactio's somewhat looser federative model that "they're actually retracting from that, they are going back. And the people that I speak to, at least, have said this to me in person" and his preference, at least for carrying through transparency, is "to make things transparent and clear at the smallest entity and then work on bringing things together, rather than trying to do it all in one go".

In terms of self-reflection on the future of Hizmet in Germany Karakoyun said: "I think there are some internal challenges that we have to overcome now, Hizmet especially in Germany". Among these he lists the need for "emancipation from the discussions in Turkey" and "When say what we are, which we are – German Turks", "we have to focus on our issues and we have to focus on our issues on which we have been working from before 2016 as well". Thus, beginning with these organisational developments "Hizmet more and more started to become something German" and "Especially with the third generation German Turks like me, something like a German Turkish Hizmet began to develop".

Speaking out of the perspective arising from his role in Switzerland, Özgü also sees the events of 2016 as pivotal, arguing that "after this 2016, after this coup event, Hizmet did begin to change. The main change has been after that". Özgü's projections of future Hizmet trajectories are based not only on what he says is already happening as a by-product of interaction with the wider social and political environment, but also as conscious construction. Therefore, notwithstanding what may be the orientations of some among the new wave of Turkish asylum-seekers, Özgü says:

> Now we try to develop a Hizmet with Swiss structures, but now because of Turkey, I am active for fifteen years in Hizmet, but I didn't know much about Hizmet in Turkey. But I think Hizmet Switzerland is not like Hizmet Turkey. There is also a clash of values, in Europe and also in Switzerland with these people, because people in Turkey they have all these Turkish reactions, and all this understanding of culture, and I think this will clash with this understanding of democracy. But in Switzerland I am sure that the people who are here, also as asylum-seekers, they will also understand the meaning of democracy.

At the same time, despite this emphasis on the national, in relation to the interchange between Switzerland, Hizmet globally, and Gülen in Pennsylvania, Özgü acknowledges that "We have our global connections, that's true. I was also there. I went there, but just as a dialogue responsible person and as an *abi* I was also there", and Özgü's observation on this is that "What I have seen there is that we don't really talk about the countries, about things like what shall we do in Switzerland, but Hizmet global issues". In other words, "we don't really talk about education, dialogue and things like that with the other countries – or our education things – in Pennsylvania, but to talk about international things". Such international things include "about how can we help the people in Turkey because we have to help them financially, to support them financially in Turkey, and that's also a global issue. And these global issues they talk about in Pennsylvania".

In fact, the issue of national Hizmet emancipation is, for Özgü, articulated not only in relation to Turkey, but also that "another difficult thing was to emancipate ourselves from Germany". This is because originally Hizmet people from Switzerland went to Germany to share experience because "Germany is very huge and there is a very big Turkish Hizmet community there and they are very active". Therefore, as Özgü says, "most of the initiatives in Switzerland, we copied them from Germany". But as Özgü says, "Switzerland is not like Germany". As a concrete example, Özgü cited that:

> To open a private school in Switzerland was not the best idea, because also state schools they are very good, and those private schools in Switzerland they are very expensive. You have just forty students in those private schools. But we copied that from Germany because in Germany they founded schools and that's why we 'needed' also private schools in Switzerland.

As Özgü says, "We are Hizmet Switzerland. We don't want to be just part of Hizmet Europe, or Hizmet Germany" because "Switzerland is its own nation and has its own history. They are not just German". And this is not only a matter of the French- and Italian-speaking parts of Switzerland because, as Özgü explains: "we have another understanding of democracy here in Switzerland that's different from in Germany". And such developments across the board are important for the integration of Hizmet in the wider Swiss society for whom, even though it is part of "an international network" at the same time, "Hizmet Switzerland is part of a known entity ... we have our own meetings; our own thinktanks; and our own associations". As an example of this, Özgü cited the foundation they founded in 2018 for asylum-seekers, in relation to which he said:

> It has a very good structure and we have our own activities, and we didn't copy the same thing from Germany. They have their own associations with their own structures and we in Switzerland, we have our own activities and structures. And of course it is very important to found these things as Swiss associations and with Swiss culture, with Swiss thinking, understanding and everything.

In relation to the future of Hizmet, Özgü in Switzerland stated that, although he was many times in other countries, "I prefer to talk about Switzerland, not about Hizmet globally or in Europe, because I don't really know Hizmet in the other countries". And here, in line with also the broader culture, Özgü thinks that in the future "Hizmet will be more democratic, it will have more democratic structures, because the people who grew up in Switzerland, they grew up with this thinking of democracy – to vote about a referendum issue. Brexit is in each two or three years here! It's not new for us!" And people of Özgü's generation are socialised within this. So, he says: "I think that people in Hizmet who grew up in Switzerland they want more democracy in Switzerland, they want more participation in Hizmet, they want to have the authority".

If Hizmet is indeed becoming "de-centred" from Turkey, Gezen says that "I hope the Danish Hizmet volunteers will largely focus on their local issues. So, integration issues; radicalization issues; you know, young Danish Muslim kids/boys who are not well educated, solving those kind of problems". He acknowledges that "This may be wishful thinking". However, if Hizmet does manage to do this "Then there is a huge potential for Hizmet in general, not just in Europe, but also globally to contribute to solving local issues". In relation to links across Europe, he thinks, "It's going to be difficult to find a big European Hizmet that gets together like maybe happened before". What he thinks likely more to emerge in three to five years' time is a loose linkage across Europe when "there will probably be a local Danish Hizmet in contact with other local Hizmets in other European countries where they will probably arrange, once or twice every second year gatherings or meetings where they can share ideas and projects inspired by Gülen" and, in the meantime, one can make informal bilateral contacts as needed.

In relation to a move back to Turkey, he says that "I can't say that for sure. I really hope it will happen – also if you listen to Gülen he is still saying the same", although Gülen is also saying that "This has forced ... people in Hizmet to move out of Turkey and to really go out to work and create peace in the world". In fact, Gezen went so far as to say that "I am hoping, and if something is going to be foreseen, that it will stay 'de-centred', that it's going to be more and more local focusing on Danish issues. That's why there were critiques of the informal structure after the coup that I am definitely reading with interest to see how things are moving". Although there are serious human rights issues in relation to Turkey which should not be overlooked, an out-of-balance concentration on these and on the issues arising from them would, in Gezen's evaluation, mean that "we would not be what the vision was about in terms of spreading peace around the world. We would become a group that was focused upon a really small area of what matters right now". In contrast to a focus on Turkey, Gezen argues that what is needed is a broad vision:

> I think rising nationalism, populism, you know, the issue of what is truth and what is not truth in the sense of media coverage is our major issue, and our major issue is not only what is happening in Turkey. What Erdoğan is doing, like what Trump is doing, and other populist leaders is what we should, you know, work against. I don't think that the major focus for the Hizmet right now is Turkey alone.

In relation to options about how one might frame the future self-understanding and external projection of Hizmet, some have started to characterise its presence and activities in countries outside of Turkey as a "diaspora", although Gülen himself has questioned this. Others argue that Hizmet should simply think of itself as being where it is, in relation to which Toğuşlu affirms that he thinks "This is the idea", while also noting that "If you say this in a one hour speech, if you say it in a few words, everyone understands". But the challenge is how to work it out specifically and concretely and, as Toğuşlu says, the challenge at the moment is that there is "a kind of struggle for survival because people are trying to escape not only from Turkey but also from other countries in order to get asylum. So, with this survival, even though you cannot recognize yourself as a diaspora, but as a kind of 'diasporization' ".

In summary, in relation to these pivotal transitions, Toğuşlu expressed the sense of disorientation felt by many Hizmet people when he said that "I think there is a rupture with what is going on now at the local level, and what is going on now at the global level. At the local level I think we lost a little bit, at the global I don't know exactly what is going on".

What Toğuşlu was highlighting here was the issues that of what he called a "translation of words" which has already happened in comparison with "the translation of the whole vision of the movement" which has not yet seriously happened—in other words, the hermeneutic challenge as explored in more detail in Weller 2022, Sect. 5.3. In the light of this, Toğuşlu explained that "I think we need something new, coming from the Hizmet principles, but we should put it within the European context, and within the European context every country has different historical dynamics and legacies, we have to adopt, and with these Hizmet principles to make a kind of mix". On the one hand there are "so many universal values that we can share" but there are also "many values distinctive to the history of the country" and therefore "Hizmet will more and more get the new approaches and values from cultures and values from the cultures and countries in which it is operating. Then, maybe, it will create a new synthesis or something like that".

In Sects. 2.2, 2.3 and 2.4 of this book it was noted how the vast majority of Hizmet activities emerged with an organisational focus around the meeting of needs in relation to the overcoming of ignorance through education; of divisive conflict through dialogue and of poverty through relief. The pedigree of this lies, as previously noted, within a broader Islamic inheritance mediated through Turkish and Kurdish culture via the teaching of Nursi who identified the three evils or three enemies which are not to be seen in terms of people, but rather as things that undermine humanity around education, relief of poverty and dialogue.

One of the historical dangers identified by many Hizmet interviewees has been that of adopting what might be called a "copy-paste" approach in a too simplistic attempt to transplant into Europe what worked in Turkey because the balance in such needs varies across both space and time. And similarly, when looking at the future of Hizmet across Europe, it is arguably also important to avoid falling into such a "copy-paste" trap when considering what might, in the end, be quite varied nationally focused translations of the key Hizmet themes and recognising that what might emerge might not be a single European developmental trajectory, but potentially trajectories of multiple Hizmets.

6.2   EDUCATION TO TACKLE IGNORANCE

As discussed in Sect. 2.2 (and also in Weller 2022, Sect. 2.6), a commitment to education has been one of the key characteristics of Hizmet, including within its development in Europe. Speaking about Hizmet as an international movement, HE3 from the Netherlands went so far as to argue that "This educational factor or feature" is "one of the pillars of the movement" which "functions as a means of social and cultural engineering of the movement". And Keleş explained the way in which Hizmet originally fulfilled an educational need in Turkey:

> You had the state Kemalist school system that was ideologically anti-religion, or you had a state Imam Hattip school that was religious, but detrimental in terms of the Diploma and everything else that it gave you. Hizmet created a school system that was ideologically in line with the secular laws; that taught the national curriculum; that had a religious ethos, so it wasn't anti-religious in its ethos, but also gave them a great Diploma. It provided a great service – a "third way" so to speak between the state secular and state religious (Imam Hatip) schools, tapping into a genuine need. And that's why it was appreciated.

With specific regard to Europe, Yükleyen and Tunagür (2013) argue that "At its inception, the Gülen movement in Europe did not specialize in education" and that "The emerging religious field when his [Gülen's] followers first arrived in Europe was based on mosques", in relation to which Yükleyen and Tunagür's comment was that "religious communities begin with activities for which Muslims have a demand" (p. 228). Indeed, generally and Islamically speaking, the establishment of a mosque in places to which Muslims migrate has traditionally also been seen as something of an Islamic duty. But Yükleyen and Tunagür's argued that because, in Europe, there was already more competition in that regard "the Gülen movement specialized in education, where there were no competitors" (p. 228). In the first instance, this was concerned with focusing on the needs of the children and young people from the original Turkish migrant diaspora. However, as HE3 notes:

> In the field of education, compared to Africa, Central Asia, and Turkey also, in the Netherlands and in other European countries, the educational system is at a good level. What is your niche in that environment? – this is the point, I think. There are schools initiated from the Gülen movement here – for example, the Cosmicus school, although they have another name at the moment. After the coup the board of the schools has changed the names of the schools.

And, indeed, as time went on, the educational offer of Hizmet extended beyond that of Turkish children so that HE3 noted, "I think that this is the niche that the movement participates in within the Netherlands, and in Belgium also, to have the children of Moroccan, Turkish and other cultural and ethnic backgrounds". In addition, things are also already extending and developing beyond that so that HE3 now notes that "I see the mix of some Dutch children are also participating in the schools, because the teachers are partly Dutch teachers of origin, and the schools have a Dutch name, not a Turkish name. And this is the transformation the movement's schools, educational activities have now". As HE3 says:

> Schools are supported, and fairly successful here. They are part of the local Dutch school communities: the schools are not of the movement. The schools are a part, formally, of the local Dutch school communities. In Rotterdam, it is one of the twenty-nine schools of that community. In Amsterdam, it is a part of the Montessori School Community. The movement supports and helps the school to be successful. But formally it is a Dutch school, not a Gülen school, and this made the school successful.

Therefore, while in the field of education the focus in the Netherlands has until very recently been on migrant children and migrant groups, "in the last year we see an opening to the other groups – also the Dutch groups – it is a process". Once again this underlines the need for clearly contextual developments rather than for "copy-paste" approaches of any sort.

In Belgium, as in the Netherlands, Hizmet educational initiatives were initially focused on meeting the needs of Turkish migrant children and their families. A flavour of the historic context for this is summarised in the following interviewee testimony from EH1 who first came to Belgium from Turkey as a teacher:

> When I came to Belgium in 2010, in Ghent, I was a teacher in one of the Hizmet weekend courses for small kids, I think the ages were between twelve and fifteen. In Turkey, all people, not only the Hizmet part, know the importance of education very well. And every parent wants their kid to be well educated and to have a good education. But in Belgium it was not the case. So I had, like twenty kids in the room, and I just asked all of them, "What do you want to be? What do you want to study? And what do you want to be in your life?" And nobody responded to me that I want to be teacher, a want to be an engineer, or a want to be architect ... One response was I want to open my own kebab shop and the other was to be a worker in the factory. And all the answers were similar to that. And also like the workers who work in a specific factory earn more than a teacher, let's say.

EH1 recognised of these young people that, overall, then "they had their arguments. So, the context in Belgium was completely different from the context in Turkey". Nevertheless, in this context, EH1 says:

> I see the positive value of Hizmet in Belgium, in a country where Turkish people are the second biggest minority (and the Moroccan people are the biggest minority), I think just giving that vision, of what is the only chance to be successful or make good out of your life, you need good education, you need a better education. I think Hizmet people gave these people of Turkish background the sense that education is the most important thing you can do in your life ... There are, I think, ten schools which were opened by the Hizmet participants in Belgium. I think this is the most concrete and obvious added value by Hizmet to Belgium. And Belgium is a special case, like people who had migrant backgrounds don't have a good educational level in Belgium ... And this is a big failure for Belgium. And I guess when some people – in this case Hizmet participants – explain their projects to the Belgian authorities, one can see why they allow Hizmet to open schools in Belgium.

As Tascioglu acknowledges: "So, it's an advantage in Belgium that the state system organises and supports cultural and educational activities as well. If it's like a good project and it speaks to an audience, to the public, it gets help from the state and that's the same for the Netherlands and for Germany". In contrast to this, the events of July 2016 in Turkey have not been without their impact on perceptions of Hizmet schools, especially among the wider Turkish population which historically have been the main source of students. In relation to the schools in Belgium, interviewee HE1 noted, referring to 2018, that:

> Yes, last year, in the first few months, it was the same thing – that Turkish people withdrew their children from the schools. But in Belgium there are always waiting lists for schools, and within a few months they got the other kids (mostly Belgian with Moroccan origins): like around 30% of people were Belgian with Turkish origins and seventy per cent is mixed. So, they didn't suffer a lot in Belgium. I know some places where some families withdrew their children from the schools and within a few months they wanted to enrol back again because their kids were not happy in the new schools. The conditions were not the same and, unfortunately it was not possible to re-enrol these families because the schools are in full capacity in Belgium.

However, following that initial withdrawal, Tascioglu noted that "Because the schools were so popular, there were already waiting lists and after this year, all the people on the waiting lists for these schools could be in the schools", but also that one of the consequences of the immediate hiatus was that "Most of the kids in the schools right now are Belgians of Moroccan origins, but there are also a wider diversity of ethnic backgrounds".

In Switzerland, whereas some years ago, Hizmet's provision of supplementary education addressed similar migrant-related issues as to those in Belgium, Özgü now comments that "Hizmet also now has no more supplementary schools and is no more active in education in Switzerland". For him very personally "that's the worst thing I think" because such initiatives had been Özgü's personal route into higher education and ultimately to a career in law. But as noted earlier in Sect. 3.6, the events of July 2016 and following undermined the economic models of these schools. Similarly, in Germany, as Karakoyun explained it:

> We have the problem that many Turkish people who were engaged in our schools, our teachers, parents, pupils left the schools since 2016. So, you

have to deal with it. So, you first of all have to deal with this, with the big problems that you have. Of course, there are big financial problems; there are big leadership problems at the moment; there are big discussions going on because of the Turkish heritage of Hizmet and because many people are in the crisis situation and with their trauma, not everything is going healthily. Not all discussions are healthy because everyone has a problem. Because someone had to quit his job, someone lost his institution, and so on.

In some other parts of Europe, things to do with education have continued in a more "traditional" Hizmet way, albeit with educational services being offered now more to asylum-seekers and refugees rather than to labour migrants. Thus, in Spain Hizmet newcomers have been active in educational initiatives and have self-organised an online education platform called Academy Vision which holds classes that engage nearly ninety students in all, supported by around thirty volunteer teachers (largely from among the parents of the students, although also including some from Japan, Germany and Belgium) in studying mathematics, English, Turkish, Spanish and universal values. With logistical support from Casa Turca, they also organise seminars for adults on topics as varied as entrepreneurship, dialogue concepts, health issues, child education and psychological sessions. Naziri comments on this that, on the one hand, "This example and initiative, for me, is, once again, a good proof of Hizmet as a group dedicated to education and values", although noting that once those running this initiative find a more settled existence with regular employment, "There is a risk that this project … is not sustainable" as in due course the people concerned will not be as available as they had previously been. At the same time, out of its awareness of this potential issue, Casa Turca is "now working on writing some projects so that we may find funds to maintain it and even to expand it".

In the UK, Hizmet was not so exposed to this particular issue because it had previously only developed one school—the North London Grammar School (formerly known as Wisdom School). In comparing the situation with regard to schools with that in Germany, while noting that there was only one Hizmet school in the UK, Keleş also observed that "But the reason for that is more straightforward, I think, it's money! So, in Germany as far as I know, they have more money, they have more donors, they have more Turks. So that's one thing. They can outspend us, the Germans!" However, even though many Hizmet schools have been founded in

Germany, Karakoyun from Germany is critical of the use of what he calls a "copy-paste" approach of which he also says that "I think it is very Turkish" and that:

> I think the European way is a little bit different. If you sent someone here, they would say what kind of problems does this society have; what is the biggest problem; and what can I help in terms of it being solved? Is it a school or starting an inter-religious dialogue by bringing together the natu-ralists, the humanists, the Christians, the Muslims of this country, by teach-ing them in conflict management and in inter-religious and inter-cultural dialogue, what has to be my job here? And not "copy-paste". I think many Turkish initiatives were based on "copy-paste": this is why we have twenty-five schools in Germany. But, well, you said it, in Turkey it was the right thing because there was not good education; in Ethiopia it was also the right thing because there was not good education. But in Germany you have a state that is one of the richest in the world and that is organising education at its best, everywhere in the country for free, absolutely free, and you will say, I will also do!

In relation to the creation of the North London Grammar School in the UK, Keleş says that, in many ways, it is "more reflective of Hizmet schools in Turkey and in Central Asia, which were schools providing excel-lent education". However, while "it was easy to do that in that context" because "you had the workforce, and the rest of the educational system wasn't so great", with regard to the UK setting, as Keleş puts it:

> Who are we going to compete with – Eton? The Prime Minister already comes from Eton? Are we going to provide a school to compete with Eton? Do we think that people who send their children to Eton would ever consider sending their children to North London Grammar school, even if your education was on a par with them?

Therefore, there are issues with replication in itself, but also in terms of how to demonstrate success since, as Keleş asks, if this is what one projects "what does it say about who you are?" Overall Keleş cites this as a concrete example of what he calls "the difference between internalizing the meth-odology of your teacher, or the methodology of a particular line of thought, versus reproducing the product of that methodology that is time bound". In interview discussion about this, the idea emerged that a radi-cally contextualised application of the basic Hizmet commitment to education could be a translation into the education of kids on the street in a knife crime context, in relation to which Keleş reacted:

> That's it, that's a need. Now you provide that, right, you provide a community centre that deals with knife crime in any London borough, now, do that, and then you become you are delivering a service that people appreciate. Do it authentically, do it from your heart, do it from your values, and then that becomes something that people then want: that's a service you provide.

From these accounts one can see that, while the notion of educational initiatives remains an important one for Hizmet in Europe, how to give concrete and appropriately contextual expression to this continuing Hizmet value is leading to new, interesting and challenging questions. Indeed, these questions are also now being framed in relation to Hizmet's own educational needs in Europe, not just in terms of educated citizens of migrant background, but precisely as Muslims and Hizmet participants in Europe. Thus, for example, whereas in the past, Hizmet has on the whole not been involved in educating children in relation to Islam, there are signs of this beginning to change. For example, Balcı confided in interview that "I have never spoken to anybody about this – but I am always thinking that Hizmet is going to start for the first time in the West, Religious Education for our own children. Hizmet has never opened Religious Education facilities, but the need is there". In illustrating this need Balcı spoke about his own challenges as a parent of a seven-year-old daughter attending a Church school and coming home with all kinds of questions in relation to which "I feel myself challenged". Thus:

> Let me tell you a beautiful story. This was two years ago. She was in the Reception, only the first year, and then she was going to a secular school and not a Church school, presumably no Religious Education. So, I was carrying her on my shoulders, and we passed by a church. And she said, "Daddy what is this building?" and I said. "This is a church, honey"... "Wow, I love churches" she said. So, I was shocked and said "Why"? And she said, "cross bun!". And I didn't know what is "cross bun". And she said, "cross bun, they're in churches, cross bun". So, I said well I am going to see what this is, so I Googled and realised it was "hot cross bun". This is what they teach in the school about hot cross bun, and I assume she asked her teachers what is this? – and they said this is distributed in the churches. I said, we can do "cross bun" because they sell it in Tesco. But I then realised that I had never

brought her to a mosque. She wouldn't say I love the mosque. So, I said there is a challenge here that I had to deal with, you know. So, I looked for a beautiful mosque – and our mosques are not always the best places to visit, and so on, and as Hizmet people we do not always go into mosques. But there was a beautiful mosque, a Pakistani mosque in Wimbledon, and I had heard something about what is this place and so on, and thank God people were happy with children because in Turkish mosques they don't like children. But then I realised, you know, that the coming generation is going to have a huge challenge with these issues.

In reflecting on this Balcı notes that "Inter-faith dialogue is something that we know, but whether through only dialogue we can teach our young children about our own religious identity, it's a question mark". And if it is a question now when his daughter is seven, he notes that with teenagers there will be "another huge challenge out there" and then "what will I do, what will I do?" in relation to which he concludes that "we need communal support bases, which we lack". This is potentially significant for the future of Hizmet in the UK and in Europe more broadly because what Hizmet was doing in its original Turkish context was meeting an educational need and what Balcı identified through the story about his daughter was about identifying a newly emergent need for Hizmet in an environment such as the UK. What is more, such a need is also reinforced by the arrival of Hizmet asylum-seekers. Thus, Balcı shared that:

> We are going to open nurseries, particularly for Muslim children, because a lot of new families came who knew nothing about how to cope with the challenge of living in a predominantly non-Muslim, secular environment. So, they will need guidance, and when they look for guidance, they will most probably prefer people who came from Turkey, because they will say these are still keeping the ideal and authenticity.

And this is being planned even though up to now "That is something we have never done" citing Manchester in the UK as an example of where some newly arriving businessmen are being advised to invest in nurseries. Therefore, if it is the case that a focus on education has been one of the orientating things for Hizmet and has been reproduced throughout the world, these new initiatives signal yet another potential evolution of that basic orientation. In Turkey the need was for schools with an emphasis on, especially, scientific excellence so that pious Muslims could fully participate in, rather than finding themselves in practice often excluded from, modern society. Hizmet schools did not offer religious education, albeit they were informed by a particular ethos in terms of being influenced through Hizmet teachers. So, in relation to this newly identified need for religious education, Balcı identifies what he calls "an opportunity space" arising from the fact that due to the impact of July 2016, there is a "trend of highly skilled Hizmet population coming to the United Kingdom" and in relation to whom Balcı says, "We don't know what to do with them, because it's largely non-English speaking, but very highly qualified" including about twenty graduates from what he calls Gülen's "own university" out of perhaps a total overall of one hundred and twenty graduates, whereas "Five years ago, we had none". Therefore:

> This is an opportunity, but they need to learn English and they need to start dealing with the real challenges of the Western world, instead of third century, fourth century theological discussions. There is a huge human potential here, but we have to be able to mobilise them, financially also support some of them in publishing, for example. Books do not make a living, do not make money. They have to be supported. In the long run we will be, but then we might have, we might be late.

In fact, Balcı went on to identify a special aspect of both this broader Hizmet educational need and the potential opportunities to address it in terms of the traumatic impact of July 2016 on the lives of the children of Hizmet asylum-seekers and refugees, and the seriously challenging question arising of how far these children might be at risk of inheriting an inter-generational trauma from which they cannot escape. Thus, Balcı entertains what is, perhaps, counter-intuitive thinking around education as compared with how Hizmet education developed in Turkey, in which he says, "I foresee – and it has already started in this country also – that some of us who are coming from Turkey are going to become tutors of Qur'anic education".

Balcı also refers to emerging challenges at the other end of the age range from that on which Hizmet's educational initiatives have traditionally focused. Scholars of what sociologists of religion often call New Religious Movements (Barker 1989) point out that, typically speaking, such movements engage young adults more than any other age group. What then often becomes challenging for such movements is when those within them have to start thinking more about generational transmission to their young, as well as about generational transition from older original leaderships to newer ones. In relation to this, too, Balcı shows awareness when he states that:

I am looking to the growing age of Hizmet also. The point is this: we have never worked on retirement schemes because we never believed in retiring because as long as Hizmet was able to continue and financially able to support its volunteering population, we didn't actually need retirement schemes. We did have hospitals, we did have dorms where people, even at the age seventy, could do something. So, we were actually providing jobs. Now Hizmet is not doing that and won't be able to do that in the western context for at least two more generations. But Hizmet has a huge growing older population who are not going to be learning local languages easily, who won't be able to work other than, you know, simple jobs like distributing pizza and so on, which need no qualification. But you cannot do that at the age of seventy.

Creatively, in relation to this challenge Balcı makes the connection with the challenge of children's needs and the possible foundation of mosques because:

You can teach in a mosque at the age of seventy, where the students will be also speaking your language. And that is quite a satisfactory profession because, by way of your religious beliefs you believe you are going to meet your God, and at the age of seventy, or even sixty to sixty-five it will be the best of, you know, occupations to deal with divine issues.

At the same time, in relation to this Balcı comments that "But we don't have mosques"—although more precisely, as noted in Sect. 3.2, in the UK there is one mosque in north London that, as previously noted, is identified with Hizmet, and so Balcı goes on to say:

So, I have been lobbying here, the leadership of Hizmet in the United Kingdom to think about opening more, you know, mosques because our children will need it, and looking at Pakistani – particularly Bangladeshi and Somali people – they need it. Their kind of mosques and most probably you have heard the last survey, you know fifty percent more than fifty per cent of the society believes that Islam is incompatible with British values. I'm not sure when you ask them what are British values, what they would say. But still there is a perception out there that needs to be changed.

Commenting on what Balcı had suggested concerning Islamic education, Karakoyun from his own perspective in Germany said, "I think that's true". Indeed, he went on to say that "And not only we need it" but "also

Muslims who are not organised in Germany (and who are perhaps eighty per cent of the Muslims in Germany) need it". This is because, especially in Germany:

> The Turkish mosques are Turkish. They are even the long arm of Erdoğan, and who can better integrate the newcoming people into Germany than people like us who were born in Germany and sharing Islamic values, and bringing together Islamic values with the German *Grundgesetz*. I think we have to take more responsibility in this issue.

Thus, Karakoyun notes in relation to Germany also that "We are now in active discussion about whether Hizmet should launch something like an Islamic academy. So maybe within the next one or two years we will see steps there. So it is rather concrete even". Taking similar ideas further, Balcı confided that is his own personal "retirement project" is that "I am planning to open a *madrassah*, an online *madrassah*, because off-line is off!" and in relation to which he explains that:

> I'm getting prepared, I'm just making readings. I'm trying to learn what has failed, why the *madrassahs* particularly in India, Pakistan, Afghanistan etc are failing so gravely our religion. So, I am making readings about their curricula, and why they are failing people, why it's taking so long to be knowledgeable about religious issues and so on. In the long run, in five to ten years I'm hoping to establish a small digital Madrassa where I can teach people on challenging issues.

In relation to such a *madrassah*, Balcı underlines that he wants it to be dialogic in that "I need Christians, Buddhists, Jews, you know, I need them to come and teach in the *Madrassah*". And it is the significance of this affirmation that leads into the next section's discussion of Hizmet future trajectories in relation to dialogue.

6.3 DIALOGUE TO TACKLE CONFLICT AND PROMOTE INCLUSIVE INTEGRATION

Whenever and wherever one encounters Hizmet organisations throughout the world, dialogue has always been one of Hizmet's three key themes. Such dialogue is intended to address disunity and division. As Keleş explains it historically:

When Hizmet came out with dialogue … it provided a platform and it brought the secularists and the religious, the Sunnis, and the left and the right: it provided a great service that was needed. Now dialogue they didn't know that they needed it, which is why they were so surprised at what came about through it. But, actually, they realised that and as a result they appreciated it, and the state started to copy what you were doing which showed there was an appreciation there at some level of Hizmet.

Comparing a country like Belgium where education has remained a central and probably primary Hizmet activity, interviewee HE1 noted that "Of course, the countries like Spain, Italy, Poland, like where there is almost no Turkish background or community existing, these are active in dialogue activities". Or, comparing Belgium and Italy, as Tascioglu noted "the inter-religious dialogue that we do here in Belgium is completely different from that in Italy because of the presence of the Vatican". In relation to such national contextual factors, Toğuşlu, who has lived and worked in both France and Belgium, cites the contrasting example of these two countries.

So, I think this structure coming from two different countries it changes what Hizmet does in these countries, I think. So, for example, in France, religion is less visible in Hizmet activities, but in Belgium although it is very neutral it is a little bit neutral. Dialogue activities – especially inter-faith activities – are there and Hizmet people organise many inter-faith activities in France, but not like in Belgium, it is a country where this does not really create a problem, even though it is a secular country, and especially in education. So, these sorts of differences, I think, affect directly the movement's existence in these countries. We have to contextualise where Hizmet is involved and its activities. It is important, I think.

Spain, of course, has a particular history of Christian-Muslim and Jewish relations, including both negative periods such as that of the Inquisition and some more positive ones such as the so-called Convivencia. Although Naziri commented that there are a lot of Spanish people today who are sceptical about such a period in their history, the idea of it can at least in principle still be quite evocative as, for example, in relation to the role that it played in the United Nations' initiative on "The Dialogue of Civilizations" of which, as Naziri pointed out, "It was interestingly promoted in 2005 by Zapatero, the Socialist Party here in Spain, and Erdoğan". However, although himself citing this, Naziri was also keen to underline that "we are not comparing it to these standards of the 21st century". Therefore, in and of itself Naziri reflects that "It doesn't say anything. It was just an historical fact, and that's all right". So "It was like, good" but "I just focus on today" because the "historical reality that we are facing today is completely different".

Coming back to the distinctive kind of focus on dialogue adopted by the Dialogue Society in the UK, Keleş (in Weller 2015) recalls that when it was being set up: "I specifically remember discussing issue of identity and where we wanted the Dialogue Society to be. We wanted to give it an identity that could accommodate different types and forms of dialogue about different themes and topics" (p. 245). In relation to this, he went on that "We knew that our work would include interfaith dialogue but also that corporate identity needed to be wider than that as a time would come when form of dialogue may be more extensive or would need to be more extensively or differently framed" and that therefore "We were very conscious of the dynamic nature of Hizmet's mode (not aims) and the dynamic or unsettled nature of dialogue itself: hence the name and logo". As Keleş said "Because 'dialogue' is so elastic a term, defining and clarifying the work of a dialogue organization is all the more important for establishing corporate identity and achieving targets" (in Weller 2015 p. 246).

Indeed, the Dialogue Society has been concerned to make a useful contribution in regard not only for itself and its own immediate work but also with the aim of clarifying (and perhaps also making more measurable) the wider field of dialogue by initiating a number of projects aimed at establishing dialogue studies as a distinctive field under the banner of an Institute of Dialogue Studies. These include the founding of a Dialogue School; the establishment of an MA in Dialogue Studies with the University of Keele that was run between 2011 and 2017[3]; the publication of books on *Dialogue Theories* (Sleap and Sener ed. Weller 2013); *Dialogue Theories 2* (Sleap, Sener and Weller Eds. 2016); the 2013 founding of *The Journal of Dialogue Studies*[4]; along with, as previously noted, the important publication of its book on *Islam and Dialogue* (Kurucan and Erol 2012).

This kind of emphasis on dialogue in the wider societal sense contrasted with the Netherlands, where, from the beginning, Hizmet organisations and groups were engaging much more specifically in inter-religious dialogue, including textual dialogue around the Bible, the Qur'an and so on. Inter-faith dialogue was also very much a focus in Denmark, where Gezen says of its Dialog Forum that it "has mostly been known as a Muslim association" and that, overall, its orientation has been that "we want to be in dialogue with Christians, Jews and other denominations, where we have to be together to build this society together, we have to be in peaceful coexistence. So, it was inspired a lot by what Gülen started to do in Istanbul when he initiated dialog activities". Indeed, in Denmark, the Dialog Forum built on its pioneering dialogue work by engaging in what Gezen cites as being "highly successful" joint grassroots developmental work together with the Jewish community in Denmark.

This Muslim-Jewish initiative now exists as an association in its own right called De Nye Stemmer (or New Voices). It encourages and supports young Jews and young Muslims to visit schools and communicate around "what it means to be a minority, and what it means to live in a country where you are a minority, and showing that Muslims and Jews can live together". As a joint initiative this contrasts with some of the traditional approaches taken by Hizmet to engaging in dialogue in Europe where, historically, as Karakoyun said in relation to Germany: "For example, when I started Hizmet, when I said 'look there is such an institution and they want us to co-operate', the former *abis* said 'We only sit at the table if we have prepared it ourselves'"—an approach that he summarised as being informed by an understanding that "We don't sit at a table that was prepared by someone else because we don't want to be instrumentalized" with Karakoyun commenting on this that "Well this is a very Turkish way of thinking and I didn't care about these fears". By contrast, Karakoyun thought it important for Hizmet to recognise that:

> We are not inventing inter-religious dialogue. It has been running in Germany now for fifteen or twenty years. Let us join in activities that are already running. Let us make them better and richer and more influential. Of course, we can also do our own, but let us not do as if we have invented dialogue. Hojaefendi also says dialogue is important, but he didn't invent it. So, we have to be humble. And if there are local institutions that are already doing it why shouldn't we sit at their table and participate and be part of it. And this is what I did.

Therefore, as in Denmark, in Germany Hizmet participation in broader collaborative initiatives in dialogue have become more common, with Karakoyun explaining that "And this is why in Berlin we are part of The House of One" (see Sect. 3.3). In relation to the Netherlands, too, Ablak acknowledged that, arising from collaborative work with people of other religions in inter-religious dialogue that "We had lots of support from those dialogue friends" during the post-July 2016 reactions and threats she experienced and "That helped me a lot in that hard time". Thus, while in the Netherlands the Turkish diaspora mostly supports Erdoğan, Ablak celebrated the fact that:

> We got a lot of support from our Jewish and Christian friends in this hard time. Especially our Jewish friends understand the best about what we are looking to do. So, my friend who was just a child when the Holocaust happened said "It's very hard for you. It's harder than what we went through in the Second World War because our enemy it was Hitler. Everyone knew our enemy was not one of us. But now, your problem is that Turkish Muslims, and Erdoğan, he is willing to destroy you although he is one of yours. So, you have a bigger problem than we had in the Second World War. I thought, "You can't be serious about that?!" But then, you know, I can't trust Turkish people. Someone talks to me and it flashes in my mind: is he or she an Erdoğan supporter, and what will he or she think or me when he or she knows.

In Switzerland, each individual Canton very much has its own culture and tradition, in relation to which Özgü comments that those "like Zurich, Geneva, Berne, and Basel are very open-minded". In nearly all the Cantons Özgü says of the Hizmet-related asylum-seekers that "Most of all they have got well connected with the Church, the Catholic and Protestant Churches and all the other Churches which are really open to the asylum-seekers". This was confirmed by the asylum-seeker AS1 who, in a 26 February 2020 written interviewee update subsequently sent to the author explained: "Firstly we immediately established a working group to contact local people and introduce ourselves, at the same time to determine as a non-governmental organization our shortcomings". But interestingly, from this beginning, rather than trying to establish their own institutions, asylum-seeker AS1 explained that "I was able to join some Intercultural and Interreligious Working Groups which are esteemed institutions in the eyes of local people in Bern".

Among other examples of engagement in inter-religious activities given by AS1 were those of an OffeneKirche (Heilliggeist Kirche) event on climate change that included climate-related prayers in accordance with Islamic rituals "which was wonderful and attracted great attention from locals and also from official media SRF". There was also a common Ashura-Day celebration with the Christcatholics/Old Catholics in which "We made the Sunday Church Service together and after that had the

Ashure Dessert with the Church Community. They were fascinated and made note of their agenda to do it again in coming year". With Jewish people there is an initiative called Respect through which "We try to be together in each other's special days". Finally, there is a discussion group of Swiss Christians and Hizmet participants in their premises at the Culture Centrum in Bern where "We try to meet regularly every month and held a discussion about different religious themes to understand each other better and closely".

But they have also included trying to educate other asylum-seekers by, as AS1 explains it, asking "local intellectuals to introduce Swiss opinion leaders and important characters" such as Karl Barth and Nicholas of Flüe (Bruder Klaus)—of whom AS1 said they had "a very similar mindset with Bediüzzaman Said Nursi and Yunus Emre" in order "to encourage them to adapt to the Swiss society more willingly". At the time of writing, AFS1 said that "Next week Swiss Reformed theologian Leonard Ragaz, one of the founder of religious socialism in Switzerland, together with his wife Clara Ragaz, will be introduced". From within Switzerland itself, and interestingly, given the historic tendency of perhaps the majority of people associated with Hizmet in Turkey towards at least the centre-right, Özgü adds that, in terms of dialogue "the other thing is that maybe one can get well connected to the left-wing movements".

Overall for Hizmet in Europe, HE2 from Italy was of the opinion that "For different contexts, I think that for every country and every national or regional context we need people, or maybe institutions, who will be working or interesting in 're-innovating' Hizmet". As an example, he cited Tevere in Rome, as:

> A distinctive institution. I am not saying this, but the Japanese Ambassador said this. At that time he said a "unique" institution, because at that time in a Catholic city, Muslims decided to invest into inter-faith dialogue because we are here and we would like to give a response. And as the Journalists and Writers Foundation was an important inspiration connecting to a Catholic minority in Turkey, now as a Muslim minority we are trying to reach out to Catholics who are in dialogue – Jesuits, Franciscans, Focolare. The document *Nostra Aetate* in 1965 invites Muslims and Christians to promote together social justice, peace, freedom and moral values. And to some extent Tevere tried to give a response to this.

Given the relationship of Hizmet initiatives to the values that underlie and inspire them, but also the commitment to engage with local contexts, just as in the case of Hizmet, in approaching its dialogue initiatives one can expect to find similar patterns albeit as Tascioglu suggests, with its forms being specifically inflected according to each national context:

> Maybe I can say that the work of Hizmet changes according to the context. According to each country there are different realities, different political realities, different democracies, different institutions. It's very flexible because in the centre we focus on the human being and we then try to find a way to work within the context of a country. So, it is normal that for every country there is a different outworking of Hizmet.

6.4   Helping to Relieve Poverty Developing into Supporting Human Rights

As has also been noted, the relief of poverty has, together with education and dialogue, been the other one of the triad of foci for Hizmet's work, as originally inspired by Nursi but also as further developed via the teaching and call to practice of Fethullah Gülen. In working this field, Hizmet has, both historically and generally speaking, tended to focus more on direct response to the concrete presentation of human need rather than on the kind of structural and systemic injustices which give rise to much of the poverty that presents itself. Overall, of the three historic and characteristic foci for Hizmet activity, it is perhaps fair to say that the relief of poverty has probably been the one that has received the least attention in Europe. This might in part be because, while poverty of a real kind certainly exists in Europe, it is generally more of the relative than absolute kind as can be found in the Two Thirds World. What has, however, perhaps also been observable in Europe has been what one might call a "stretching" of this original focus on poverty in terms of its injustice and the human suffering that it brings, into a more inclusive understanding of human social rights that also encompasses other matters, and in relation to which there is evidence that the impact of July 2016 throughout the world has fed into a greater sensitivity among Hizmet participants.

For example, in Denmark, a new Hizmet development is Ius Humainum which explicitly focuses on Human Rights and within which, as Gezen explains, "Young lawyers and university students studying law are planning projects that focus on human rights including a long term focus on certain projects". In Switzerland, based on Geneva being a recognised centre for international organisations and activities, Özgü cites the International Human Rights Advocacy (IHRA),[5] of which he says:

> And this focuses on global issues. For example, if someone is getting kidnapped by the Turkish authorities in Azerbaijan, we apply for them at the United Nations or the Committee Against Torture, and other human rights things. And that's a global issue. We can't just talk about it in Geneva. We have an association, we have there our advisory board. We talk with them, but we need also an international global meeting to talk about issues there. And there are now many global issues, and human rights is a global issue, and the thing with asylum-seekers is also an international thing, because the people from Turkey they go to Greece and then want to come to Europe. That is also a global issue for us to talk about.

In relation to migration issues, Toğuşlu says:

> We discuss many times, should we raise our concerns for the topic. Most of the time, we don't. I have found it a little bit problematic, if it is against our principles. I saw many of my Belgian friends, they are against what the Belgian state does in terms of migration policies. Why can't the Hizmet people do the same thing?

Toğuşlu argues that "this political participation: our understanding of politics is, I think, again related to the identity issue". In challenging Hizmet about this he acknowledges that with local integration and indigenisation can also come dangers:

> What I mean is that we try to make the movement a French movement, or a Dutch movement, or a Belgian movement. Up to some point, it's OK, but as a person coming from Turkey, I am not defending a Turkish position, I'm not defending a Turkish identity. But we have a bit of experience with this being anchored to a local identity, a state identity especially – it creates very, very problematic issues. So, I would prefer a kind of maybe a set of principles we hope to follow, whether in China, or Tajikistan, whether in London or in other countries we have to follow. We have to give our focus on these principles, and not on these local identities. We have to be careful: for example, if it is against my principles.

And in fact, recognition of this tension led Toğuşlu to pose the sharply self-critical question for Hizmet of "if I am against my principles then why do I remain in the movement to struggle with these kind of issues rather than to find something else and follow my principles there?" This is quite a radical (in the proper sense of dealing with the roots) questioning and is perhaps a reminder that a movement that is no longer in "movement" in effective becomes dead. So, even where issues are still in process—as with the place of women—as long as a movement actively continues to wrestle with issues, at the least it is still alive. In conclusion, in relation to the challenging nature of these issues Toğuşlu added the comment: "The people have hope also. Without hope I think you cannot live".

6.5   MEETING NEEDS AND KEEPING THE BALANCE

In reverting to the situation of Hizmet overall, Keleş poses the fundamental question of: "What are we about? What is our project about? And that was a problem anyway, because, you know, the things that you said at the beginning: education, dialogue and unity to overcome the three ailments and so on, all of this made sense". The three Hizmet value foci remain relatively constant even if differently expressed apart from perhaps in the case of the relief of poverty which, as argued in the section above, might well have been the most radically further developed through a gradual transformation into what seems to have become a broader concern with what might broadly be described as human rights. In the end all three of these foci are shared human concerns, and religions (including Islam), are fundamentally concerned with the human. But because these needs take different shape in different places and at different times, what Keleş argues has to be avoided (when stated negatively) is the danger of providing a service/*hizmet* that people do not want or need. This not only in principle important but also because the danger of a disconnect in this can negatively impact on the motivation of volunteers. People start questioning what is being done, and if one cannot make sense of it, motivation is lost.

There is, as Keleş puts it in relation to the future roles of Hizmet in the UK: "So the question of whether Hizmet will be able to grow out of this, is actually about if this process helps us to break away from these unnecessary sensitivities and question our values in relation to the need of this country" in which, in summary, "The values and the principles are still very relevant. It's the *how* we now interpret them". In the light of this, Keleş advocated that:

We have to make two lists: what does this society need, without us? What are we going to do, what can we do? We need to compare these two lists, and when you look at that, that's where Prevent comes out, you know – integration, religious literacy, religious absolutism, you know, minorities, ethnic minorities ... that's one list ... extremism, and so forth. And there's other things on that list such as climate change, and various other issues. Brexit now is on that list. Now, what can we do?

In further reflection on this, Keleş accentuates what might in future need to be done more collaboratively:

Well, there seems to be very little that we can do uniquely about the environment. There is, but not at the top of the list – based on our characteristics, our abilities, who we are, there's other things that we can do. Religious literacy is one of them: religious absolutism is one of them and teaching a religious curriculum that deals with this issue about absolutism and belief versus religious knowledge and the uncertainty of religious knowledge. And things around Prevent, we can do a lot, and things around mentoring we can do that type of thing. And we can do that by our educational model, making it more open in terms of its identity, and perhaps a more diverse ethnic audience. So, you are not now looking to be a grammar school, which is more elitist. Do you see?

But while in all these matters there was already a dynamic of development that was in play before the events of July 2016, Gezen highlights that "How much researchers are aware, I am not sure, but the coup attempt has really affected the Hizmet movement a lot, to a very high extent" and that, with this impact, there is a danger not only of imbalance between the three foci, but also of between European and Turkish foci. It is not that Gezen thinks what is happening in Turkey should be ignored because he says: "What is happening in Turkey is heart breaking" and that "Hizmet participants shouldn't forget what is happening in Turkey and all the unjustly imprisoned people; especially women and infants". But nevertheless:

I am just saying that if you have a portion of work – if you have ten balls – and you have to use this some way, I'm saying that maybe eight or nine of them should be for the local community, and one ball should be used to address the issues in Turkey. Right now, that's my perception. Right now, I feel that it's the reverse. I feel that nine of the balls are being used for looking at the issues of Turkey and only one of the balls is focusing on local issues.

As Karakoyun expresses it, since the arrival of Hizmet asylum-seekers "we have people who permanently talk about the developments in Turkey, about what is going on there, and want to help the people there and say that Hizmet now should have the only aim to rescue the friends in Turkey". But in contrast to that Karakoyun says:

> the second group are people like me who say, yes, of course, it is sad what is happening in Turkey, we have to work on it. But we also have to care for Hizmet in Germany and what has been developed here for over twenty years because there are schools, federations, cultural centres, Islamic centres, business institutions. So, there is a lot of what Hizmet is doing here for Germany. So, you can't now say to people born here, now make your education institution into an institution that is working for human rights in Turkey.

Toğuşlu also expressed the view that, especially in the post-July 2016 period, "we missed a little bit of the balance … we put too much for the people coming from Turkey. I know there is a huge problem there, but there is also an awareness that the movement should continue its activities in dialogue, in education, and this shouldn't be stopped". Because overall there are only finite resources, this creates an uncomfortable tension in terms of the realistic prioritisation of resources which after July 2016 have become even more limited. In relation to this, Toğuşlu affirms:

> Yeah, exactly. So, it creates huge amount of problems within the movement. The people coming from Turkey feel alone here, and the people from here ask why aren't continuing our activities like dialogue, like education, and that we are killing ourselves if we put our only emphasis and focus on these people who are refugees.

What is more, this has occurred in the context of what might be called a relative "deprofessionalisation" of Hizmet in these same countries arising from a sharp reduction in the financial and human resources previously coming from Turkey coupled with a growth in need in terms of meeting immediate asylum-seeker needs of Hizmet in Europe. As illustrated by Özgü, in relation to Switzerland:

> before the coup attempt we had around fifty people who were professional Hizmet, and after that we just had five, because financially we couldn't handle that. And now in Hizmet, non-professional people are more active than

before 2016. In our meetings most of the people are no longer professional. They work in another thing outside of Hizmet. It is no more a professional thing, Hizmet in Switzerland.

At the same time, Toğuşlu's overall judgement is that "It is not about resources, but we have lost this motivation, I think, within the movement. So, maybe it is about our energy: you have to go back and forth between the newcomers in Turkey and you have to look at what you can do for the community here in Belgium". Overall, in concrete terms, as Karakoyun says:

There is a limit to time, money and people, because, for example, just as an example in a small city in Germany, there are maybe ten or twenty people of Hizmet who are active there. They are all active in the education institution, for example. And now there are people coming from Turkey, asylum-seekers, and they want to work on Turkey issues.

And, therefore, all in all, "So, on the one hand they have to help, because it's our duty. They are our friends, they are not guilty, they are innocent. And on the other hand, but we are for twenty years now in Germany saying we are German Turkish, not something that is based in Turkey. We are a German Hizmet movement". And in the face of this, Karakoyun says "it's not easy for us. But we try to keep a balance".

In Denmark Gezen said that the context following July 2016 has additionally underlined the importance of "discussions and some debates about what the main focus is and what the second focus is, and what should we be focused on". In Gezen's view, "there is a focus on issues related to Denmark but not enough, since the major focus is still on Turkey" in relation to which perspective, he explained that "I have a relationship with Turkey due to my parents, my ancestors. Yes. But I am highly concerned with what is happening in Denmark" and went on to say:

I am born and raised in Denmark, because I am concerned with my own country, Denmark. And I think this is something that is going to grow and it's a big issue within Hizmet. People like me – I'm almost forty, but I was born in Denmark, a have three kids, and I am going to probably be in a cemetery in Denmark until my resurrection one day – and I don't see Turkey in the same way.

At the same time, Gezen says, "This doesn't mean, we are not concerned with the undemocratically and unhuman purge and witch-hunt on Hizmet participant around the world"; rather: "it means the Hizmet participants around the world are becoming more and more concerned with their local issues too".

As a result of these tensions between the trajectory towards greater localisation, but also the trauma caused to Hizmet by what happened in Turkey and has been brought to Europe in very direct human form by Hizmet asylum-seekers, in practical terms a kind of "division of labour" has been established in a number of European countries. Thus, in Spain, as distinct from the work of the Arco Forum, the Casa Turca has moved to "have a contract with another NGO, association, lawyer who are very specialist, let's say, on these issues, on the asylum-seeker issues". Naziri explained that this was necessary because: "we are seeing that there were many huge errors, mistakes, in the first interviews that they had in the airport (an enclosed space resembling a jail)". This is partly, as Naziri says, because there is a lack of appropriate translators in which sometimes the government or an agency working on this for the government sends people who are from an Arabic background thinking that they can communicate via Arabic, or sometimes someone who has only Level 1 Turkish. There is also the issue that, while the majority of asylum-seekers are from Turkey, and there are already some difficulties for people external to that context understanding it, overall it is even more difficult to understand the situation of a Hizmet person from, for example, Senegal. Also, sometimes, a few pro-Erdoğan Turks are sent and who, "instead of doing their jobs ask, 'Why did you do that, the coup?' " But there is also the overall problem that, in Spain, "very few people are familiar with the Turkish case" and "silly things are happening in Turkey that you are sometimes unable to understand it from sitting and living in the liberal European countries. You can't understand this and what it will take in this persecution".

In a number of European countries, the pressures arising from this multi-layered situation risk distorting Hizmet's historic and ongoing work. Therefore, there is now an additional and new organisation called Solidarity with Others, which aims to work on the level of the European institutions and focuses only on human rights violations in Turkey and the victims among Hizmet. In the UK there is a similar differentiation of roles between the Dialogue Society and London Advocacy, the latter of which has a special remit following July 2016. Headed up by Balcı who explains that the London Advocacy initiative is one of "the large family which Özcan established in the past as a network of organizations" and of which Balcı explains that:

> London Advocacy was established, I assume because of my background in Turkey, and my nature or character. I wanted to raise awareness about the human rights violations, the persecution of Hizmet people back in Turkey, and also the spill over effect of that persecution also in other countries, not only Muslim countries, but also European countries. So, I wanted to raise awareness here in this country on a public level.

In relation to London Advocacy in the UK, Balcı says that it has "two wings". One is focused on legal cases in Turkey because:

> There are lots of ex-judiciary members of the Gülen movement who managed to flee the country: these are lawyers, former prosecutors, and in some cases bureaucrats from the Justice Ministry and so on. They have come together, using a loose network of What's App links and so on. They are doing a good job by means of guiding people back in Turkey how to apply for review of their decisions and so on.

There is also the opportunity to connect with the "potential of former bureaucrats" who are "much better educated compared to the general Hizmet population" and "Some of them speak English also". But Balcı also notes the challenge that some of these newcomers have brought with them "some Turkish bureaucratic manners" which are not appropriate in the UK. Some came from very high positions in Turkey: "So, from time to time, I am meeting a former lawyer, a judge and so on".

However, many of them also have relatives in prison in Turkey and Balcı spoke of an example of only the day previously when he was trying to persuade someone to testify when Amnesty International was asking for a speaker: "But she is afraid that if she spoke, it would influence her husband's case back in Turkey and so on. So, we need about five years to mobilise those people". He also cites some police officers who have doctorates, for example, and who, at present "are not actively involved in Hizmet. They're just trying to make a living", although in relation not which Balcı said, "I told them why don't you establish a school, you know a security training school (they have their asylum, you know) why don't you do something you know, rather than working in a fish and chip shop?"

6.6 HIZMET IN EUROPE WITH AND/OR WITHOUT FETHULLAH GÜLEN

In the context of comparison between Western Europe and the USA, Yükleyen and Tunagür argue (2013) that "The activities of the movement are highly adaptive to local socio-politico-economic contexts" and thus "Gülen activists address these contextual differences at local level, and are in turn shaped by them" (p. 224). However, this "adaptation" is not merely something in terms of sociological observation. Rather, the principle of contextualisation is something that has been strongly articulated in the teaching of Fethullah Gülen himself and has been actualised by Hizmet's forms of presence and activity across the globe, including in Europe, and in the various countries within it. In relation to this, Alasag explained of Gülen's perspectives that he had always recommended:

> Act according to your own context and have friends there and ask their advice, and if you want to develop something and take an initiative, never do it alone, do it together with Dutch people as they know this society. And if you want to develop something to help people, such as an educational initiative or whatever, do it together, do it in dialogue with others, cooperate. And that you can achieve dialogue if you organise it in dialogue, therefore find partners. For example, if you want to develop a something that will help the society, you have to do it together with other groups. If you do it only for the Hizmet community or taking an initiative alone, by yourself, you can only answer your own need.

In the light of this and reflecting on the future of Hizmet in the Netherlands, Alasag said: "At this moment we are only focusing on Holland there are some meetings on European level through which a couple of times a year I see people in Belgium and we discuss some issues, because we have also common challenges and sometimes we need advice from other people". With regard to the situation as it is now, he says, "We have now much more experience. We are now twenty years later and have organised so many things and developed a kind of a Dutch Hizmet" and, as a consequence, "the things we need advice about have been much reduced".

At the same time, when there is need they have contact globally: "So, for example we need to help the people in Turkey. For this we need to co-operate and we find each other easily, no problem. But I sense there is a difference on the level of co-operation". Therefore Alasag also says that "I think Hizmet will be local but will also stay global in a way, but it will be very much different from how it is today. For example, it is global in the sense that we are a big network and we know each other" and that "it will stay global in the sense that there is Skype, there is social media, people are moving, people are co-operating, people are meeting". Thus, Hizmet in Europe and internationally is increasingly becoming what might be called a "networking of experience" rather than a differentiated programme of common things. Nevertheless, when looking further into the future, Alasag also acknowledges that "After twenty years I don't know what will happen".

Of course, one of the big questions asked of Hizmet, including in Europe, including already from before the events of July 2016, but with increased urgency since, has been that of the future(s) of Hizmet without Gülen's physical and living presence. This is explored more generally, and in more detail in relation to the inheritance of his teaching in this book's complementary volume (Weller 2022, Sects. 6.2, 6.3 and 6.4). But it is also a question that has some specific and particular relevance to the European context. To attempt to answer the question in an appropriate and accurate way requires an understanding of the relationship between Fethullah Gülen as a person and Hizmet as a movement in terms of how best to articulate, both for themselves and for others, the nature of relationship between these initiatives and the person and/or example and teaching of Gülen without such articulations leading to potential misunderstandings about the nature of these. It is a sensitive and debated issue at the moment, and is also connected with the question of critical reflection on the past and especially on Turkey—both in terms of general change within Hizmet—but also then the question of where Gülen positions himself in relation to these debates.

In relation to this, as external observers and analysts, Sunier and Landman (2015) note that "It should be emphasized that even Fethullah Gülen has himself has no statutory power of decision in matters concerning the movement at local level. Gülen's influence manifests mainly through his charisma and stature as an important Islamic scholar" (p. 90). In order to try and reflect something of this kind of understanding, the present author has sometimes previously used such formulations as "Gülen-inspired initiatives". However, as critiqued by Keleş even such a formulation can be misleading in that "it can give the impression that a person reads a book by Gülen and becomes inspired" (in Weller 2015,

p. 250). For example, the Dutch author Gürkan Çelik, in a number of places, calls Gülen a "servant leader" (Çelik and Alan 2007) and HE3 says that: "I think there is a change at the moment: Gülen was never in a position that he tells things from the U.S. and from Turkey that the people here had to do what he says and said. He is the leader and his ideas are always dominant in the things that the movement do/have done." However, HE3 also underlined that "His position is more an inspirational one, he was/is guiding and sharing his ideas.....He is not a command and control leader."

Rather than providing an answer to this conundrum that would itself also likely be simplistic, Keleş points to a number of dimensions of how inspiration can work, as follows, as:

> As impetus: in other words to that one should get up and do something, being responsible as a human being; as a general framework – that what one does should be of value to the society in which one lives; in terms of general principles – that work that one does should be based on certain inclusive positive and proactive principles.

From this, Keleş argues that while there is no single way of being inspired, example and practice is key: whether it is the teachings infused with the example of commitment and emotion as demonstrated in Gülen's sermons; or the example and practice demonstrated by Hizmet collectively; or a Hizmet participant individually. While many people may first have connected with Gülen's "practice infused teachings," many others may have come into touch with Gülen's example and with Hizmet practice before recognising the source of the teaching behind it. Nevertheless, what is clear from what has been described and discussed in this book is that the varied manifestations of Hizmet across Europe have formed part of what could be called a patterned but also a differentiated picture: patterned because of the typical focus of these initiatives and organisations on matters of either education, dialogue or relief from poverty (now developing into a broader concern with human rights); but also differentiated because from the descriptions and discussions of Hizmet in each of the European countries examined where it is clear that there is no single absolute organisational blueprint that exists to be rolled out.

Critical to the future is the reference to the question of the nature of the connection, the interaction and the dynamic between the local in Europe and to the person and teaching of Gülen. Of this, HE3 says that "The people here, they bring some reports of their activities, and they tell what they do here in the Netherlands, and the same in England, in Belgium and in Germany, to Gülen". From within the Danish context where, as previously noted, right from its beginnings, the Dialog Forum was acknowledging its inspiration from Gülen, Gezen nevertheless explained that:

> Other associations around Europe were interested in having Gülen as Honorary Chairman, but we didn't want that because it doesn't go with the Danish context. I would personally be against it, because you can be inspired by Gülen but having him as honorary president is more than that. So, from the beginning we said you can be inspired by Gülen, but you can also be inspired by other people.

In relation to the question of Gülen's role with regard to these pivotal times and future trajectories of Hizmet in Europe, Toğuşlu offers the respectful, but cautiously critical, observation that "I think that Fethullah Gülen also lost a little bit these debates, is what I see". In addition, within these important debates within Hizmet "we lost a little bit of 'balance' because people got upset. So, this is what I feel as a problem". Of course, in recognising the collective trauma of Hizmet, it is also important to recognise that Gülen himself is likely also traumatised, which is something the present author observed from interviews with Gülen and the time spent in the Golden Generation Retreat Centre in Saylorsburg and is discussed in Weller 2022, Sect. 5.1. This is because it would appear that, while in other historical episodes in which he and his close associates had become wanted people things had happened to him and to a small number of close associates, but now they are happening to a very large number of other people in some senses *because* of their very distant or even only assumed connection with him.

As Toğuşlu noted, "This is maybe the first time that Fethullah Gülen and his students or his friends experience such a kind of feeling. There was state brutality, OK, but it never before came in such a massive and general way. So, in this sense, it's a first experience". Such a reality is a very big burden to carry and it affects how one looks at things, in relation to which Toğuşlu observed of Gülen that "He feels still a little bit guilty and blames himself for what is happening nowadays. And so I think he lost a little bit his orientation and guiding for the people", one of the consequences of which is that "Now in the last four or five years, the Turkish speeches coming from Gülen, his focus was on Turkey. This debate, this discussion with the AKP, with the Turkish government, with the Turkish state. He probably felt he should moderate the people to stay strong in the movement".

In relation to this, Toğuşlu observed that "the people living in Turkey need such a kind of thing, which is understandable" but of himself that "I don't need that in the same way because I am living in Belgium". However, a consequence of what has happened in Turkey is that "you have lost your focus from what you are doing, onto Turkey" and that this has affected not only Hizmet people in Europe, but also Gülen himself, of whom Toğuşlu says that "In that sense I think he lost a little bit also". At the same time, Toğuşlu quickly went on to say that "Maybe he is misguided by the people from his environment. So, this is another option".

Despite this, Tascioglu approaches these matters from the perspective of a theodicy of testing the faithfulness of Hizmet people:

> I have a lot of confidence in these new generations. The Hizmet movement has a very profound basis in Europe. So, all the sponsors, the establishments and the businessmen who support, even with the coup they kept on supporting. It was like a very difficult test for them. So, for most of us we were successful in our tests.

And that:

> So even after he is gone, every country has an applied system that economically and theoretically now works independently. We have different contacts in our countries and also with the states and if we continue in this way, I don't see a reason why things should change or go back. So, the ball is on our court and we just have to play a good game!

Referring to research into the development of religious groups more generally, interviewee HE2 also says that:

> There is a period of charismatic leadership. And then there is a crisis, and out of that they reach out and ask how can we organise the community so we are good for the future. And this I see is independent from the religious, the metaphysical or anything, I will not say secular, because for me it is very religious. But it is a very human dynamic.

In relation to the need for ongoing learning informed by self-criticism, HE2 noted: "But I ask myself the question, about the future, or survival, or sustainability of the institution, what can we 're-invent' now, based on our experience, what we have been learning and what will be the future needs of the city and society, and for this there are too many things to do!" In conclusion, Toğuşlu argues that such a renewal can be based on a continued recognition that "what Gülen says is important, but at the same time he taught with these issues in the nineties and eighties" and so also very clearly that now "we need new relevance in terms especially of the Islamic faith in a European context".

6.7   Confident Engagement, Islamic Self-Criticism and Human Focus

Hizmet across the world and in Europe finds itself situated in an overall context where "Islamist" movements aspire to be "modern" in the sense of using science and technology, but generally do so out of a relatively simplistic and shallow engagement with Islamic tradition, with many key Islamist figures never having been trained in classical Islamic scholarship but seeking rather to engage direct with their understanding of the Qu'ran. But contrast, in its engagement with the contemporary world, Hizmet draws upon Gülen's formation as a trained and properly "traditional" (rather than "traditionalist") Islamic scholar who has especially championed education as a liberative opportunity to be embraced by Muslims. As a result of such an approach, individuals engaged in Hizmet organisations have, in general, been empowered to negotiate tradition and modernity in a balanced and creative way. Indeed, in many ways one might evaluate one of the most significant contributions made by the teaching of Gülen and the practice of Hizmet is that, generally speaking, in the contexts of modernity and pluralism, it has enabled individuals to be Muslims on the one hand without apology, but on the other hand also without heavy insistence on "Muslimness" over against "humanness".

Such liberative pathways can be identified in the personal biographical stories told by a number of the Hizmet interviewees. For example, looking back, Ablag summarised that "More than once I felt ashamed at the low quality of the ideas of our preachers when I visited the mosques" but then "A friend invited me. I felt that they could be an intellectual, a modern person and a Muslim". Such considerations are also underlined in the biography of Karakoyun who first came into contact with Hizmet in Germany when he was fifteen or sixteen years old. His parents had always been believing people but he explained that, as a teenager, he had a lot of questions such as "Who am I? Where am I going? at is my belief? Where do I belong to?" In his searching around and through these questions he connected with a lot of different Islamic movements. Until he was fourteen, Karakoyun recounts that he had visited the Qu'ran schools of the Süleymanci movement, but he felt that these concentrated on only formal things such as reciting the Qur'an properly, and although he recognised the importance of that, he also thought, "yeah, I am always reading the Qur'an, reciting it, but I want to understand it, and what can I take from it to our days". Then he visited some *sohbets* of the Millî Görüş movement. But in that context it seemed that he was "always listening to someone who is seeing the 'other', the German, the West, the Christian, the Jew, the American as an enemy". This was very problematic for him in relation to his day-to-day experience because he had grown up in a little town in Germany where his family had been the only Turkish family, and in his school he was the only Turkish boy, and therefore he had a lot of very good German friends.

Overall, because what he was hearing seemed to be in contradiction with his personal experience he reports that he thought "something is going wrong there". Against that background, he was invited by a neighbour to a *sohbet* of the Hizmet movement that was organised by an engineer who came from Turkey. And Karakoyun noted that in Germany at the end of the nineties, there were not so many Turkish people with an academic background. Therefore, "He was the first Turkish person I met with an academic background and he had very interesting things that he said at his *sohbets*" which included "about dialogue, about integration, about Muslims in a modern world; about learning, reading and then practising; and then even teaching to others; taking responsibility – so all the things you know about what makes Hizmet Hizmet". It was, though, only "later I realised these came from Fethullah Gülen and his teachings". Following this, Karakoyun explained that in 1998, "We organised a journey to Turkey and there we visited the institutions and spoke to a lot of people, and from there on you can say I was part, was engaged in the Hizmet movement". Thus when Karakoyun finished university in 2005, he took on a job in a Hizmet dialogue institution, and in 2008 he was tasked with founding a new institution in Berlin.

At the same time, while the individual journey to a living and personally appropriated Islam is something one can find in many Hizmet stories, Hizmet organisations and groups in Europe were, for a variety of reasons, not always so transparent either about their connection with Fethullah Gülen and the wider Hizmet or even about their fundamental inspiration from Islam. Ongoing discussion about this and evolution in relation to it has been initially discussed in Sect. 5.4 on transparency in general; Sect. 5.5 on relationships with the state and civil society; and Sect. 5.6 on relationships with other Muslims. As interviewee HE3 from the Netherlands puts it:

> The characteristics of the movement here in the Netherlands and I know also in other European countries, the movement has a religious, an Islamic background, and almost everyone confirms this, also academics inside the movement. The movement is a religious one. But, inspired from Islamic religious elements – like love, tolerance, moderation, forgiveness, and Sufism – identifying the Islam in Anatolia.

However, at the same time, "When we look at the activities of the movement here they are all social – education projects, and projects for aid, and to help poor people here and lots of activities for women, for participation and for integration". Thus, the connection between the religious inspiration and social engagement is not always evident and, in relation to the question of how, especially in organisational terms, to actualise its Islamic identity in an appropriate way, Toğuşlu says, "We are still thinking about how to make it really, really visible. But it shouldn't be a kind of Islamic organization giving Qur'anic courses, but some Islamic something should be there".

Significantly, Toğuşlu linked this discussion with the need for a contextualised self-criticism, prompted especially by a more widespread and greater degree of reflection on the questions arising from what happened to Hizmet in Turkey and the associated ones of whether some things could have been done differently and/or better there and also as discussed in relation to the limits of this in Weller 2022, Sect. 5.5. In relation to this, AS2 acknowledged: "There are a lot of things we could have done better. Maybe we made a lot of mistakes – not a lot of, but it is possible. And we are criticising ourselves, what did we do? And when the Turkish people don't believe us, we ask, 'Why don't you stand with us, what are our mistakes?' " In relation to this, AS2 explained that "one of the criticisms is that we have not integrated enough with other people" and that because of this "the Hizmet movement got a very big kick". AS1 also expressed reflective questions about what happened in Turkey that have not gone away and can leave at least some Hizmet people in quite a conflicted inner struggle:

> But, of course, we need answers about how these things happened. But whether or not we find an answer, we have to continue again with our thoughts. But it's disturbing – if someone did that, I am also thinking we shouldn't walk together with these guys whoever they are, whether these were close to Mr. Gülen, or not, they were just close to the government in Turkey, or they were some agents from the government. People are looking for answers, and I can just say they have had hesitations.

At the same time, within the generality of Hizmet there remains the feeling that "they know this is a good movement, doing very good things for the public, for the people who need help, and this goodness should continue, to feel themselves spiritually better". Because of this, in a spirit of Islamic self-criticism, AS2 sought to find a new balance between a realism about all temporal organisational forms, combined with a positive focus on what these forms are at least trying to bring about, with the option identified either critically to continue to engage in such or not, as the case may be, which he expressed as follows:

> When I see something illogical, I can finish, or can try to correct them. If I cannot correct them, then I sit and watch. But for an organization, there will always be some problems. There is no organization without problems. For me the most important thing is to minimize the problems and to be transparent. So you have to look at the, how can I say it, the main idea. You have to look what can be done for humanity, for education, for good things. And you can continue after that.

All of this is very important for the future possible trajectories of Hizmet in Europe. This is because although Islamophobia is a reality in the European context and needs to be challenged at every level (and especially by those who are not Muslims), for Muslims themselves to focus only on the injustices done to Muslims whether in Turkey, Europe or elsewhere is dangerous. In his teaching Gülen has tried to emphasise that being Muslim in reaction to something is at best limiting, can also at the least become distorting and at the worst turn into something that then becomes combative towards others. By contrast, to be able to be properly confident in being Muslim one needs to be shaped not by reaction but by the sources of Islam, by an emphasis on that which can be universally shared with people of other religions and none, and a willingness to engage in practical projects together, all of which entails a readiness to undertake self-criticism and to be challenged mutually and to learn from one another.

Such an approach is identified as a way of living that can both give strength to Muslims, while also offering much to the wider European society the nature of which is identified by many Hizmet people as having a greater spirit of openness to evidence than is the case in the more authoritarian and conspiracy laden nature of Turkish society. Thus, AS2 observes:

> Of course, not all of the people in Europe are the same, but most of them, especially Switzerland are questioning, looking, searching, reading. They don't believe the things in the television unconditionally. So that is very important. So, in Europe, the Hizmet movement will shape, I think, from now on if we can evaluate this chance. We can do more good things and more people can have a chance to know us – Hizmet. There are a lot of people coming from Turkey to Europe in Hizmet. So, they can touch someone. They can go and say something. For example, in Germany, can go to a church and tell something. We are a Muslim, we love you also. We like and respect to all people for the sake of God. God create you, so, you are honourable as an art of the God. No matter what is your belief, religion or nationality. Christians are very kind to us. Because their religion is kind in its origin. It is like that. We love you really! Our belief is like that.

Kerakoyun underlines that "In Turkey this is very different. There is nobody who is self-critical, who is reflecting on itself. Everything was great; we were always the best; nothing went wrong; we never made a mistake. So, nothing has to change – we have to go on like we did always". And while this was something that Kerakoyun was identifying primarily as a Turkish mentality, he also said, "you could find it in Hizmet as well". But, by contrast, as AS2 put it, if Hizmet is ready to embrace self-criticism then the European context also provides a great opportunity for it:

> The Europeans or Canadians or Americans can see us directly and search us: what are they doing?! What kind of people are they? Do they have a secret agenda? And they will see there is no secret agenda, that is the way they live their life. So, I think, they will be more friendly to us after that. So, in Europe, our future, Hizmet's future will be better, I hope so. It is not very

clear, it is not certain, but I think so and hope so. If we are good at representing ourselves and Hizmet then it will be better. But if we are not good at representing and if we don't integrate into the country we live and if we don't introduce ourselves then most probably they will hate us. There is a Turkish proverb ... "man is the enemy of the unknown".

In parallel with the actuality of, and arguably growing need for, a more explicit actualisation of Islamic identity, is a re-emphasis in the contextual realities of Europe on the centrality and priority of the human, as also discussed more generally in Weller 2022, Sect. 6.6. As Naziri put it:

> In Islam, before being a Muslim, to be a human is very important. If you are a human, you are very, very important in Islam, because God created you as a human. No problem whether you are Muslim or not. It is the connection between you and God. It doesn't interest me. You want to be another religion, it's not important. I couldn't say bad things about you. But I am Muslim: I love my religion, I love my God, I love my Prophet Muhammad very much. But maybe you are a Christian, I don't know ... Your image doesn't change ... accordingly whether you are Muslim, Christian, Jewish or any other religions. I respect the man for his honesty, diligence and good character, but not for his beliefs. Religion is something between God and man.

Perhaps also partly reflective of the laic tradition, with which Tascioglu has engaged in Belgium, he says: "I don't want to focus on different religions or different backgrounds. I just want to approach people as human beings". Taking another example, when explaining the history of Hizmet in Denmark, Gezen in fact notes that its Dialog Society was built on the idea of "human first" which he said was also in line with the approach of the Danish Christian pastor, educator and philosopher Grundtvig, who said: "Human first, then Christian". This emphasis—which Gezen points out can also be found in the Danish philosopher Løgstrup—resonates with Gülen's similar approach that one is "first human, then Muslim", and of which Gezen says that it is such an approach that "makes it possible to live as a Muslim in Denmark, because of the interpretation I get from Gülen". At the same time, it was Gezen's opinion that "we have to make new plans, new projects, and this position must be a new chance for Hizmet to represent itself truly, and more widely", learning the lessons from a relative lack of integration with others in Turkey to the situation now in Europe, so that "We have to connect with them and we have to tell

Hizmet logic and Hizmet way more and more, because I think before that we have not been very good at telling about ourselves, Hizmet".

Concurrently, in internal Hizmet discussions, Gezen explains that "When I meet people I try to remind them that we should use our resources to do what is said in the Qur'an and *hadith*, and in the *sunnah*, that we should contribute to the countries we live in, and that people should find solutions". One of the consequences of trying to find a perhaps better dynamic between a more explicit acknowledgement of Islamic roots and inspiration, combined with a strong emphasis on the human, is perhaps a new readiness, rather than to claim uniqueness, to identify shared values that can exist within various societies and to learn from these other experiences of trying to translate values into concrete actions. As the interview HE2 from Italy said:

> We are constantly learning from the Italian society and I am very happy it because, you know, if you are willing to learn and if you open up your channels to get something in. But in some cases, sometimes I see people, here or there, even though it is very contradictory to Islam, even though it is very contradictory to the teaching of Said Nursi, I see unnamed, implicit pride: "Hizmet is a very good thing, and we have so many things to teach and people should find out and we teach them". I mean they don't pronounce it, it wouldn't be rational, but I simply construct some attitudes, some grammar they use, some socially constructed language.

By contrast, HE2 points out that, including in relation to some of what are seen as the core characteristics of Hizmet, "There are so many things that we are learning from the society including some things that could be celebrated as being like Hizmet – for example, volunteering. In Italy, five or six million people volunteer regularly" but that in order to benefit from this, "the dialogue of life, dialogue of collaboration means give and take all the time". In relation to the wider learning that is taking place within Hizmet, AS1 said, "we always said this movement is very good on principle and thoughts. Yes, it is true. But we are not alone. This does not only belong to us. This does not belong alone to the Islam people or in Turkey", which theme is also discussed further in Weller 2022, Sect. 6.6. In summary, the interviewee AS1 says that:

> What I am saying for my people here is that we are just at the beginning. Maybe at the end we can say, "Ah, this was it" when we hopefully integrate in this society or otherwise. And anyway this whole western part is very far

away from Turkey in the way of living together in society. Of course, there are some criticisms about other parts but, if you look at it, you can see the results here. We are refugees here. Not the British people are refugees in Turkey, or Germany in Iran or in other parts of the world. Hopefully this education will be very good for us and we will graduate in these countries, and hopefully our sons and daughters and children will grow with these goodnesses, principles of the Hizmet movement – plus, this is not enough for us – and the western mindset. And hopefully a good model for the country where they are living plus dreaming further in the world.

6.8   FROM COPY-PASTE INTO CONTEXTUAL REINVENTION

Although—or perhaps precisely because—this is the first monograph written taking an overview of Hizmet across Europe since the events in Turkey of July 2016, this book can make only a preliminary contribution to a story that, first of all, is continuing; and second, even in relation to its past four or five years, remains to be told in a fuller and more detailed way, both by those who seek to live it out in practice and by those who seek to analyse and understand it whether as "insiders" or as "outsiders". In terms of where Hizmet in Europe has come from and is possibly going to, Keleş makes the summative observation that:

> It's like a PhD thesis, you know, there is that idea of it being circular. It makes sense. It made sense in Turkey and outside of Turkey in the 1990s. At the level of ethics and principles, it still has a lot of attraction, and it still makes sense. But it needs to be re-invented and re-produced and re-understood at the European level, to understand what we mean for Europe – because Hizmet ultimately did something that was needed, and it was something that society knew that it needed.

Over the around two decades in which this author has had some experience of engaging with Hizmet, it has always struck the author that it is a phenomenon that does, first of all, make space for others to interpret and critique it in a way that a lot of groups of all religions would not really be willing to do. Therefore, while it is possible to critique Hizmet for not always being fully transparent in that interchange, its *relative* transparency in this regard is something from which other religious groups and organisations might usefully learn.

Secondly, the degree of transparency that it achieves comes from its Muslim and Islamic roots. One does not have to depart from these things in order to welcome the engagement of the critique of others; indeed, it is part of the teaching emphases of Fethullah Gülen that it is precisely because of what should be learned from Islam that one should be open to embracing such critiques. And for those of us who are outside Islam or Hizmet, the fact that we do not always take the opportunities afforded to us and the invitations made to make our honest (including properly critical) input is not the fault of Hizmet, but is rather a matter of our scholarly and/or religious/ethical responsibility and/or failings.

One of the by-products of engaging with and researching Hizmet over a couple of decades is that the present author is sometimes asked by Hizmet people or groups for future recommendations. Generally speaking, this is an invitation that the role of a scholar makes one reluctant to accept—not least in this instance where personally and/or professionally one does not have then personally to live with the consequences of such recommendations, in the same way as do people who are within Hizmet. However, as noted earlier, as part of a distinct role as part of the Dialogue Society's Advisory Board the present author has, on occasion, either individually and/or as part of the wider Board, made recommendations that have impacted upon the development of Hizmet in the UK.

In relation to any wider recommendations based directly on scholarly and research work, there are among scholars a variety of positions on the legitimacy or otherwise of that. Whatever position might be taken in this regard, as Chryssides (2004) notes when reflecting on questions arising even from the fact of engagement in the field of study:

> Am I disturbing the "ecological balance" of the religions I study? I think the answer must be yes. Does it matter? Yes, it probably does, but to ask the question, "Should I help to effect change in the religions I study?" is really to ask, "Should I be studying these religions at all?" The only live question is, "How much should I be changing them", for changing a religious community by one's presence and one's study is inevitable, even though the change may be small.

Whether such a perspective would be contested or not what would, however, likely be seen by the vast majority of scholars to be legitimate is for a scholar to try as fully as possible understand what is going on within a movement (in this case Hizmet) that is being researched; and, when setting that within a broader analytical framework, as far as possible to be in a position, in a responsible way to hold up an "informed mirror" of the movement to people both within it and to those beyond it.

Having lost Turkey—according to one's approach as a starting point, a power base and/or a reference point—a fundamental evaluative question arises from that fact as to what Hizmet in Europe might thereby be losing and what it may also be gaining. To some extent this is also something that still cannot fully be answered because it is still in process and it will take some more time of accompanying this process in order more fully to be able to see and evaluate the trajectories of what is happening. This is especially because of the presence of the "third layer" of arrivals from Turkey, although of these HE3 says: "I think if the political pressure in Turkey will continue for a few years, the new people here from Turkey after the coup, they or their children have time to think better and to decide that they are from here, part of the Dutch society. This is a process of ten or twenty years".

What perhaps can be said summatively is that, while clearly having strongly Turkish roots and having continued for many years to have had a very strong Turkish inheritance, for many years prior to July 2016, Hizmet had already been at least as strongly engaged in Europe as in Turkey especially through its initiatives in education and dialogue. At the same time, although there have been clear commonalities of foci rooted in common values and of themes through which those values are historicised, there have also been distinctive developments in terms of varied inflections within which Hizmet has been trying, with varied degrees of success, to take seriously its diverse national and local contexts in Europe. In any diasporic and/or minority situation there is both opportunity and/or threat. As a minority, in terms of "threat", it is possible either to become so "rigid" that one risks becoming an island in the wider society; or, by contrast, one can become so "permeable" with the risk of losing all distinctiveness. In terms of opportunity, there are the learnings that can be achieved from new environments and the possibility to make properly distinctive contributions.

The post-July 2016 travails and debates within Hizmet in Europe accentuate and bring to a head what are not new issues and questions concerning how far Hizmet is a Turkish movement; or how far is it an Islamic movement; or how far is it a civil society movement, and/or in what combinations and how all of this is to be understood and articulated. These issues and questions have been there in at least incipient form from when Hizmet started spreading into various parts of the world. But Hizmet's crisis in Turkey and the overall consequences and reverberations of that into other parts of the world have sharpened those pre-existing questions and issues and made them more insistent.

Gülen's close associate Haylamaz explained the dynamic of Hizmet from its beginning that "Only perhaps the major principles were taken from Hojaefendi. For instance, one of those principle was to establish contact with other people. People took on this principle and put it into practice in their own way. It was an ongoing interaction". El-Banna (2013) refers to what she calls the Hizmet's "strategic adaptavism" (p. 66), in relation to which Sunier and Landman (2015) have argued that this transformation has gone so far that, even following Gülen's earlier settlement in the USA, "Hizmet transformed into a typical NGO" (p. 87). The events of July 2016 and what followed have arguably, at the very least, been disruptive of any more evolutionary "strategic adaptavism" through the collective trauma that it has brought to Hizmet and the effects that flow from that now, but also (as discussed in Sect. 4.5 and in Weller 2022, Sect. 5.2) potentially into the coming generations of Hizmet.

However, each of these kinds of understandings of what occurs in Hizmet process of change and transition tends, as one can see from the way in which they are structured and expressed, to assume a conscious and relatively linear process, including in the relationship between Gülen and the various expressions of Hizmet. By contrast, and in critique of such understandings as being too one-dimensional, is an argument made in a recent important doctoral thesis by Keleş (2021). By tracing the dynamics of change in relation to Hizmet and Gülen's handling of, and engagement with, human rights questions and issues particularly around apostasy and around women, Keleş has, by detailed reference to these two specific examples, evidentially and analytically demonstrated the necessity of a complexified understanding of the inter-relationship between Hizmet and Gülen. And he has done this by "reversing (or flattening) the leader/follower, producer/consumer, originator/disseminator and mind/body paradigm" that pervades much of the literature in which, among both what he calls "critical" and "sympathetic" scholars, "Gülen is conceptualized as the producing-mind and Hizmet as the disseminating-body" (p. 146).

In relation to these overall dynamics, it nevertheless seems that, at this point in time, at least while he continues to live, the person and teaching of Fethullah Gülen will remain an important and likely a continuingly key point of reference for Hizmet in Europe. Whether and how far new impulses will come from him and his teaching on the other side of his more "passive" role of being a point of relative unity around which Hizmet can still coalesce, and his more "active" role in providing advice to Hizmet people on how to overcome their trauma is as yet to be resolved (and is discussed in more detail Weller 2022, Chaps. 5 and 6).

But in relation to Hizmet in Europe's possible further future trajectories, the multi-level impact of the trauma of the events of July 2016, combined with the need to deal internally with what this book has called a "three-layered" Hizmet, in context where lines of wider communication and consultation both with Gülen and with various national foci for Hizmet have at the least experienced some disruption, means that the diverse national socio-religious contexts in Europe, and the responses of Hizmet to them, are likely to play a still more important role in shaping the future of Hizmet in Europe, while that of Turkey, relatively speaking, continues gradually to recede more and more into the background.

In such a context, however, Toğuşlu identifies two fundamentally possible trajectories. The first he calls "A kind of disaporization, withdrawn totally in itself". The second is one in which:

> The movement is maybe ready to become a transnational identity, moving away from its Turkish identity – I am not saying totally its Turkish identity for me – but somehow it becomes one of the identities and not the dominant identity. It becomes one identity, whether Spanish Turkish or Italian Turkish, but maybe eighty-five per cent should be Belgian, Dutch or American or whatever. So in that sense that movement becomes transnational: that means that the people from Senegal to the Congo, from Egypt to Turkmenistan, from Australia to Brazil, they become really a part of the movement

Of this latter trajectory, Toğuşlu says, "in that sense maybe this is really a renewal, like a phoenix becoming again from its ashes: that we die, but at the same time we begin a new kind of identity in which maybe we renew again our principles as well, I don't know. We change everything". At the same time, although he places some emphasis on what lies within the agency of Hizmet, Toğuşlu recognises concerning such possible future trajectories that "It does not depend only on the movement"—in other words which trajectory is more likely to happen is not something that is only down to the agency of Hizmet. Rather,

> If this state pressure continued, for example, for another ten years, with this alienation from the Turkish society and maybe from the Muslim communities as well because the movement is struggling with the state. So, in that sense, this is a bad scenario in which the movement becomes weaker and weaker – and at the same time it could offer new opportunities, becoming smaller, and maybe rethink again.

As things currently stand, Toğuşlu thinks that Hizmet is poised between these two basic trajectories and that "I think the movement is in between now and in the next five years we will see clearly where it is going". When echoed back to him in interview that his overall position might be described as being that "one should try to focus on wherever one is, but that, actually, quite a lot does depend on what happens or does not happen in Turkey", Toğuşlu affirmed, "Yes, exactly". Indeed, when it was put to him in a stronger version that it almost depends on that, and that this is not something that Hizmet itself can necessarily influence, he responded: "Definitely … imagine two weeks later everything is finished, OK, and then people who want to can go back to Turkey" but that following on from that would be "Again, two options – not that kind of disaporazation but Turkishness again will be very, very strong: it will be dominant and will dominate the whole of Hizmet people around the world".

In such an evaluative judgement on the interplay between structure and agency, it might be that Toğuşlu's own discipline of sociology is playing a particularly strong role. However, he also makes clear his own normative position through the clear and, for some, perhaps startling statement that "The Turkish experience is only one experience of Hizmet" or, as interviewee HE3 put it even more pithily, "A Hizmet without Turkey is OK!" and that because of that, if Hizmet did refocus on Turkey, then in Toğuşlu's evaluation, "I think that the movement would miss something in terms of becoming really, really transnational". In relation to this current period, Toğuşlu says: "Even the Turkish state pressures, if the decision-makers, especially Mr. Gülen says we become really transnational, and the decision-making processes, all of these structural changes should be adopted in a mutual consensus. In this sense I am optimistic". On the other hand, "if this polarization, if this Turkishness still holds sway, I am not very optimistic, I am a little bit in this sense pessimistic".

In summary, the tendency expressed here by Toğuşlu, and as broadly found among many of the other Hizmet interviewees in Europe, is that, somewhat ironically, and also very painfully, it may be precisely through what has happened in July 2016 and its aftermath that there may now be the possibility of current initial trajectories in due course arriving at something that could in future also "from the outside" be more truly be described as "transnational" than is currently the case, as well as more genuinely experienced as such from the "inside". At the very least, if it is true that such a development might already have been in process, as a more purely evolutionary one it would likely have taken a lot longer to come about. However, this has now accelerated because of July 2016 and its aftermath.

At present, overall, the situation in Europe is one that the present author would find it hard to express more clearly and accurately than in the words of Tascioglu with which this chapter and book will now draw towards a conclusion, namely that "We are trying to start new projects"; that in trying to draw upon the additional personnel and experience brought by Hizmet asylum-seekers "we still need a couple of years to get those emigrants adapted"; and that, overall, as things stand at the moment, "it is clear that we are still not fully back to our game yet, that we still have wounds". While taking this woundedness very seriously, it is also the case that because, as this book has shown, Hizmet continues to wrestle with many issues concerning itself and with changes and continuities in the human needs in relation to which it aspires to offer service rooted in a religious and spiritual vision, Hizmet remains alive. And because it is still alive, there are ways for it potentially to reinvent itself for the future. As HE3 says of when Erdoğan goes, "The dynamism in the movement will come back in the future, I think". But also:

> The movement has to be proactive to show that it is not only the religiously-oriented movement, not only the Turkish-oriented movement. The projects and programmes that they did are mostly good, and people here appreciated almost all the activities. And they will come back, I think, and the movement, its people, need some time, some several years and it will be OK, I think. It will be such a kind of process that movement's people have some feedback from the society, from the people inside and outside the movement – it needed that.

For any continued distinctiveness and vitality of Hizmet in Europe, the creative way forward will likely not be one based on any combination of the receipt, preservation and transmission of the substantive body of Gulen's inherited teaching, pregnant though that remains with matters that will remain important into the future; the veneration of his person and/or practice, inevitable as that is likely to be given the inspiration that he has brought to so many lives; or the "copy-pasting" of historical Hizmet initiatives, as valid and important as they have been for their contexts and times. Rather, it will be a case of working with what this book and its companion volume (Weller 2022) argue is at the very heart of what Gülen's person, practice and teaching have offered to the world which, at its heart, is to be understood as a dynamic methodological call to continuously renewed and contextualised engagement with religious and spiritual sources that are centred on love and on the human.

NOTES

1. https://www.hizmetbeweging.nl/hizmet-overleg/landelijk-hizmet-overleg/, n.d.
2. https://www.hizmetbeweging.nl/wp-content/uploads/2017/07/De-Nederlandse-Hizmet-Visiedocument.pdf, n.d.
3. http://www.dialoguesociety.org/courses/dialogue-studies-ma.html, 2021.
4. http://www.dialoguestudies.org/, 2021.
5. https://www.iahrageneva.org/, 2020.

REFERENCES

(All web links current at 20.11.2021)

Barker, Eileen (1989). *New Religious Movements: A Practical Introduction.* London: HMSO.

Çelik, Gurkan and Alan, Yusuf (2007). Fethullah Gülen as a Servant Leader. *International Journal of Servant-Leadership, 3* (1), 247–265.

Chryssides, George (2004). 50 Years Unification: Conflicts, Responsibilities and Rights. Paper presented at 2004 CESNUR international conference at Baylor University, Waco, Texas, June 18–20. https://www.cesnur.org/2004/waco_chryssides.htm.

El-Banna, Sanaa (2013). *Resource Mobilisation in Gülen-Inspired Hizmet: A New Type of Social Movement.* New York: Blue Dome Press.

Ergil, Doğu (2010). Anatomy of the Gülen Philosophy and Movement. In Gürkan Çelik and Martien Brinkman (Eds.), *Mapping the Gülen Movement: A Multidimensional Approach. Conference Papers. 7 October 2010, at Felix Meritis, Amsterdam* (pp. 17–31). Amsterdam: Dialoog Academie and VISOR, VU University Amsterdam, Institute for the Study of Religion, Culture and Society.

Keleş, Özcan (2021). *The Knowledge Production of Social Movement Practice at the Intersection of Islam and Human Rights: The Case of Hizmet.* Unpublished Doctor of Philosophy in Human Rights. January 2021. Sussex: University of Sussex.

Kurucan, Ahmet and Mustafa Kasım Erol (2012). *Islam and Dialogue: Qu'ran, Sunnah, History.* London: Dialogue Society. http://www.dialoguesociety.org/publications/dialogue-in-islam.pdf.

Sleap, Frances, Sener, Oemer and Weller, Paul (Ed.) (2013). *Dialogue Theories.* London: Dialogue Society.

Sleap, Frances, Sener, Oemer and Weller, Paul (Eds.) (2016). *Dialogue Theories 2*. London: Dialogue Society.

Sunier, Thijl, Landman, Nico (2015). Gülen Movement (Hizmet). In Sunier Thijl and Nico Landman (Eds.), *Transnational Turkish Islam: Shifting Boundaries of Religious Activism and Community Building Turkey and Europe*. (pp. 81–94). Basingstoke: Palgrave Macmillan.

Watmough, Simon and Öztürk, Ahmet Erdi (2018). From 'Diaspora by Design' to Transnational Political Exile: the Gülen Movement in Transition. *Politics, Religion and Ideology 19* (1), 33–52. https://doi.org/10.1080/21567689.2018.1453254

Weller, Paul (2015). The Gülen Movement in the United Kingdom. In Gurkan Çelik, Johan Leman and Karel Steenbrink (Eds.), *Gülen-Inspired Hizmet in Europe: The Western Journey of a Turkish Muslim Movement* (pp. 239–251). Brussels: Peter Lang.

Weller, Paul (2022). *Fethullah Gülen's Teaching and Practice: Inheritance, Context and Interactive Development*. Cham: Palgrave Macmillan.

Yükleyen, Ahmet and Tunagür, Ferhan (2013). The Gülen Movement in Western Europe and the USA. In Matthias Kortmann and Kerstin Rosenow-Williams (Eds.), *Islamic Organizations in Europe and the USA: A Multi-Disciplinary Perspective* (pp. 224–241). Basingstoke: Palgrave Macmillan.

Index[1]

---

[1] Note: Page numbers followed by 'n' refer to notes.

Printed by Printforce, United Kingdom